The Saga of San Francisco's Wild Western Addition and Me

By

Robert Leland Speer

ISBN: 0615863795
ISBN 13: 9780615863795
Library of Congress Control Number: 2013903417
Speer Publishing, San Francisco

Table of Contents

Dedication

My Parents

Leland and Frances Speer

My Domestic and Life Partner

John Wong

My Best Friend

Ming C. Gee

My Muses

Cathy Furniss

Roger Walsh

Joseph Lordi

Andrea Speer Tatlock

1.

Prologue

Upon buying in 2004, a National Historical Landmark building circa 1870s with my partners John Wong and Ming Gee, I became further involved in the anthropography of the city of San Francisco. Primarily, my observations were in the Western Addition neighborhood, where we have lived since 1975 and where this purchased building is located. After we sold the building in 2008 and the tenants moved out, we were shocked to read in the *San Francisco Chronicle* about the tragic and sensationalized death, in the Fruitvale Bay Area Rapid Transit Station in Oakland, of the paternal grandson of a former tenant. Because the grandson, Oscar Grant III, was an African American, and he was shot by a white BART policeman, named Johannes Mehserle, the murder became a cause célèbre. Grant's untimely death—at the age of twenty-two on January 1, 2009, at two o'clock in the morning—became an impetus for this book which was begun in June of 2009. The events surrounding Grant's death will be expanded further in a later chapter. The purpose of the following narrative is to project and reflect on similar twentieth century developments seen elsewhere in urban expansion, social evolution, and redevelopment, through those seen in this particular area of a major American city.

San Francisco is a unique American city. Because of its fertile bay, with an outlet to the Pacific Ocean, it offers a direct gateway to Asia. The wealth of natural resources, which abound from the surrounding land mass, has made the port a source of great wealth with worldwide commerce. The gold rush of the 1849 created an instant metropolis with agriculture, the maritime industry, and silver discoveries following to augment the growth of the city. Today, the San Francisco Bay-based innovative high technology industry, ever-growing biotechnological industry, and banking firms continue to provide important sources of new income. The city is also ideally confined by topography to a narrow peninsula, versus urban sprawl. In many other ways, San Francisco is like other cities in its growth patterns, which are dictated by local politicians when dealing with the changing local, state, and national politics and policies.

As a real estate broker, neighborhood leader, and appointee to policy-making clubs, boards, and committees, I have direct knowledge of the changing anthropography of the city, especially in the Western Addition. My great interest in architecture might be a distraction for some readers, but I believe that it adds an extra dimension to the development of a city and its populace. Additionally, for a comparison, I have added a personal note in referencing the changes to the place where I was born—the greater Kansas City area (Kansas and Missouri), as well as changes to my personal life in the Western Addition. To illuminate the changes I have observed has not been without angst, but it has also provided a great sense of fulfillment. From my forty years of personal observations, I hope that the reader will be more enlightened about urban development—both physically and sociologically. As you read on, you will discover an amazing and wild journey of the late half of the twentieth century and beginning of the twenty-first century.

2.

The Evolution Of The Western Addition

The Western Addition is more than the vague original geographical area in San Francisco. It is a tale of urban development which is continually evolving. The original addition to the city would eventually become many separate neighborhoods with one remaining greatly-reduced Western Addition neighborhood. In the twenty-first century, the San Francisco Association of Realtors designates District 7 (North) as consisting of the subdistricts; Marina, Pacific Heights, Presidio Heights, and Cow Hollow. Whereas the rest of the Western Addition is designated District 6 (Central North) as consisting of the subdistricts; Anza Vista, Hayes Valley, Lower Pacific Heights, Western Addition, Alamo Square, and North Panhandle.

After a long, peaceful habitation by the Ohlone (Costanoan) Native American people in this verdant paradise, followed by the deadly (epidemics and relocation) conquest in 1776 by the Spanish, and then the Mexican occupation in 1834, and finally the American occupation in 1848, this area eventually became part of the new American city of San Francisco. The Western Addition was the land west of Larkin Street, which was annexed in 1855 and 1856 by the City of San Francisco through three ordinances, sponsored by Mayor Van Ness. The northern border was the Golden Gate portion of San Francisco Bay and the southern border was Duboce Avenue, ending at the diagonal main, commercial thoroughfare, Market Street. As Pacific Heights would develop later in that century on the hillside overlooking the bay, the lower, less hilly, sand and scrub land—California Street on the north and Oak Street on the south—became generally referred to as the Western Addition. At the outer-western edge of this area were several cemeteries such as Calvary on Saint Josephs Avenue and Laurel Hill on Masonic Avenue. Beyond Lone Mountain stretched the foggy and colder so-called outside lands that were mostly sand dunes with indigenous plants, which ended at the expansive Pacific Ocean. The original 1847 city plan, with a grid pattern by the surveyor, Jasper O'Farrell, and elaborated on by William Eddy in 1851, was extended. A new network of additional north-south cross streets was created and the east-west downtown streets were continued in straight lines over or through any hill, in the way. The grid block lots were laid out using a Spanish measurement based on the *vara*, which could be expanded on or constricted depending on the owners' financial condition. Thus, houses could be added onto and out buildings built on the lot. Also, lots could be combined for grander structures. The corner block lots often had commercial space on the ground floor and flats above. The standard *vara* lot was 25 feet wide by 100 to 137.5 feet deep.

After California became a state in 1850, a legalizing process for property ownership was put into effect as quickly as possible to evaluate all of the earlier existing claims to land. On California's admission to the United States, Senator William Seward stated, "The unity of our empire hangs on the decision of this day." A plaque on the Pioneer Monument on lower Market Street proclaims such. The California Consolidation Act of 1856 reduced the overall size of allotted land to the City of San Francisco to the present county borders, which total 46.7 square miles. Thus, San Francisco is unique in being both a city and a county. Gradually, the increasing number of wealthier San Franciscans, mostly of Western European ancestry, saw this area as a place to relocate away from the booming heavy industry, the expanding commercial district, and the smaller downtown lots. Formerly, in the 1850s and 1860s, Rincon Hill and South Park were the earliest enclaves of the wealthiest industrialists, merchants, bankers, etc. However, in 1869, the second Street cut of Rincon Hill (a precipitous leveling) caused many of these socially elite residents to move away in the 1870s and 1880s to the more desirable Nob Hill, Russian Hill and Western Addition. Homestead associations in the Western Addition were established to negotiate saleable land to all new buyers. Often the parcels, in the form of blocks, were bought by owner-builders, building contractors, and tract builders such as the Real Estate Associates. But other parcels were purchased by an owner to construct his own home, with the assistance of a carpenter, draftsman, or architect. The land speculation that had started with the discovery of gold in 1848, and silver discoveries including the Comstock in 1859, greatly accelerated new construction into the open countryside in the 1860s. The completion of the transcontinental railroad in 1869 brought a desirable quicker and comfortable route between both coasts.

Before the Van Ness Ordinance, there were, in the "new" Western Addition, only a few existing houses, shacks, roadside taverns, and small farms (often close to the few fresh water ponds). With extension along the previously laid-out streets, several privately owned horse-drawn streetcar lines, in the 1870s and 1880s, provided quick access to the area from downtown and Market Street (the main commercial transportation artery). By the 1890s, many of these lines were electrified. The splendor of the era of Queen Victoria was quickly realized in lavish elaborate row houses, villas, and commercial district buildings. A common feature was the bay window, which added extra space and more sunlight. The mostly wooden buildings of redwood were balloon-frame construction, which could be quickly built and individualized with many custom decorative elements. There was a proliferation of many styles, which often overlapped. But the most popular styles were the Italianate in the 1870s, Stick-Eastlake in the 1880s, and Queen Anne in the 1890s. Parks, such as Alamo Square, Hamilton Square, and Jefferson Square, and wider streets were laid out to provide for a more genteel environment. Van Ness Avenue, California Street and Divisadero (Devisadero) Street were made even wider to accommodate a good flow of traffic and grander buildings.

By 1900, most of the Western Addition had been completed with an intermingling showcase of mainly imposing brick and masonry buildings. The end of this era was also much accentuated by the large flamboyant Queen Anne houses, with their landscaped side yards and convenient neighborhood stables, making this district even more glamorous and desirable. Much of the economic growth was based on periods of boom-or-bust, but the port location and rich resources of California provided a magnet for a quickly increasing population. Also, with the completion of the transcontinental railroad in the 1870s, more people had immigrated to San Francisco, and business expanded from coast to coast. During the Gilded Age (1880–1905), San Francisco became the seventh-largest city in the United States and was considered one of the most glamorous of cities—if not infamous.

In April of 1906, the great earthquake and fire destroyed many buildings. The major damage was from fires started by home coal-burning stoves and fireplaces, as well as the broken gas lines, which particularly devastated the older core of the city. Under Kansas-bred General Frederick Funston's orders, the military dynamited Van Ness Avenue so the destruction was restricted to the east side, down to The Embarcadero waterfront.

Thus the Western Addition became the repository of much of the finest Victorian housing left in the city. Another major effect of the earthquake was the sudden importance of Fillmore Street, which became the vibrant new center of the commercial activity in San Francisco, when the displaced downtown merchants opened in any available space possible. In 1907, iron arches, anchored on all four intersection corners, outlined with electric lights and a large globular electric light hanging from the tops of each; were erected at thirteen intersections from Clay Street to Golden Gate Avenue to give a spectacular luminary appearance at night to this newly important business district. Theaters, hotels, and an amusement park, called the Chutes occupying the entire block between Fillmore, Webster, Eddy, and Turk Streets, further made this a destination point for people to visit and shop. Also, many Japanese Americans, who were located primarily in the originally wealthy South Park and secondarily in Chinatown, relocated permanently to the area to form a Japanese district called Nihonmachi, or Japantown. Unlike Chinese American immigrants, they could buy property and enroll their children in public schools. Soon their children became a large minority presence in the neighborhood public schools. A larger number of Japanese immigrated to Los Angeles, to an area now referred to as Little Tokyo. By 1915, the Panama Pacific International Exposition signaled an incredible rebirth of the magnificent "Phoenix" city, with a newly constructed downtown built through insurance claim payments and private investments, without government assistance. This revitalization overflowed somewhat in the 1920s and 1930s, spotting the Western Addition with the construction of twelve units or more of wooden apartment buildings, with Mediterranean style stucco facades, and reinforced-concrete high-rise apartment towers. A few houses were torn down and replaced with scattered commercial buildings and Edwardian homes of varying styles.

After the great earthquake and fire of 1906, the existing Jewish population greatly increased with immigration from Russia and Eastern Europe. The Jewish population also increased with the movement of Jewish people moving into the Fillmore District from the devastated district South of Market Street in San Francisco (This area was formerly referred to as "south of the slot" where a streetcar cable line, which fitted into a slot, divided the length of Market Street). These immigrants joined the much earlier immigration from Germany, England, France, and Poland. The earlier immigrants had already established thriving mercantile operations throughout the city much earlier and had become quite prosperous, and lived in many different districts. This concentrated, invigorated community added more synagogues, schools, theaters, and various small/medium sized commercial operations, such as kosher butcher shops and bakeries. Additionally, more social service groups were founded with stronger socialistic, and sometimes communistic, orientations.

Also, a few Chinese Americans opened Chinese restaurants and laundries. Since they were, however, much segregated in their residences by the exclusion laws, they were determined to rebuild their early concentrated community in Chinatown, centered on Grant Avenue (earlier called Dupont Street). Many civic and prominent business leaders were unsuccessful at trying to relocate the Chinese Americans to South Beach. In spite of these racist efforts, a new and expanded Chinatown was rebuilt on Grant Avenue. The buildings were rebuilt with pseudo-Chinese decorative elements added on to give the area an oriental flavor. All Asian immigrants were screened at the immigration station built on Angel Island from 1910 until 1947. Earlier, they had been screened at the Custom House building near Portsmouth Square.

The much smaller African American community continued to be scattered sparsely throughout the Western Addition as well as older locations throughout the city, such as the southwest side of Russian Hill at Larkin Street and Broadway. Early city leaders included William Leidsdorff, who was a mulatto from the Danish West Indies and who established the first city hotel in 1846. He also established the first steamship run between the earlier settlement of Yerba Buena and Sacramento, and was a member of the first American town council. In contrast, at the end of the nineteenth century, Mary Ellen "Mammy" Pleasant (1814–1904) established herself at 1661 Octavia Street (Bell Mansion), which has since been demolished. It was a house used for "the relaxation and pleasure" of gentlemen. In one version of her life story, she said that she was born as a slave to a Voodoo priestess. In 1848, she became the wife of John James Pleasant, whose father was a governor of Virginia, and possibly also her father. She often passed as white because of her father's background. As an abolitionist, she was deeply involved, from 1857 to 1859, in directly helping John Brown establish the activities of the Underground Railroad. She was able to amass a large fortune with the assistance of Thomas Bell, a "friend," using his banking background and her tips and guidance. After the Civil War, she was called "the mother of the Civil Rights Movement" in California after she won a discrimination lawsuit against a city streetcar company in 1866. Her lawsuit set a precedent in the California Supreme Court and was used in later civil rights cases, such as an 1893 case over segregation in housing.

Upon the event of World War II in 1941, the Fillmore Street area went through a dramatic alteration. Many African Americans immigrated, to San Francisco to work in the rapidly expanding war industry. In juxtaposition, the West Coast Japanese Americans (many of whom were American citizens) were abruptly evacuated and taken to remote internment camps in the western deserts of California, Utah, and Idaho. Many of them abandoned or sold their properties cheaply. This blatant racist decision, upheld by the United States Supreme Court, had a particularly devastating effect on a whole generation (Nisei) that was vacated from the Japantown area. (The total number of Japanese Americans interned nationally was approximately 120,000.)

An enormous and vital war industry developed in the Bay Area, particularly in the shipyards of the Hunters Point district as well as in the East Bay Area across the bay from San Francisco. The thirteen lighted arches on Fillmore Street were torn down in 1943 for scrap iron to support the war effort. Interestingly, the United States had sold much scrap iron and steel to Japan before the war. Many African American families immigrated here from the South, often from Texas, Oklahoma, Mississippi, Alabama, and Louisiana. They were attracted by the high wages paid. "The Fillmore" became a vibrant center for their jazz clubs, restaurants, churches, and hotels.

The Booker T. Washington Hotel, on Ellis Street between Fillmore and Webster Streets, was the only hotel where "Negro" entertainers were allowed to stay in the city! Ironically, President Millard Fillmore, for whom the street was named, signed the Fugitive Slave Act in 1850, which forced the return of all runaway slaves to their masters. The effect of this racist act contributed significantly to the Civil War. The generous wages offered to these new immigrants provided them with money to spend freely in their clubs and personalized service industry, as well as the ability to buy fine new clothing for themselves and their families. Some of the more enterprising families purchased homes, income-producing buildings, and commercial buildings. The vacated housing of the Japanese Americans was often just occupied, bought, or leased at low rents. In some instances, the remaining furnishings were used, or items such as paintings on scrolls were thrown out as being useless!

After World War II, the Jewish population started to move to the many western suburbs of both San Francisco and the surrounding suburban communities. Some of these neighborhoods had instituted anti-Semitic clause restrictions. The Jewish community, however, kept many of their stores in operation and continued to own rental property, which they began to rent to more people of color. In small numbers, Chinese Americans, with state exclusion acts repealed in 1948, started to move in and buy property, but preferred other neighborhoods according to their personal financial status and citizenship status.

At the same time the African Americans started gradually expanding, from around Fillmore Street from Sacramento Street, to Duboce Avenue. For example, the historic Third Baptist Church, organized in 1852 as the first Negro Baptist Church, by 1966 had completed a large new church on the site of a large Italianate Victorian Villa that had an observatory on top (southeast corner of McAllister and Pierce Streets). The church was designed by architect William H. Gunnison, and was built in the form of a white stucco-covered modern building with a graceful, pillared, circular, entry portico and a lofty rectilinear tower. The complex included a large sanctuary, a youth center, and an administrative building. One block away, another large lot had an even larger Italianate Victorian Villa with a centered square tower, which was demolished to become a parking lot to be used in the future for church educational facilities. Known leaders who have addressed the congregation include former President Bill Clinton, Adam

Clayton Powell, Jr., W. E. B. DuBois, Martin Luther King, Jr., Andrew Young, Jesse Jackson, Ralph Abernathy, Benjamin Mays, and Benjamin Hooks. Many other African American churches also enlarged their presence through larger congregations that acquired older existing churches and store fronts. The ministers were the most important factor in publicly voicing to the city their concerns and the issues of their newly arrived members. The *Sun-Reporter*, newspaper, founded in the late 1940s by its publisher, Carlton Goodlett MD, became a powerful force in forming the views of the African American community.

The whole demography of the Western Addition underwent a major metamorphosis and became the first multicultural neighborhood in San Francisco. After World War II, a large number of Filipinos, because of their supportive war efforts, joined their already-existing small community. Some Japanese Americans returned, and Japantown was reestablished. But many others disbursed to the Richmond and Sunset Districts, as well as the new suburbs of the San Francisco Peninsula and the East Bay region. During the time through the 1960s, jazz clubs provided lively underground entertainment with *The Fillmore* district becoming the *Harlem of the West*, with such famous personalities as Billie Holiday, Ella Fitzgerald, Louis Armstrong, and Duke Ellington. Newly opened soul food restaurants and black Chicago-style barber shops catered to the new African American majority. A professional class evolved from their ranks to provide new services. Real estate brokers of all ethnic backgrounds helped both the more frugal and the more successful African Americans acquire homes and buildings. All of this activity brought a curious mix of events. One club owner, who was also an African American owner of a large Classical Revival-style mansion, circa 1900 on Alamo Square, related to me how, in the 1950s, she hosted a group of Baptist ministers in San Francisco for a conference. Leola King locked them up in her club, the Blue Mirror on Fillmore Street, for two days with a good supply of fine food, liquor, and "ladies of the evening." She said, "They went away thinking of San Francisco as a heavenly place."

Following the district overcrowding during and after World War II, the result was a more concentrated African American neighborhood. Further African American family relatives relocating from all over the country, added to the increased density. In the 1950s, the San Francisco Housing Authority (SFHA) constructed public housing consisting of four enormous, concrete, eleven-story apartment blocks to house much of this increased population. These buildings were all closely located together on cleared land between Eddy, Turk, Laguna, and Divisadero Streets. The SFHA, as well as the San Francisco Redevelopment Agency (SFRA), was funded by a combination of federal financial aid under Title 1 of the Housing Act of 1949, through the Urban Renewal Administration Housing, and bonds issued by the California Home Finance Agency and the city. Most of the apartments were two and three bedrooms. They were the latest in modern construction techniques and provided a safe and modern living space. During this period the city also enforced de facto segregated housing primarily through renting to only African American tenants in the Western Addition. In the 1960s, a similar annex, a monolithic reinforced concrete eleven story tower, was built between Webster, Buchanan, and Turk Streets, and Golden Gate Avenue. Buchanan Street was replaced with a landscaped mall with a playground. By the end of the 1970s (in less than twenty-five years), the buildings in the Western Addition had become blighted and were a source of criminal activity, which negatively affected the surrounded areas.

Because of interior court yards and no parking, the police had a difficult time apprehending criminals. Many African American families that could afford to move did so to protect their children and families from the ongoing abuse and intimidation by criminals living in the area, and their drug dealings. The housing authority was lax in maintaining the buildings and had little on-site management or security patrols. A continual open-door policy of periodically replacing one incompetent director with another made the situation even worse. In similar fashion, their work crews would show up at the premises during the day time and proceed to do as little work as possible. The elevators were often vandalized and nonfunctional because of lack repairs. There was no attempt made to upgrade the landscaping or to paint the exteriors. The result was the warehousing (i.e., concentration) of the poor people!

As if this problem was not enough, George Christopher (the first San Francisco Greek American mayor, and, at present, the last Republican mayor from 1956–1964, who was also a major local-dairy distributor) was displeased with the slow pace that the similarly funded organization, the San Francisco Redevelopment Agency (SFRA), had been proceeding. In 1958, he replaced former Mayor Robinson's termed-out commission appointees with his own. Everett Griffin, a wealthy chemical engineer, who believed strongly in Christopher's grandiose and well-funded plans to modernize the city with a business-like approach, was appointed president of the commission. Griffin decided to replace the current director with M. Justin Herman, a Harvard University graduate. Since 1951, Herman had been the western administrator of the federal Housing and Home Finance Agency. The HHFA was the federal funding organization for urban renewal. He was confirmed by the new commission in 1959. He quickly moved to energize the urban-renewal projects in various areas of the city. In 1956, the first of the two redevelopment districts in the Western Addition was established to demolish the buildings in a two to three block swatch from Franklin Street west to Saint Josephs Avenue (later to be called the SFRA A-1 Project Area). The surrounding areas were added in 1964 as the SFRA A-2 Project Area.

At the same time, massive redevelopment areas were developing in the downtown district. The Yerba Buena Center (YBC) was planned to replace the residential hotels that were mostly occupied by retired pensioners in the middle of downtown (south of Market Street) with a gleaming, modern convention center. This development plan also consisted of hotels, parking garages, and a sports stadium, but the stadium was never built. The torturous battle of the low-income tenants and the powerful downtown interests has been well documented. The replacement of the old, centrally located food and produce market near The Embarcadero, on the waterfront, was another battle of many powerfully vested interests. This proposed SFRA development (Golden Gateway Center and Embarcadero Center) was a new city grouping of modern high-rise apartment complexes, high-rise office buildings, and hotels. This entire completed complex is in a garden setting with ground-floor, retail, and commercial store operations. The only other planned residential development at that time was the Diamond Heights Project on a sparsely settled hilltop near Twin Peaks. This SFRA-completed development incorporates a shopping center, market-rate detached homes built by Joseph Eichler, some scattered market-rate condominium complexes, as well as scattered SFHA public housing. The public housing was controversial from the beginning, and is still controversial to this day, because it is a source of criminal activity. Due to Mayor Christopher's influence, a Greek Orthodox Church was built there.

The SFRA actions in the Western Addition were to isolate and move quickly to eradicate buildings there. This immediate action, through eminent domain, sped the removal of many

African Americans, as well as others. The destruction of much of the existing housing, both residential and commercial, was widespread. In many instances, outstanding, mint-condition Victorian mansions, apartment buildings, and commercial buildings continued to be rapidly demolished in the 1960s and 1970s under Christopher's second term as mayor, and during the succeeding administrations of Mayor John Shelley (1964–1968) and Mayor Joseph Alioto (1968–1976). Mayor Christopher, who had aligned himself with downtown interests to move forward, significantly won reelection in 1959. Curiously, public outrage of his opponent's claims that his administration protected an obvious presence of the large, growing homosexual population, by not throwing them in jail, helped him win. Later, an even more enlightened city attitude toward the gay movement would have a most dramatic effect on preservation in the Western Addition as well as affecting other neighborhoods and the historical preservation movement in general.

During this period, large tracts of land were cleared. Herman, the SFRA Executive Director, was essentially the West Coast equivalent of the New York City housing czar, Robert Moses. As a memorial to Herman, a plaza in front of The Ferry Building was constructed next to "his" modern freeway along The Embarcadero, which had been stopped earlier by irate citizens at Broadway. This memorial was similar to an Egyptian pharaoh having a pyramid constructed around him, near his two greatest accomplishments, which were the Golden Gateway Center and the Yerba Buena Center. Wealthy residents of Telegraph Hill, Russian Hill, and the Marina District were very politically and financially influential in persuading Mayor Christopher to effectively stop the freeway at Broadway. Thus, the freeway did not continue farther along the bay to the Golden Gate Bridge. The Western Addition population, lacking the same political clout, was impacted by Herman's freeways with entrances and exits from Gough, Franklin, Turk, Fell, and Oak Streets. Only through major objections of effective grass-roots neighborhood groups was worse damage stopped, and the projected extensions of the freeway system were not built through the Golden Gate Park Panhandle and into the resplendently beautiful Golden Gate Park.

The Western Addition however, did not escape from the brutal destruction of its infrastructure with the expansion of Geary Street as an expressway from Van Ness Avenue to Masonic Avenue. The newly named Geary Boulevard continued west as a median-strip-

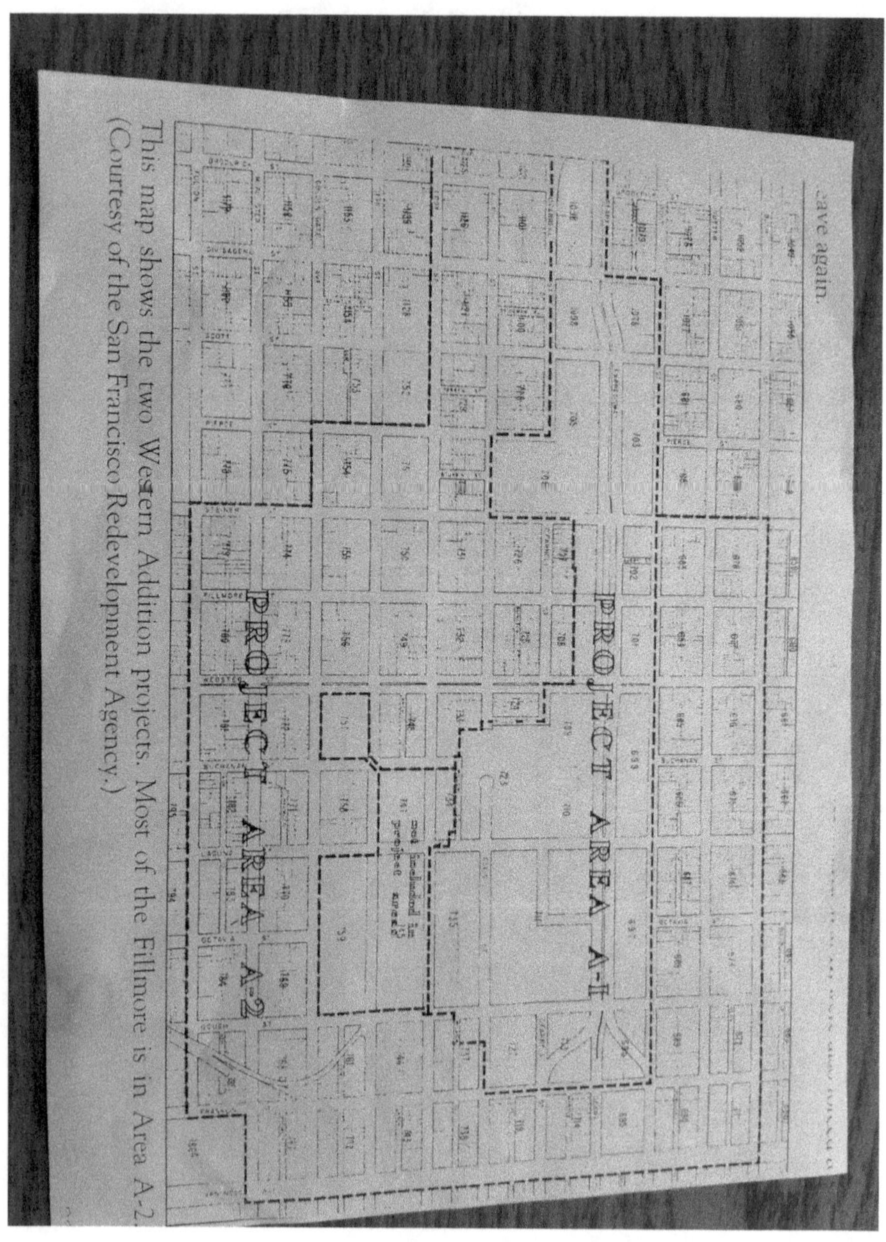

This map shows the two Western Addition projects. Most of the Fillmore is in Area A-2. (Courtesy of the San Francisco Redevelopment Agency.)

divided six-lane road to the Pacific Ocean through the Richmond District. This expressway through the Western Addition was eight lanes with a divider strip and two street-level lanes at the six-lane Fillmore Street underpass. Thus Geary Boulevard was to become a major dividing line, both physically and financially.

The street had been named for the popular John Geary, the first mayor of this new American city in 1850–1851, prior to being the last elected *alcalde* of Mexico in 1849. Later, he was appointed the third territorial governor of the Kansas-Nebraska Territory for six months, from 1856–1857. As territorial governor, he eventually favored the position of the Free State Party, i.e. the abolitionists, as well as the free soil enthusiasts, over the pro-slavery faction, which was concentrated by the actions of the residents of the neighboring state of Missouri. He then returned to his birthplace in Westmoreland County, Pennsylvania, where he became the sixteenth governor of that state from 1868 until his death in 1873.

The redevelopment area in the Western Addition was divided into the A-1 Project Area and the A-2 Project Area, which often became an indefensible, political *No man's territory*. These areas have been previously delineated. The A-3 Project Area is the famous historically landmarked Alamo Square District, saved by many dedicated preservation-oriented neighbors. They formed a neighborhood group in 1968 to protect this irreplaceable treasure of historically significant properties surrounding Alamo Square, which was called the Alamo Square Neighborhood Association (ASNA). The A-1 Project Area (essentially the center of the surrounding A-2 Project Area) was to include a modern Cathedral Hill on the east, a new Japantown in the middle, and Kaiser Permanente Hospital on the west. The complicated dynamics of this urban redevelopment plan will be explored in detail later on. The A-1 Project Area was essentially a large vacant parcel to be developed in whatever manner the redevelopment agency wished. The A-2 Project Area, approved in 1964, was more residentially and commercially mixed but would be formed by violent turf wars between neighborhood groups and the greedy special interest individuals/groups influencing the SFRA. The A-2 Project Area was approximately 277 acres.

The approximately 1,824 families and 2,698 single-person households were displaced and given certificates-of-preference to return after the new housing was finished. In many cases, these certificates were sold to secondary parties. Prior to redevelopment, the population was approximately 14,700 people. The agency identified and acquired 1,019 substandard structures, of which ninety-seven percent were demolished. Out of a total of 1,180 existing businesses, the agency relocated or otherwise removed 1,145 businesses. There was much manipulation and profiteering during this period by people of all ethnic backgrounds. The basis of several family real estate fortunes, and newly expanded construction companies, was established during those years. An example was Chester MacPhee, who was a real estate broker. As a good friend of Mayor Christopher, he was appointed, in June 1958, as Chief Administrative Officer of the city. By October, both the *San Francisco Examiner* and the *San Francisco Chronicle* newspapers exposed his relationship as a shareholder in Del Camp Investment Corporation, which bought, at cheap prices, properties that were privately owned buildings slated for future demolition. Using unethical and illegal manipulation, the corporation sold these properties to the SFRA at inflated prices. Newspaper articles that followed, in January of 1959, further exposed his vested interest in Citizen Savings and Loan Association, which was heavily investing in slum properties throughout the city. He resigned before any more articles appeared in the two leading newspapers.

Also, much of the basis for this wholesale destruction through eminent domain was sensationalized by specially slanted newspaper articles and staged photographs of grim poverty in the bleak slum-like settings of tenement-type housing. Some buildings were allowed to become even more dilapidated for the purpose of influencing neighbors to sell more quickly. The anger, from both the African American community, as well as the citizens who owned or treasured the older architecture and the diverse population of the Western Addition, occurred immediately. Under the slogan of "Black Removal," some newly activated civil-rights activists, as well as the opportunistic individuals seeking personal gain, fought or defended the SFRA. Even without the political and financial resources to fight the bureaucracy, the preservation community, many who were gay members, fought bitterly against many of the plans of the redevelopment agency. Sometimes they were successful, as in the case of the Beideman Historical District (somewhat compromised later), the Cottage Row Historical District, Endicott Court, and the Alamo Square Historical District.

Under the inept and detached leadership of the next mayor, Mayor John Shelley (who was purportedly often drunk), and his Irish American-backed political machine, the SFRA continued the same unregulated, forceful direction during his single term in office from 1964–1968. Not campaigning for a second term, this former U.S. Representative from the city had felt suddenly "unwell" and offered his support to Joseph Alioto, who had the support of the labor unions, etc. Shelley had built himself a home in the Twin Peaks area near the SFRA Diamond Heights development, with the rumored assistance of city employees. The African

American racial anger, generated by the Watts Riots of 1965 in Los Angeles, spread to San Francisco, as well as other cities. These disruptive events had a sobering effect on many San Franciscans, who would not consider venturing into the Fillmore District. The now even most exclusive, distinct, Pacific Heights (the gold coast on Broadway between Divisadero and Lyon Streets), which had been originally part of the Western Addition, became even more isolated. Mayor Joseph Alioto (1968–1976) approached the direction of the development in the Western Addition in a much more effective and conciliatory way. He was wealthy from his trial attorney business. His interest was, however, more focused on the Yerba Buena Center (the new convention center) and the Golden Gateway Center (site of the former city food market). An article in *Look* magazine implied that the mayor was a front man for the local Italian Mafia. After a lawsuit, which he won with a large settlement, the magazine would eventually cease publication. Alioto had a good relationship with the African American community and supported making them more actively involved in the daily operation of the redevelopment agency. This wild state of affairs was the background setting for our arrival into this tumultuousness mix of continually changing city policies in the Western Addition!

3.

Our Arrival

In the month of February in 1975, John Wong, my partner, and I moved to our English Arts and Crafts-style house, circa 1912, on Eddy Street between Divisadero Street and Broderick Street in the Western Addition, ***featured on this book cover.*** The house was perfect for us and was barely affordable at a purchase price of $53,500. With savings, including gifts of U.S. savings bonds from my grandmother and money borrowed from John's nursing credit union, we were able to get together a ten-percent down payment. The only willing lender, Citizens Savings and Loan, carried an eighty percent of loan-to value; a fixed, first Note and Deed of Trust for thirty years at 10.25 percent interest with monthly payments of $377. The sellers carried a ten-percent of loan-to-value; a second Note and Deed of Trust for three years at 8 percent interest. My father in the Midwest could not understand our paying so much for a house in a *marginal* neighborhood. During the first winter, with the typical heavy rains but mild weather, the hip roof leaked into the pitched-roof attic. The front flower box on the second floor leaked onto the living room window seat below, and the back of the house had many leaks from two different-level flat roofs. We placed empty five-gallon paint cans strategically throughout the house!

Our main source of happiness was the creating of a beautiful home. Also, being young and being in love made a big difference. The blazing log fire in the living room fireplace, and a functioning, central, forced-air gas furnace added more luxuriant features for us. Of course, the house was sparsely furnished from our most recent occupancy of a one-bedroom apartment in a building on Nob Hill, which was owned by John's family. But thirty-eight years later, we could claim that our home is adequately and artistically furnished. We initially fabricated furnishings by using a cheap, hollow-core door on two saw horses, covered by a linen tablecloth, as our dining-room table. Later, we replaced this makeshift table with an English-Regency Honduras mahogany table and eight chairs, circa 1910. John's income as a psychiatric nurse paid for expenses, with the monthly first-winter utility bill costing almost as much as the mortgage payments. In spite of some so-called friends not visiting because we lived in the Western Addition , and the additional snide comments of paying too much money for a *black* neighborhood, we were pleased with our neighbors and the splendid weather—little fog during the summer and mild winters. In spite of a rock being thrown through one of our front windows within two weeks of our moving in, the constant problems from the Public Housing Projects that we had not anticipated, and the devastating, mysterious arson fires occurring in a couple of nearby buildings around us, there was little to deflect us from our now treasured home. When John said, "I think we made a mistake," I reassured him that everything would be all right. Like many couples, we continued to have our differences through usually inane situations. Being a psychiatric nurse, John was probably the more empathetic partner. Although we might have some other minor problems, we, at least, did not need to worry about the additional needs of nonexistent kids (for better or worse?).

John and I fell deeply in love after a short courtship. We first met at a hippie party in a Victorian attic flat in Japantown in 1969, with the latest Beatles tune *Sergeant Pepper's Lonely Hearts Club*

Band playing. John was wearing a white nurse's uniform and a string of Buddhist beads over his short, muscular body. He looked very oriental with his goatee and mustache, which was enhanced by an ivory dragon-covered cigarette holder and his wonderful smile. He was eight years older but actually much more lively and worldly than I. However, I was a quick learner. I was also short, like my parents, and considered myself somewhat avant-garde. My physique was slight, with a twenty-eight-inch waist; long, ear-length, light-brown hair, touched up with lemon juice; a mustache like my father; gold, oval *granny* eyeglasses (at the age of ten years my parents finally recognized my need for spectacles); and I was very interested in exploring the hippie world. That evening, as I remember, I was dressed in form-fitting, butternut-colored leather bell-bottom pants (which I thought were quite provocative), tan suede boots, and a cream-colored silk shirt. The walls of the flat were covered in tinfoil, and all the drugs of the period were available—mescaline, "acid" (LSD), marijuana, hashish, and alcohol. A group of outrageously dressed drag queens, known as the *Cockettes* (West Coast *Rockette*s), who became famous later, were performing. Later, John would be responsible for calming me down after a scary, hallucinogenic, acid trip from one party.

At that time, I lived in a Victorian apartment located on California Street at Fillmore Street in the Western Addition. When I first moved in, I was approached one evening by the local drug dealer, who asked me, "Are you interested in being one of my regulars?" I was not interested. The building even had a tenant who introduced herself as a witch to me. Her husband taught at the exclusive private Town School for Boys, and they had two beautiful, blond-headed small children. The wife did indeed convince me, with her piercing green eyes, of her potential for witchcraft. I continued to see John through my next move to a one-room basement apartment with a communal bathroom in a brownstone Romanesque Revival-style mansion on Pacific Avenue. This building was located in the exclusive Pacific Heights neighborhood near Lafayette Park. Curiously, at that time, a modern apartment building across the street had an active bunch of expensive hookers and was close to Sally Stanford's (the most famous former Madam) brick Classical Revival-style mansion, circa 1905, on Pacific Avenue. Lafayette Park was my favorite place to be sunbathing in my tight, navy-blue Speedo swimsuit, to cruise the good-looking guys, and to pen something that would be famous someday.

From there, I moved, in 1970, with John into a post-earthquake (1907) North Beach building owned by his family. His mother lived with us in a flat of four rooms (two bedrooms) that was behind and attached to their building on Upper Grant Avenue, which consisted of two commercial stores on the ground floor and two flats above. The top six-room flat had been the family home, where John had lived since middle school. Across the street was the famous, predominately gay bar and restaurant the Savoy Tivoli, which featured clever revues, including the prototype for Steve Silver's *Beach Blanket Babylon.* Some of the actors were Gilda the good witch, MM candies, Christmas tree, etc. Behind his bar, Freddie Kuh also operated the lively Old Spaghetti Factory (original use) restaurant, which was decorated with his eclectic collection of objects, such as theatrical decorative sets and spaghetti manufacturing machines. John commuted from our flat in his jade-colored Volkswagen to Agnew State Hospital (near San Jose) for the *mentally insane* which was perhaps the prototype for Ken Kesey's book, *One Flew over the Cuckoo's Nest*. During this time, our gay world was similar to being members of a special fraternity. We frequented our favorite gay bars, dance clubs, and restaurants. The gay and lesbians celebrated with the now-famous Gay Pride Parade in June of 1970 to commemorate the Stonewall Uprisings in New York City the previous year. Halloween was always a madcap festival of fun and frivolity. Lively private parties and visits to hear rock music at the Fillmore West Auditorium and Winterland Auditorium (a former prize-fighting venue and then an ice-skating rink) in the Western Addition were other marvelous diversions.

During the intervals in between, I began working at the *Time-Life* magazine offices in the Flood Building (a monumental office building of Renaissance/Baroque detailing, designed by Albert Pissis in 1904) to make some money by selling their books on the telephone, *so I could continue to compose and write poetry, plays, a children's book, and short stories.* I particularly excelled in selling the art, nature, and cookbooks. According to our female office manager, African American households would order the books without any intention of paying for or returning them. On the other hand, the Hispanic American households seemed interested in purchasing them for the advancement of their children's' education. My favorite telephone call-incident occurred, when a woman started talking about knowing the *Time-Life* publisher Henry and his wife, Clare Boothe Luce. She said, "We were at their Upper East Side penthouse (New York City), and we all dropped mescaline, and Henry went out on the enclosed glass terrace and said 'these cacti are the most beautiful things that I have ever seen.'" A famous character named Rio Dante, who performed with Charles Pierce (one of the most famous and funniest female impersonators in the world), was a favorite coworker in our telephone operation. Also, there was a mysterious older gentleman, named Marko, whose father had been a famous author about Gypsy life in Hungary in the 1920s.

At nine thirty at night, I would go back to our North Beach flat, and I would usually eat my dinners at cheap restaurants along the way, such as Tad's Steak House around the corner, for $1.95 strip beef steaks, or Woy Loy Goey restaurant in Chinatown for my favorite $1.10 tomato/beef chow-mein. I continued to write, in spite of multiple rejection slips, and still hoped to write the greatest whatever. My father, a pediatrician, sent me *Roget's International Thesaurus* as a Christmas present. I am sure that he hoped I was not a complete embarrassment to the Speer family.

In 1972, John and I moved into another of his family-owned properties, a Renaissance/Baroque Arts-style Edwardian apartment building, circa 1915, of twelve units at 1145 Pine Street on Nob Hill. Our three-room sunny apartment, with views of an interior palm courtyard, was an improvement over the beatnik/hippie atmosphere of North Beach, which brings back the memories of drunks and dogs that were alternatively defecating, vomiting, and urinating on our front door steps on a sunless narrow alley. We still went to North Beach for entertainment. Coming home over Nob Hill at four in the morning, after all-night partying, and having a snack of raw fish salad or a bowl of juke (rice soup) at the twenty-four-hour Sam Woh restaurant in Chinatown, we happily felt exhausted in the morning sunlight and went to bed until twelve noon.

The Sam Woh restaurant, in a narrow three-story building with the kitchen on the main floor, was the private, upstairs stage for the eccentric and entertaining waiter Edsel Fong, who smilingly insulted his customers, who seemed initially shocked and repulsed, but later laughed; but we nevertheless gave larger tips. I usually ordered the raw fish salad, delivered on a dumb-waiter from the ground-floor kitchen. Across the street from our building at 1144 Pine Street was a modern apartment building of the 1960s, which had replaced the Fair Mansion (silver mines and the Fairmont

Hotel). But the real claim to the house history was that the last owner Sally Stanford had entertained the first United Nations delegation, in 1945, with the addition of her Jewish "girls," who would appeal to the middle-eastern delegates, taking care to not explain the heritage of the "girls."

On John's birthday, I took him to the grand Alexis Restaurant, on the top of Nob Hill, for a fabulous dinner. We had been there several times for pre-brunch and late evening cocktails, such as French 75s (champagne and brandy). The restaurant was much like the expatriate imperial white Russian bars in New York City. The ambience of this restaurant had an exotic Persian flair. From this apartment, John and I took the Grand Tour of Europe in the autumn of1973. After two months, we returned to find our apartment door wide open. We had been robbed, and I suspected the crazy apartment-house residential manager was the culprit. With foresight, we had placed our valuables with friends. In this Nob Hill location, like many neighborhoods of the sexually liberated 1970s, was provocatively, openly gay, complete with the exhibitionists' behavior of nude posturing in their street-front bay windows.

In spite of this exciting life of bar-hopping, meeting new people, and attending wild parties, some financial stabilization came with my part-time jobs. Finally, I got tired of the overwhelming number of rejection notices, with both a Bachelor's and a Master of Arts degrees, to enter the field of real estate for a more economically rewarding occupation and the freedom to travel more comfortably. After a month of intensive educational courses at the local branch of Lumbleau Real Estate School to earn a sales agency license, I became a real estate salesman. From this career change, I was able to obtain a real estate commission that went toward buying our home. My real estate career began in 1974 with a reputable firm called Roman Realty in the foggy Sunset District of the earlier-designated outside lands of sand dunes to the ocean. Jerry Bernstein, who was from Brooklyn and the son of a kosher butcher, had also just joined the company. He, his wife, and I started our promising careers at Roman Realty, as Realtors. He became quite wealthy and was the proud father of three children. He was shot and killed in his office (Bernstein Realty) in 1998 by a disgruntled client. Jerry was dead at the age of forty-three years—a real tragedy!

In the spring of 1976, with my newly acquired broker's license, after my advanced two-month course with Lumbleau Real Estate School, I established my own real estate firm. Roman Realty had rejected my proposal of becoming a partner. My initial corporation stock investors were several recent northern Chinese immigrants, via Hong Kong and Taiwan. I shall always be extremely grateful for their assistance. The name of my firm is Robert L. Speer and Associates, Inc. My many *colorful* associates over the years to date would make an interesting book. My first office consisted of a front reception room with my future secretary separated from my private office by a frosted-glass wall in a vertically mahogany-paneled frame (very 1960s). The location was on the sixteenth floor of the magnificently massive Russ Building in the financial district. My newly hired, taller, older, plump, and adorable English secretary, Miss Olga M. Treusein was a formidable presence. She would say, "I will sit on you if you do not agree with my English Spelling vs. American English." She was usually wrong. Her parents had been in the English civil service in Singapore and were murdered in a Japanese camp during World War II, while she was studying at Cambridge University in England. She encouraged me to join her fascinating English Speaking Union group. So I did join and shall be always fascinated by the mutual ethnic superiority of this exclusive club experience. At this time, I started wearing a suit with a white shirt and tie, and have continued to do so throughout my entire real estate career.

The historic Montgomery Street Russ Building skyscraper with Gothic ornamentation was built in 1927. The architect was George Kelham. I enjoyed my time there, but I decided that the downtown, commercial real estate world was too restrictive with its *Old Boy* network. I was also more interested in selling residential, historical buildings in the Western Addition and the Haight-Ashbury. When I was at Roman Realty, many of the realtors had been appalled that I would sell property and hold Sunday open-houses in these *black* neighborhoods.

Although my father approved of my new profession, he was disappointed when I sold my fire-engine red 1972 Pontiac firebird and purchased my silver 1978 Cadillac Seville with grey leather upholstery. He had said, "How can you afford the payments?" I said, "The monthly lease payments are affordable." The enterprising and gregarious Frank Lembi, the owner of Skyline Realty, had said, "Speer, to be successful you need to drive a Cadillac. Tell them at Bianco Cadillac in Marin County that I said they should give you a good deal." I loved that car and drove it until 2000, when I purchased a 2001 dark green S-type Jaguar from British Motors. My father had been saying, "You should not be throwing away so much money on that old car and should buy a new car every four years." Like my father suggested, I bought a new ebony colored 2004 XJ8 Jaguar with biscuit-colored upholstery. I believe that whatever automobile I drove made little business difference, but I liked quality.

Later in 2010, the somewhat eighty-five-year-old Frank Lembi, whose family was allegedly the largest owner of apartment buildings (three hundred plus) in San Francisco, was forced into bankruptcy proceedings on two hundred of these properties, because of the Great Recession. He had always wanted me to join his firm. But I said, "Frank, I don't want to be in court every month over real estate transactions, even if you have four attorneys." I admired his charisma and even bought stock in his Continental Savings and Loan Company, which was to fail financially.

In 1979, I relocated my office to a building that we bought in the heart of the gay Castro District, at Castro at Eighteenth Streets in the Upper Market district. By 1994, I established an early Internet connection with a computer technician through a website, which became www.sfproperty.com, at my insistence. This home page has an image of the eighteenth-century Giovanni Battista Pirinasi etching of one of my favorite buildings, the Pantheon. Emperor Hadrian had constructed this temple in Rome between 118–128 CE. This building replaced an earlier temple, circa 27–25 BCE, dedicated to the Olympian gods, which had been destroyed in a fire. Our office motto is the sale of *architecturally and historically significant* buildings in the spirit of the Pantheon.

4.

Our Home

Our Edwardian home in the Western Addition is an English Arts and Crafts style house of approximately three thousand square feet, which was built in 1912 for a prominent Irish American physician, Dr. George J. Sweeney. This well-proportioned house was designed by a draftsman named Harry E. Nye, who was intensively involved with the Panama Pacific International Exposition. The two-story, brown, wooden-shingled house has also a full attic under a hip roof and a partial basement. The exterior trim is painted a cream color, and the wooden casement windows are accented with gloss-black paint. Much of the handsome original interior detailing is intact. The house consisted of six rooms with servant quarters at the rear of the house, and it originally had a slate roof, which was replaced later with asphalt shingles. The inset entrance door faces east onto a square open-covered front porch, which is approached from the south by eight steps, which were both constructed of maroon, white, and black mixed-colored terrazzo. We felt this alignment encouraged good Feng Shui. The house is oriented so that during fall and winter, sunlight streamed in when the sun was lower on the horizon. Then during summer, the sun is overhead and the backyard is brightly lit and the interior is filled with a soft, glowing sunlight. The combination of this dramatic light, along with occasional annual summer fog banks floating in from the Pacific Ocean, produces a particularly dramatic luminosity.

The interior on the ground floor consists of a central square entry hall with three-quarter wainscot paneling and crown moldings finished in mahogany-stained original-growth redwood. The same nine-foot ceilings and golden oak floors exist throughout the house. From the entry hallway radiate the main floor rooms and a squared staircase, which flows gracefully to the second floor. During the winter and spring, sunlight streams through the windows and a free-hanging Chinese wooden carved panel, projecting beautiful, elaborate patterns on the staircase walls. A powder room had been created by the previous owner from the original hall clothes closet, underneath the staircase. To the left of the square entry hall is the living room, which can be separated by a heavy, sliding pocket door. The large south-facing living room has the same crown moldings but knee-high wainscoting paneling, which is much lower than the entry hall. This room features a coal-burning fireplace with a substantial mahogany-stained redwood mantel. The room also has a series of vertical front and side horizontal casement windows that conveniently pivot in the middle so the exterior glass can be cleaned. These windows allow generous light and ventilation into the room. To the right of the hallway are the entrance doorways to the dining room and the kitchen The dramatic formal dining room features an original, branched, brass chandelier with frosted-glass shades, a built-in, leaded-glass paneled china cabinet, the same three-quarter wainscot paneled walls with a top detailing (combining the basic lower Celtic-pattern frieze, applied gilded-gold oak fleur-de-lis reliefs, and gilded, egg-dart molding), a wallpapered panel and a wide, crown molding. The ceiling and side wall panels are covered with spectacularly colored William Morris-patterned wallpaper accented with small areas of sky blue sparkling with four-inch gold stars. The dining room has a large east-facing, square bay window with three casement windows and a view across the driveway of a sixteen-foot trellis covered with bright purple, pink, and magenta fuchsias. Next to the dining room doorway is the doorway to the original kitchen, and also the servant's quarters, which consist of a bathroom, living area, and bedroom. A back door leads to side porch stairs, detailed with lattice, to the garden. Throughout, the hardware is solid brass and the door knobs are beveled glass.

The second-floor plan has a sunny, south-facing master bedroom with a fireplace and a well-proportioned, painted mantel. This bedroom is located above the living room and featured a large flower box above the square bay window below. Two smaller bedrooms are at the rear, and one of these bedrooms still has the original coal-burning fireplace. Originally, there was a rear laundry room off one of the bedrooms, and an enclosed open-air deck with a glass greenhouse for orchids off the other bedroom. In the upstairs hallway, there is a Victorian English-style split bathroom with a toilet room and a separate bathtub room, which was still popular at the time of construction.

All of the walls are the original plaster, reinforced with horse hair, over wood lath. The lighting was originally serviced by heavy-gauge copper wiring, sheathed in heavy insulation, which was reutilized in the house. The original gas lines to the light fixtures had been capped off many years previously because they were unnecessary. Most of the original hardware and light fixtures, including push-button switches, are still in place. There is a partial basement under the back kitchen and servant quarters, and a high crawl space in the front. The foundation is built with a sixteen-inch wide brick layering, a four-inch thick old-growth Douglas fir mud sill as well as the same Douglas fir balloon-frame supporting timbers, which are all oversized from the normal construction techniques at that time.

The originally dilapidated, detached garage with the original track sliding carriage doors is at the rear of the lot, and it is serviced from the front street by a paved driveway with a middle grass space. Eventually I filled in this middle grass space with paving blocks that had been brought to San Francisco as ballast for sailing ships and used to pave the original muddy downtown city streets. A neglected surrounding yard, including a set-back for the front yard, has some of the original existing mature plantings, such as the vibrant purple bougainvillea vine on the front of the house, established rose bushes, lilacs, and several trees, both ornamental and fruit producing. The spaciousness of this garden is particularly attractive to me, with my Midwestern roots. The large lot size, which was 45 feet wide by 137.5 feet deep, is larger than most other housing in San Francisco and is almost a double (earlier Spanish measurement) *vara* (25 feet by 137.5 feet) lot.

5.

Our Autobiographies

JOHN WONG

John Wong was born July 14, 1935 (Bastille Day), the second-oldest child, but the first son of the second wife. He had grown up in a crowded family-owned two-flat building in Chinatown, on John Street. This one-block-long street later was called "Coffin Street" by the Chinese because of the Cathay Mortuary located there. All six siblings slept with their parents in one bedroom of the four-room flat at the top of the building. Their father worked hard to accumulate a modest amount of money and bought the building from an Italian American family with the assistance his older, adult daughter, who was an American citizen. He had been financially devastated earlier in the stock market crash of 1929. However, he was not bitter, and went back to work in the prestigious Richelieu Hotel dining room to accumulate money, which he safely deposited with the Bank of America. In 1948, when the Chinese immigrants were allowed to buy property without the usual earlier ploy of using the name of a surrogate owner or native-born relative, he purchased, in his name, a residential/commercial building, circa 1907, in North Beach on Upper Grant Avenue. The family occupied the third-story, six-room flat. The building also had a roof deck above the attached, separate, small, two-flat building behind on Bannam Place. The other units, including the basement, were either rented to family members or to the two commercial tenants.

Earlier Chinese Americans were often taunted and abused physically by the Italian Americans on the north side of Broadway. John's father related that their queues would be yanked at or bodies beaten, but insulting remarks always went both ways. The Chinese soon learned to run faster and a few carried threatening chopping knives, which were rarely used. The Italian Americans were mostly able to artificially contain them on the south side until 1943, when the Federal Chinese Exclusion Act of 1882 (first US immigration law to target one ethnic group) was repealed. His father had come to the United States originally in 1896 under an assumed name, or a "paper name", of an existing Chinese American citizen, and had various jobs before buying a small, twenty-four seat counter and booth café in the Tenderloin district, which he could call his own, in 1943.

John's mother was the second wife and a picture bride. His father had sent ship-passage money for her to immigrate to the United States. She was to be the mother of six children (one died in infancy) and a stepmother to eight children. During World War II, his petite, attractive mother worked patriotically in the shipyards as a broom sweeper in a war production plant. She was proud of her bib-overall blue jeans, red bandanna wrap on her head, and her black, metal lunch pail. She also worked in Chinatown sweatshops, often bringing home garments to be sewn. Before and after the war, she and the older two children also helped out at the Larkin Café, next the Larkin Theater, which showed art films and much later porno. While her husband cooked American-style food, she helped peel potatoes and wash dishes. One older sister was a waitress at various hotel dining rooms and the café. When she got married and moved away, the other older sister became the sole waitress at the twenty-four-seat café. John often helped as a cashier to count the evening receipts using an abacus, which his father had taught him how to use. The handsome, tall, blond haired, blue-eyed Caucasian theater manager was a frequent diner here and John excitedly conversed with him about the mysterious "white" world. He would invite John to see for free, such movies as the Russian *The Battleship Potemkin*. John also enjoyed watching his father cook and was rewarded with tasty meals, such as pan-fried liver with onions, meat loaf, and roast turkey. In the early morning, John accompanied his father to the city wholesale produce market to procure bruised vegetables and fruit that were not acceptable for the retail grocery stores. Only left over bread from their cafe was brought home and meat was a rare home luxury. Every Sunday, a live chicken capitulated from its back porch cage to the dinner table. They gradually adapted to their heavily Italian North Beach neighborhood but their schools outside of this area were still much segregated by neighborhoods.

John went first to Commerce High School, which had a high number of African Americans who were the children of the recent immigrants coming west to provide labor for the war industry. After transferring to Galileo High School, John graduated with honors in 1953. He also received the Bausch & Lomb Honorary Science Award for scientific scholarship. John's family was quite close-knit and everyone, including often untraditionally married daughters and their spouses, came for the freshly killed chicken dinner every Sunday. His father was a member of the small Lew Family Association. His mother was a member of the much larger Lee Family Association. So John's family celebrated all the Chinese special occasions in both family association buildings. Vendors in markets and stores would know his family when his father's name was mentioned. Family members felt both captured and captivated by this exotic Chinatown community on lower Grant Avenue. In contrast, their visits to the bustling department stores on Market

Street, such as The Emporium, and the nearby grand movie palaces, such as the Fox, Warfield, and Orpheum, were always special events. All expenditures were considered carefully and were precious. All of the children from John's father's family with his second wife went on to college. In 1957, John graduated from the University of California at Berkeley with a Bachelor of Science degree in public health. His older sister graduated with a Doctorate of Medicine from Howard Medical School in Washington, D.C., He joined the U.S. Navy Reserves and served the required two years of active duty.

Then he returned to his North Beach home. Not knowing how to, and perhaps not wanting to, work in a Public Health vocation, he soon was engaging in the Bohemian/Beatnik lifestyle of North Beach. After a telephone call from his sister, a doctor now and psychiatric resident at Agnew's State Hospital for the mentally ill on a large, sprawling, self-sufficient farm-like setting near San Jose, he went to work there and concurrently went to school for his RN degree. During his early nursing years, he lived in the lower four-room flat on Bannam Place. He soon melted into the North Beach milieu. He painted his flat black and covered the floors in a wall-to-wall orange shag carpet. With a black wooden platform for flamenco dancing and a beat-up upright player piano, he held many, mostly impromptu parties with the latest popular and jazz music playing in the background. Wearing his black beatnik clothing or Levis, he cooked many large pots of spaghetti and tomato sauce, spiced with marijuana, and offered a plentiful number of gallon jugs of Mountain Red, a California wine. It was "open house" at John's place late in the evening after the local bars closed. When his widowed mother, who spoke very little English, vacated her large Grant Avenue flat for additional income, she and John moved into the upper two-bedroom flat on the one block long Bannam Place. I moved in with them in 1969.

John then transferred, in 1972, to Langley Porter Psychiatric Institute at the University of California San Francisco (UCSF). The transfer from one state institution to another was due to the passage of a State law called the Lauterman-Pettis-Short Act of 1967, which required that the mentally ill be transferred from concentrated institutional housing to housing in their own local communities with access to counselors. The concept at that time was that the mentally ill could be treated with medicine in a friendlier environment. In 1978, he was accepted to work at Mount Zion Hospital as the evening charge nurse and was within walking distance to our home. He reluctantly retired in 1992, shortly after the hospital was bought by UCSF, due to being overloaded with several nursing roles, which effected his health. A year later, the psychiatric unit was closed and the famous 1950 building designed by Eric Mendelson was utilized for oncology care.

ROBERT LELAND SPEER

My paternal background began with the 1765 arrival in the future United States of America by Robert Speer (originally Spier, Spiers, Speere, Spear or Spyer for the Scottish lookout in the church tower watching for an English invasion), who was a United Presbyterian escaping the *troubles* in Ireland (Ulster) specifically County Tyrone. He purchased farm land (220 acres in Adams County, Pennsylvania) from the Penn Proprietary Land Trust. The nearby town of Gettysburg would later be the Civil War battle site that turned the tide of war against the Confederacy. Robert Speer lived from 1735–1813. He had some army duty in the Revolutionary War. The family intermarried with fellow Scotch-Irish Americans (lowland Scottish reformed Presbyterians) who had immigrated to Northern Ireland in the early 1600s. This clannish family tradition of intermarriage continued up to my father's generation. One daughter of an ancestor was the mother of U.S. President James Buchanan, who has been the only bachelor President and was perhaps gay. Robert's wife (nee Stuart) had a free, Negro, female dependent named Deff, who is buried next to both of them. Their son Stuart, like many of their children, was quite enterprising. He operated, as did his father, a profitable distillery, which extracted whiskey and brandy from rye and peaches. In conjunction, he opened a tavern popular with teamsters who came along the road in caravans of long, English-bed wagons drawn by six horses and laden with merchandise for other distant markets. The majority of the generally large Scotch-Irish families practiced both sobriety and thrift. They were strictly abolitionists. As their financial circumstances improved and cheaper land was available, our family members like Stuart migrated gradually to Ohio in the early 1800s.Some moved further west to the Kansas territory in the late 1860s.

My great-grandfather, William Scott Speer (1839–1925), served in the Civil War with the Seventy-Eighth Regiment of the Ohio Volunteer Infantry (O.V.I) and fought alongside the Eighteenth O.V.I., a Negro brigade, with General Sherman in his *March to the Sea* campaign through the Confederacy. In 1868, William Speer homesteaded a fertile 160-acre farm in Johnson County, Kansas near Kansas City. He was on many county commissions and served for one session (1902–1904) in the Kansas State House of Representatives. He was not as strident an abolitionist as the earlier New England-bred settlers from Boston, Massachusetts, in efforts to keep Kansas as a "Free State," but he strongly believed, as an abolitionist, that everyone should have the equal rights that were mandated in the Emancipation Proclamation. He had become a member of the Republican Party because of his great admiration for President Lincoln, like many other family members. His farm was near Black Bob Road, named after an early Osage Chief settler who owned land there in accord with earlier peace treaties dating from 1830. These treaties were continually broken or renegotiated. In 1854 for example, the Kansas-Nebraska Territory was proclaimed through treaties, with President Pierce, to be opened for settlement and the American Indians were to resettle farther west. A quarter-section (160 acres) could be purchased for $200. The new settlers would determine whether Kansas was admitted as a free or slave state. Thus, *bleeding* Kansas became a prelude to the Civil War, with battles between the Free State party and the Pro-Slavery party (mostly nearby residents of the State of Missouri). The free-soil leader James Lane, a radical Democrat suggested, "Any black man, slave or not, should not be allowed to live in the new state!"

My great grandfather was buried in the nearby Olathe City Cemetery in the Civil War Memorial area, where the maternal great-great grandfather of President Barack Obama is also buried (150 feet from the Speer plot). The name of the President's ancestor was Robert Wolfley (1835–1895), and he served in Company-A 145th Ohio Infantry, which was formed to protect Washington, D.C. He moved from Ohio to a farm in Johnson County in 1865 and thus, in all likelihood, he knew my great grandfather. They were both to retire to Olathe and were greatly respected by the populace.

My grandfather Newton Clark Speer (1876–1947) was one of the two sons born to the devout Julia Henderson, who was the second wife of William Scott and the sister of a man in his Civil War Company. Her brother had been in the same regiment, as William

Scott. The first wife died and only a son named Henry (1866–1954) survived two sisters in infancy. My grandfather grew up on the family farm and made regular visits to the nearby Johnson County seat of Olathe. He graduated from medical school in Kansas City (later KU Medical Center) and established his practice with his physician brother, William Louis (1879–1957), in Osawatomie, Kansas. He married the devout college-educated Clara Alice Aiken (1880–1979), whose wealth father owned several farms and a mercantile store in a small nearby town of Richmond, which was like so many other prospering early towns, located close to a railroad station. They both practiced sobriety. Her family name of Aiken is Scottish for an acorn, and she was, like my grandfather Newton Clark, from Scotch-Irish parentage. John Aiken emigrated, in 1789, from County Antrim, (Ulster) Ireland to Washington County, Pennsylvania. My handsome grandparents had four children named Robert Louis, Muriel, Frederic Aiken, and my father Leland Newton (1912–1994). My grandmother designed their two-story colonial-style home, which was located next to a city park where John Brown's original log cabin had been relocated. My father missed the important visit in August, 1910, of President Theodore Roosevelt, who gave his famous New Nationalism speech. The central issue was government protection of human welfare and property rights. On December 6, 2011, President Barack Obama gave an economic speech, reprising many of Roosevelt's themes, in the Osawatomie High School. My grandfather moved his family, in the early 1922, to Kansas City, Missouri, and his medical practice to the Armourdale district of Kansas City, Kansas, which had a large concentration of railroad yards. Besides general practice, he was surgeon for the Kansas City Terminal Railroad, Griffin Wheel, Fiber Box, and Railroad Ice. He was an excellent physician and quite popular with his patients. He left the care of his children largely to his wife and was hostile to religion. My father went to high school in Kansas City, Missouri, and then graduated from the University of Kansas at Lawrence.

My mother's side of the family arrived in the future United States in about 1700 from Amsterdam, Holland, with Frederick Iceler (c.1680–1796), who was from one of the many individual principalities that were later incorporated into Germany. He spoke five languages. In America, he settled on the south branch of the Potomac River in Virginia. Frederick raised his family on a prosperous farm there. In 1745, he with one son traveled by wagon to have their grain milled at grist mill some distance away. In their absence, a Mohawk Indian scouting party raided his household, killed his wife, and kidnapped their children (two girls and a boy). One of his daughters married an Indian chief, and from their progeny came the Prophet Teliskwatawa and the well-known chief Tecumseh, who learned from their mother to read and speak English. The son, who was captured at the age of ten years, lived and learned from his captors; but he never forgot his roots. At the age of eighteen years, while on a war-scouting party with his captors, he escaped wearing his Indian buckskin clothing. By horseback, he fled to Fort Pittsburg (Pennsylvania). William. "Indian Billy" (1735–1826) was reunited shortly thereafter with his father Frederick, who gave him five hundred acres in West Virginia. He would continue to accumulate much more land in both West Virginia and Pennsylvania. He sired ten children.

During the interval prior to the reunion with his son William, Frederick had shortened the family name to Ice and had established a second family in West Virginia. His son David Adam, from this second marriage, was born in 1767, and was the first white child west of the Allegany Mountains. Frederick established, with another son Thomas, in 1781, Ice's Ferry on the Cheat River near Morgantown, and they lived on an island in the middle of the river. George Washington used their ferry in 1784 and commented about Frederick in his diary. Thomas (1808–1896), who married a wife of the Virginia Confederacy, sold the ferry and a grist mill in 1886 to follow many other extended family members, including his five-foot tall son Thomas Jr. (1845–1930) with his five-foot, six-inch wife, all of whom had already moved earlier to Douglas County, Kansas in the 1870s. Thomas Jr. was distinguished looking with his white goatee. He chewed tobacco most of his life.

My mother's paternal grandfather, George W. Ice (1836–1924), immigrated to Douglas County to be near his brother, Thomas Jr., and other family members After George's first wife's death; he remarried a wealthy physician's widow from Texas. My grandfather, Emery Ice (1884–1927), came from this issue of the first wife. Altogether, George Ice had fourteen children. My mother, Frances Elizabeth Ice (born 1914), often relates that her grandfather, with his piercing blue eyes, on a visit from Texas, said to his six-year old granddaughter, "I can tell you're a black-eyed devil!"

My mother's maternal grandmother, Mary Emaline Eberhart (1860–1947), came from well-established Lutheran (German Reformed Church) stock. Mary Emaline's ancestors emigrated from Germany, in 1727, to Philadelphia, Pennsylvania. They first settled in Westmoreland County (Pennsylvania), where the first San Francisco mayor, John Geary, hailed from. Several of Mary Emaline's kinfolk had been soldiers in the American Revolution. German had been strongly considered as the national language because of the preponderance of German immigrants. The Eberharts, like the Speer families, began to gradually move west as new territories that offered more desirable, fertile soil for farming became available. In 1854, several relatives migrated to Lawrence, Kansas, the abolitionist main settlement in Douglas County, and settled nearby on various adjacent farms. Mary Emaline was born on her father's farm southwest of Pleasant Grove in 1860. The area that they settled was mainly the Wakarusa Creek Valley, which would be the site of many skirmishes between the free-state and pro-slavery factions fighting over the status of statehood for Kansas.

The aforementioned Mary Emaline married John George Gimblett (Welsh American descent) in 1885. John George was born in 1857, in Allegany County, Pennsylvania, and came to Kansas in 1859, with his family. This Eberhart German ancestry seemed to evolve from the Dunker religious sect. My great-grandmother, Mary Emaline, continued, as a married woman, to wear her simple grey dress and bonnet. Their daughter, Effie Mae Gimblett (1888–1929), married Emery Ice in 1911. My mother Frances Elizabeth Ice (1914) was one of their children. She was a tomboy, to the great delight of both her grandfather Gimblett and her father, Emery. Emery was a farmer, who supplemented his income as a railroad worker. Without the modern benefit of antibiotics, he died of a burst appendix at the early age of forty-three years in the Lawrence City hospital. It was fortunate that my mother saw him before he died in 1927, because he told her what a wonderful child that she was.

Her mother, Effie Mae Gimblett Ice, was left a widow with three girls and three boys in the remote rural area of the Wakarusa Creek valley. She was murdered more than a year later, in 1929, while drawing water from a creek near their cottage. The murderer was never apprehended, probably because they were a poor family. Most of her children found homes with relatives. But, my fourteen-year-old mother moved to the Lawrence home of their local postman to clean house and to take care of his older mother-in-law. Frances Ice graduated from Lawrence City High School with honors. She quickly realized, after sexual advances from the postman, that she would be more comfortable moving to Kansas City, Missouri, into another domestic job there. After a sexual advance from the old uncle of an Italian American family, she decided to go to nursing school at Bethany Hospital in Kansas City, Kansas.

During the late 1930s, my distinguished-looking and well-dressed father, Leland Newton Speer, who was five feet, six inches, with a thin, well-trimmed mustache, courted my mother. He had graduated in 1937 from the University of Kansas Medical School, as had his father. After an internship and residency, he started his own pediatric medical practice in Kansas City, Kansas. He had not been required by the medical school to bring his own cadaver, purchased from a grave robber, unlike his physician father.

On a warm day in July 1941, my father, Leland, married my attractive, brunette mother, Frances, in her white gown, at the First Methodist Church in Lawrence. He wore his formal, white, naval officer reserve uniform. Prior to their marriage, my mother was determined to succeed in Kansas City in spite of her poor, rural background and the Great Depression Era. She had graduated from nursing school in Kansas City, Kansas, and then became an airline hostess (acceptable hostesses had to be registered nurses and under 5 feet, 6 inches in height). She flew only domestically with TWA (Trans World Airlines) from 1937 to 1941, including flights on DC-2s, DC-3s, and an inaugural flight on the Boeing Stratoliner—"hotel in the sky"—with the first pressurized cabin. TWA thought this airplane was too expensive and sold their fleet of four to the U.S. government for use in World War II. Mother was photographed near ice sculptures advertising TWA because of her family name (Ice) and her beauty. She caught the eyes of many men. One airline pilot told her, "I would like to melt that Ice." A few smitten state governors with proclamations of welcome and golden keys, as well as wealthy businessmen and movie stars, were entranced by her and admired her well-trained ability as an airline hostess. She was proud, witty, secure of herself, and able to ward off advances by potential suitors. She would inspire me with her stories about the magical city of San Francisco, where she was the first TWA representative at *The Golden Gate International Exposition* on Treasure Island in 1939 for a month. She later joined a group of retired TWA airline hostesses, known as The Clipped Wings club.

My father was called up in December of 1942, to active duty from the Naval Reserves to serve in World War II in the Pacific Theater. He flew out of San Francisco (my future home) on a Pan American Clipper. Prior to my parent's marriage, he had purchased, in Kansas City, Kansas, a two-bedroom 1940s English village-style stucco-covered bungalow. My mother lived there during his absence. After his departure, in December 1942, my birth, as Robert Leland, was registered in the newspapers on January 1, 1943. Later, growing up as a youngster, my wise father said in his WASP manner. "You should only appear in the newspapers as being born, married, or deceased." My Uncle Frederic Aiken Speer, also a physician, substituted as her obstetrician, since my mother's personal obstetrician had been called up for active duty.

My uncle's wife, Aunt Jeanette, told me many years later, "You were very ornery as a child." After my birth, Frederic had shortly joined my father in the Pacific Theater. He sent my mother in a newly discovered vintage war V-mail which stated that after he looked in their camp at my father's photograph of me at that age of three months, that I looked ornery. These many treasured letters to my mother from my father, as well as my uncle, have been all been preserved. After the war, my Uncle Frederic was an acknowledged pediatric allergist and a published author on that specialty. He would later say to the author Richard Yates of *Revolutionary Road* fame, when Yates asked to marry his daughter Martha, who could have been Yates's daughter and was a student at Iowa State University, "I have many daughters; choose anyone of them as one less is not important." He and Aunt Jeanette had seven daughters, one son, and an adopted second son. At some point, my Grandmother Speer would ask my father, "Please tell Frederic about birth control."

After a difficult child birth, I became the first Speer grandson of that generation of my family. My grandfather, Newton Clark, was divorced before the end of the war from his brilliant, politically active wife, who also wrote poetry. He doted on me and my mother, and even bought me a pedigreed wire-haired terrier. Friends of our family presented me with the prerequisite sterling silver baby cup with an engraved old English letter S, which I delighted banging around. My future siblings would also be presented with their own cups.

My grandmother, Clara Aiken Speer, had been a Republican activist in the 1930s as part of the movement to oust Tom Prendergast's political machine in Kansas City, Missouri. Harry Truman was one of his protégé's. Pendergast owned a concrete company and with his political influence, his company provided the concrete to build the city hall, county court house, pavement for streets such as Ward Parkway, as well as the pavement of Brush Creek. Surprisingly, he was convicted and jailed, not for his graft, but for his tax evasion. Perhaps, unexpected future benefits occurred from these grand public works projects. My grandmother was also strongly supportive, both vocally and financially, of the United Negro College Fund, which she felt was the best direction for Negroes to take to be fully accepted. The Presbyterian Church and its missions to China and India also received much support from her. She was diminutive in stature, but a strongly opinionated woman. Her political convictions garnered much support, and she was elected, as a Republican, in 1946 to the Missouri House of Assembly to serve six terms (1946–1958) from the Country Club District in Kansas City. She assumed the role of fighting "the cigar smoking and bourbon drinking" Democrats. Being a teetotaler, she said later, "In conciliation, I once had some soda water with the *boys* at a cocktail party in Jefferson City, the capital." In 1952, she published a book of poetry, *Sonnets for Eve* dedicated to her then sixteen grandchildren.

The earlier-mentioned war correspondence from my father to my mother from New Caledonia via V-mails is filled with love and appreciation for the many received photographs of mother and me. With coupons, a check from the Navy for my father's pay, and rent from a female roommate from our Washington Avenue Methodist Church (Methodist Episcopal until 1939), my mother was able to manage with some stability during the War. She had this genteel graciousness, which people around her liked, and they offered extra care and help. She was able to get new tires and extra gasoline for their Model-A Ford coupe with ration coupons, through the kindness of an older gas-station owner, always attired in his proper Standard Oil uniform. Her younger brother, who was exempted from war-time duty for being a farmer, provided extra amounts of pork, chicken, eggs etc., to supplement her war-time rationing. She eagerly volunteered with the Red Cross to support the troops in the war effort. In 1944, my father returned to the United States on the Matson Liner *Lurline*, entering at the port of San Francisco.

Then we moved from Kansas City to Cherry Point Naval Air Station, North Carolina, for the duration of the war. My mother and father and I traveled there in our Model-A Ford, but our personal possessions traveled by freight train. My blond blue-eyed sister, Andrea Frances, was born at the nearby Camp Lejeune Marine Hospital. My father had been transferred by the Navy early in the war to serve with the Marines as their physician. Our family was housed in a two-story, brick home for the family of an officer. The purportedly gay movie star, Tyrone Power, also a Navy officer, and his wife, Annabelle, were living at the same base and my parents became somewhat friendly with them. Attached to the house were the servants' quarters, where an African American couple from Chicago, Jerothra and her Marine husband, were assigned to assist with household duties. My mother acquired, through social conversations, several local low-land North Carolina cooking recipes that we enjoyed in our childhood, such as black-eyed peas, grits, and mush. We had a particular fondness for the regional, seasoned seafood, which was new and different from anything we tasted in Kansas City.

After the war, forwarding ahead, we moved with wardrobe trunks and baggage, back to Kansas City, Kansas, in 1945, where our family increased by two more sons, George Edward (1949) and Charles Frederic (1953). Both of my six-foot brothers would mature from being swim-team leaders to professional leaders (respectively, an emergency room physician and an environmental attorney). My brothers would be referred to in the future as Baby Boomers. My sister and I were war babies, or Traditionalists. Interestingly, even with common bonding, there was a different generational sense in our outlook toward music, art, literature, etc. My sister and I experienced the horse-drawn, enclosed, Manor bread wagon, as well as milk delivered at our doorstep. My brothers grew up with television. George even asked our father, "What did you do in the evening before TV?" My father countered, "We had a radio!"

My father returned to his practice of pediatrics and was later elected president of the state medical society. Politically, he was a Republican, like his parents, and in 1972 he was elected to the Kansas State House of Representatives, like his grandfather. Surprisingly, he represented a heavily Democratic district. One of his local colleagues in the legislature was a democrat named Cordell Meeks, an African American, who served a long time in the legislature, and who my father greatly respected. My father eventually reached the rank of captain in the Naval Reserves, but thought he deserved to be promoted to the rank of admiral. He was probably right considering his Air Medal for Meritorious Achievement and Distinguished Flying Cross, as well as his quite active participation in the Reserves. After he died, in 1994, at the age of eighty-two, he would have been a tombstone admiral (a higher rank on death), if not for the changes in the U.S. Navy's procedures.

My mother, being the wife of a prominent physician and community leader, was always fashionably dressed in public settings. Mother always wore her stylish dresses or tailored suits, her chic hats sometimes with mesh veils, her stylish, high-heeled shoes and gloves. In our family setting, she was the model of the domestic image of the 1950s— taking care of her children and providing a comfortable domestic setting with her own excellent middle western cooking and unusual additions, such as avocado salads and Chung King canned Chinese food (Kansas City had only two Chinese restaurants at that time).. She was assisted early on by a young

African American mother, who quit after six months because she found a more profitable job in a local automobile plant. For a long time afterward, mother was assisted by two older Swedish American sisters who alternated as house cleaners and baby sitters. In addition to her own cooking and shopping for groceries, she frequently entertained relatives and friends at dinners for various holiday events. She devoted much time to the Woman's Auxiliary of the Kansas Medical Society (state officer), Republican Federation of Women (state president), Methodist church circle, and the Junior League.

As an invited Junior League escort, I attended (wearing a tuxedo with black bow tie) the Junior League Community Ball and Cotillion in December 1959. The hotel ballroom was elaborately decorated like a winter scene and Charles-Emile Walteufel's *Skaters Waltz* was played by a small orchestra for the dancing escorts. The debutants wore short, white, ballerina taffeta gowns with white fur muffs and hats decorated with fresh holly. I was enthralled. My dance partner was, however, the rather dowdy and uninteresting daughter of the Irish American Roman Catholic County Assessor. After the first dance, I went over to ask for a dance with my mother, who was wearing a turquoise, silk sheath gown with a large rhinestone pin. She said as we danced, "You're not nearly as good as your father." I was mildly amused because I knew dad was always socially popular as a dance partner.

Also, mother became an active participant in the Blue Birds, Campfire Girls, Cub Scouts, and Boy Scouts. I received the Eagle Scout and the God and Country awards, as well as participated in the World Jamboree in the Philippines during the summer of 1959. Mother's efforts were selfless in supporting her children's activities. She was strict, but loving. If we didn't finish our food, she would say, "You know there are children starving in China." As the eldest child, I seemed to get more spankings from both parents than my siblings. My mother's favorite threat was, "You behave or we will send you to military school!"

With mother's moxie and her own automobile—a 1953 emerald green and ivory Kaiser Manhattan, then later 1957 silver Pontiac Bonneville—she organized our annual summer moves from our three-story Tudor-style townhouse (circa 1928, on a double-tiered terrace) to the country. Our 126-acre farm was located only twenty minutes from my father's office. We all were always excited to be there and riding our Shetland ponies (Betty Boop and her off-spring Bennie) and horses (Dublin, which was my father's Tennessee-Walker), and playing with our three neutered-male *through the use of a rubber band* goats, feral barn cats, and dogs (two short-haired collies and our Saint Bernard, Prince). On an idyllic hill-top location with refreshing cooling crosswinds, we lived in a remodeled 1930s white farmhouse built around an original 1860s log cabin. Two large barns and a chicken coop were conveniently located nearby. Our nearby Meadowbrook Swimming Club provided a place to cool off in the hot, humid, summer weather. Andrea and I, both avid readers, would catch up with our reading by checking out many books from the city public library. The TV bought from our city home every year showed mostly test patterns in those early days. We played my favorite game of Monopoly, as well as other card games. Dad and Mother further provided us, at early ages, with chores to educate us about self-independence and to instill a work ethic.

The elderly Ural Stewart, who was our African American caretaker, would come up to watch *Amos and Andy* on our TV set, moved to the front lawn, and he laughed heartily with everyone.

Once, I was asked by mother to look for my missing younger brother George for dinner, and I found him sharing an opossum dinner at Stewart's nearby place in the old tack house in the horse/dairy barn! We children loved his good nature and were fascinated by his wringing the necks or chopping off the heads of our chickens, which would often chase us with their bloodied necks. Mother would put the chickens in a large, moveable, cold-storage kitchen locker for future dinners. My father was not particularly keen about chicken meat, since my grandmother had served it to him almost every other meal during the Great Depression. *Stewart* would give us his spent cloth tobacco bags so we could use them for storage of dust from our *gold mine*, which in reality was a sandstone deposit on the farm. We also dug up the bones of former dairy cows that had been buried in a gulch in the forested part of the farm. I dreamed then of becoming an archeologist!

During these teenage years, I was quite close to my father. I remember sitting with him on the front porch of the townhouse in rocking chairs one warm, late-spring afternoon and asking him about masturbation. He professionally and casually said, "I think that it is healthy." I was greatly relieved that no harm would befall me! I never asked him directly about my erotic *show and tell* activity with other boys in the Boy Scout tents on camping expeditions. Perhaps he knew about homosexual affairs from his experiences in the Pacific Theater, but he only mentioned that the very few military nurses there were quite popular. He also took a few leaves to Sydney, Australia. When I told him that I had questioned Reverend Hoon at my confirmation class, "Didn't the Bible say that Jesus drank wine at the last communion, not grape juice?" And Reverend Hoon had said, "That is a matter of interpretation!" Although the whole family went to church every Sunday, my father just looked amused about this comment and said nothing.

My father also made sure that I had a summer yard-maintenance job at the local power plant during my high school years. He gave me a small allowance over the years, but always lectured to me, "You never went through the Depression and should value thrift with your money!"

On summer evenings the family would gather in the yard to enjoy the hilltop breezes and to converse. When I was with my father in private conversations, I remember him saying, "Unfortunately the veneer of civilization is very thin and in time of crisis can show quickly the underlying savagery." Also, as a pediatrician he said, "I see in my practice every day the strong influence of family genetics; that if a mother gets pregnant at any early age, her daughter would undoubtedly also. Physical, mental, and emotional characteristics of children were often quite predictable from observing their parents." Father would comment that after he met my mother's health strong brothers, "Not only was your mother gorgeous but I could tell that she had the same positive genes as her brothers." He would comment, every so often in the enjoyment of farmhouse front yard, "That stench from the burning garbage miles away is a dangerous pollutant."

My father enjoyed his farm year-round, in his rare leisure time (usually Thursdays) restoring mostly himself, his automobiles, which included four Rolls-Royces —with the jewel of his collection being a 1926 Springfield (Massachusetts) Silver Ghost, which had been fitted with a Brewster Playboy roadster body in 1932—a 1950s Lancia, three Jaguars, as well as the cheaper Nash (1929) and Maxwell (1917) touring car, which were stored in the old horse/dairy and hay barns. Although, as a juvenile, he was a golf caddy, he thought that membership in a golf club was an extravagant waste of money and preferred "more practical pursuits".

We were to learn later, to our sorrow, our much-beloved elderly Ural Stewart accidentally shot himself to death in a small cottage a half-mile away from us. He had reached for his shotgun above his bed to protect his dog Blackie from stray dogs, and the shotgun discharged.

Several Jewish families lived near our townhome, but most of the Jewish families lived on the Missouri side. My father was often called on to perform, at *Brith Milah,* the circumcision required by religion, because then the state law allowed only a physician to perform one, not a *mohel.* Our post–World War II neighborhood blossomed and became quite lively with many large families because of an increased birthrate. These families acted as a cohesive and friendly neighborhood group throughout the Eisenhower years. Of course, like most evolving neighborhoods, there were the usual grouchy old couples and eccentric solitary couples without children. We children walked two blocks to our Mark Twain Grade School and walked home for lunch. I remember, in first grade, that I wore a Thomas Dewey-for-President button and, as a result, got a bloody nose from a Truman-for-President bully classmate. In the next election, our family was quite pro-Eisenhower-for-president; however, my grandmother was staunchly for Robert Taft. While in grade school, we had nuclear air-raid drills and hid under our old-fashioned individual school desks with an inkwell hole on the desk top. The father of a school friend of mine, who was a municipal judge, had built a suburban-located ranch-style home with a bomb shelter in their backyard in the late 1950s. Since our Northwest Junior High school was not close by, various families carpooled. Sometimes, out of necessity, I rode the bus and occasionally had to fight off the usual bullies. My father asked me whether I minded being usually the shortest boy in my class. I replied, "I always think that I am even larger than them mentally." Some of my best friends, both male and female, were much taller but my intellectual equals—especially my buddies C.H. Steele II and Donna Aldridge. Looking back on those relatively peaceful and tranquil years of 1950s, I now reflect on the sage advice of then President Dwight Eisenhower and fellow Kansan—to beware of the *Military-Industrial Complex*, which should be closely watched and controlled.

In 1957, I attended the school across the street from our home, which was highly regarded as one of the best high schools in Kansas. I was always just barely on time. Wyandotte High School was named after the county and the original settlement of Wyandotte City, which gradually incorporated adjoining towns to become Kansas City, Kansas. The local Wyandot Indians, along with other Great Lakes regional Kansa, Huron, Miami, Shawnee, Pawnee, Delaware, and Osage tribes, as well as plains tribes had been relocated again after 1830 to land west of the Missouri River. The earlier-mentioned Kansas-Nebraska act in 1854 opened up this territory to white squatters. This large city high school consists of a magnificent brick International Style W.P.A. (1935–1937) building in an expansive and tranquilly executed, landscaped campus setting. This high school was the largest west of the Mississippi River. The building, designed by the Chicago architectural firm Hamilton, Fellow, and Nedved, with associate architect Joseph W. Radotinsky and sculptor Emil Zettler, is now on the National Register of Historical Places. A federal grant of $20 million in 2005 was used to restore the building. The enrollment is now one-half of my graduating class of 450 pupils and is mostly minorities. The same architectural firm design, with the same twin, major-block towers was used for a similar high school in Little Rock, Arkansas. This school in Arkansas would later become famous for the integration of schools in the civil rights period.

The architectural details at Wyandotte High School are mostly geometrical with some brick-outlined designs and pictures shown in relief, such as athletes running on the gymnasium facade. The basketball coaches, such as Walt Shublom (c.1960s), in this gymnasium produced some of the greatest athletes in the Midwest. Basketball was introduced by Professor James Naismith at the University of Kansas (tenure 1898–1937). In this building was a swimming pool in which all the male students swam naked. Today, the now majority of African American students insist that everyone wear bathing suits. Outstanding football and track stars also emerged from the multipurpose stadium, which had an oval racetrack around the football field. The laboratories and other classrooms that faced out onto the landscaped grounds on two large, interior court yards produced gifted students that contributed greatly to the scientific advancement of society. There was a spacious social hall with two large, facing fireplaces; a large, efficient cafeteria; and even a large parking lot for cars and motorcycles. The students were a product of visionary superintendents and socially progressive, prominent businessmen, who served as school board members.

In my junior year of high school (1959), I was fortunate to be sent by my parents to an International Boy Scout Jamboree in the Philippine Islands in June. Even with monsoons and latrine trenches below our tents on the slippery hillside, I loved the camping experience and meeting scouts from other countries. In Manila, our American troop stayed at the magnificent, Classic Revival style Manila Hotel, on palm-filled grounds, that had been General Douglas MacArthur's headquarters at various points during World War II. I would have lunch there with the family of Dr. Clark Wescoe, who was dean of the University of Kansas Medical School and later chancellor at K.U. On the way to the Philippines, many of we American scouts stayed at the new Princess Kaiulani Hotel in Honolulu and the Imperial Hotel in Tokyo These travels would have profound influence for me with a great interest in Asia and the excitement/romance of travel for the rest of my life.

Our Kansas City, Kansas, grade schools, junior high schools, and high schools additionally provided music lessons, art, and science programs. Also, we were expected to take home economic classes for the girls and shop courses for the boys. I enrolled at the junior high school in metal, electrical, and woodworking classes. My mother was to be the proud possessor of three pig-shaped chopping boards from her three sons. Also I enrolled as a violinist and was probably the worst in the class, according to my music instructor at Northwest Junior High School, who brought his children to my father for medical care *thus a grade of C-*. Still, my experience contributed positively to my great love of classical music and opera!

Kansas City, Kansas, had a sizeable African American community, with many professionals because Kansas was an anti-slavery state, or *free state*, and had a close location for an *underground railroad* for slaves—mostly from Missouri across the Missouri River. The Quindaro district *earlier an established town on the Missouri River* was a vibrant center for them and even had a school for African Americans, which was called Western University, established in the 1860s. This community established banks, charitable organization, private social clubs, etc. The professional African Americans were generally treated with respect and had good relations with most Kansas City, Kansans. The schools were segregated. Most of them were divided in accordance by the neighborhood where the student lived, but they had the same quality of teachers and school buildings. The black Sumner High School and white Wyandotte High School were always competitive in a friendly manner. With the 1954 *Brown vs. School Board of Topeka, Kansas* ruling in the affirmative by the U.S. Supreme Court, the schools became more integrated. This legal decision accelerated the post-war movement to the suburbs of a large number of whites, including most of the Jewish families from Kansas City, Kansas, and Kansas City, Missouri's, central downtown areas. The majority of these families moved to the nearby, wealthier, newly built suburbs in the adjoining Johnson County, Kansas. This county was the location of the farmland that my great-grandfather had homesteaded. Kansas City, Kansas, was restricted by earlier state laws, specifically through the vindictiveness of other Kansas Legislators, not to be allowed expansion into adjacent counties.

Kansas City, Kansas, which in my youth had been a prosperous eighteen-block-long business district around Minnesota Avenue, beginning at the conjunction of the Kansas and Missouri Rivers, is today nearly abandoned. The business district is now punctuated by only a few post-1960 municipal, state, and federal buildings. The general public view in the greater Kansas City area is that Kansas City, Kansas, has become dangerous and is best avoided. The downtown neighborhoods were bulldozed by the local redevelopment agency in the name of urban renewal. Many vacated buildings were burned down by who knows which likely suspects to avoid payment of property taxes. Some biased locals muttered that it was perhaps *Jewish lightning* A few tacky ranch-style houses, or shoddy townhouses, were built in the redevelopment areas. The formerly fashionable West Heights District, near our home on Washington Boulevard still exists as an area with well-maintained homes today. This area has been designated as the National Historical District. Surrounding this historical district is a marginal district of vacant lots and deteriorating housing.

Our Washington Avenue Methodist Church still exists downtown as the same magnificent 1920s Gothic Revival "cathedral", with gorgeous ruby and cobalt blue-stained glass windows. Acres of barren land surround it, and Hmong peoples—primarily from Vietnam— now hold Christian services there. The Jewish Synagogue in the civic center was torn down in the late 1950s and replaced with a drive-in hamburger restaurant, which was also eventually demolished to become a vacant lot!

Our exclusive, private, downtown club, with city views and its delicately painted, pale pistachio-green and beige interior was the Terrace Club. The rooftop club was located in the architecturally significant, late-1940s, modern, yellow-brick style International Brotherhood of Boiler Makers building. The club is now long gone. However, my memories of the new, 1949, small, ten-inch TV in a huge, wooden console, and the bottles of booze kept by the members at the bar (BYOB) in this then *dry state* still linger. Quite a few of the members were either Methodist or Baptist, but the majority was Episcopalian or Roman Catholic. On one Thanksgiving Day at the club, my grandmother, Clara Aiken Speer, had dinner with us. The waiter came by and wanted to know whether we wanted cocktails or not. My precocious ten-year-old sister Andrea spelled out, "You mean, like g-i-n?" At home, this item was kept under the kitchen sink. In a lady-like manner, my sobriety-practicing grandmother quietly ignored the comment, and my parents skipped their regular cocktails. We children had our *Shirley Temple* and *Roy Rogers* non-alcoholic cocktails. My father decided that he was allergic to alcohol and stopped having any cocktails at the age of forty, although he never did drink that much. My mother, up to the age of ninety-eight years, enjoyed her regular bourbon and Coke-Cola in the evening. My father had invested in stock for the Town House Hotel in the early 1950s, which was a new, glamorous, high-rise, yellow-brick building. It is now a welfare hotel. He also invested in Kansas Turnpike bonds for profit, as well as to promote a more prosperous state. This turnpike is now part of the Interstate Highway System.

Certain downtown ethnic groups worked in the nearby meat-packing plants (Kansas), stockyards (Missouri), in the lower river-beds—*bottoms*—of the Kansas River and Missouri River. Beginning in the 1860s, the first butchers were the local African Americans. By 1884, Armour and Company consolidated other meat company operations. This earlier town called Armourdale would be incorporated into Kansas City, Kansas (KCK). The only other city in the world that surpassed this city in annual number of animals processed was Chicago. Later, more cheaply employed immigrants from Eastern Europe were recruited. They walked to work, retained their own distinct Roman Catholic parishes, and lived on the surrounding bluffs (Strawberry Hill). The immigrant Germans and Scandinavians, with protestant parishes, lived nearby. One of our Lutheran Swedish American housekeepers told us, "My mother would threaten if I was naughty that she would take me to live in a Catholic convent." Eastern Europeans continue to occupy the now designated Strawberry Hill Historical District. After the Vietnam War, many Hmong people moved to Kansas, mostly supported by the churches. Like in many other cities in Kansas, there are an increasing number of migratory workers, such Mexicans, moving into the remaining vacant stock of housing and downtown commercial buildings. The Amourdale, Rosedale, and Argentine annexed cities in the "bottoms" (another early annexed town like Quindaro) were an industrial and railroad center where white immigrants from farms relocated. Later, early residents included Mexicans, who worked on laying the earlier-built extensive railroad track systems and who were thought to have planted the local *loco* weed, or marijuana, alongside the track. In 1951, these *bottoms* were completely devastated by floods. But my grandfather's early 1910s, brick, medical professional building in the Armourdale district survived the flooding. The meat-packing plants were flooded, and the horrible sight and unbearable smell of the floating animal carcasses was nauseating to everyone. The consequential redistribution to small, regional meat-packing companies would signal the end of this important industry by the 1960s. The many railroad trains that had transported livestock continued to move much freight through the massive railroad crossroads. Many major companies would continue to build plants in these areas.

Even with the advances in integration made law by the Civil Rights Act of 1964, the earlier prosperous and professional middle-class African Americans left for the mostly white suburbs. Now the formerly respectable and prosperous downtown, and the expanded suburban community into Wyandotte County, is constantly in the news about homicides, family abuse, robberies, and arson. Gone are the once *black*, social, debutante balls; a *black* country club; and the elegant and emotional social pageantry of the vibrant A.M.E. (African Methodist Episcopal) and Baptist churches. The larger sister city, Kansas City, Missouri, across the Kansas River, also suffered almost as much from the integration of the downtown area and the relocation of the populace by urban-renewal demolition sponsored by their respective redevelopment agencies. The infamous pre-World War II black jazz and gangster district at Twelfth Street and Vine Street has been recreated with a few symbolic new buildings surrounded by hundreds of acres of vacant land. The whole present setting is essentially a Potemkin village at Eighteenth Street and Vine Street!

My parents lived in their townhome until my father died in 1994. Prior to his death, he enjoyed convalescing in the farmyard, during good weather. My mother only went into assisted-living in Johnson County, with much emotional resistance, after breaking her hip in 2004. At the new assisted living facility, my mother had a particularly friendly relationship with the staff, which consisted of many Ethiopian Americans. The family townhome was sold in 2013 for the paltry sum of $20,000. Fortunately, the new owner plans rehabilitate the house. The farm, with a neglected, dilapidated farmhouse, is now within the city limits of the further expanded Kansas City, Kansas away from the mostly deserted downtown. Between the cemeteries on the original outskirts of the pre-World War II city, and our farm, there are three huge multi-acre, abandoned shopping centers. In 1964, the first, the Tower Plaza Shopping Center, replaced the Farmers' Market across from the cemeteries at the then western edge of KCK. Downtown stores, such as Sears, left their downtown locations. There was even an attempt at Center City Urban Renewal from 1968–1975, which included two blocks of center landscaping on Minnesota Avenue (the main commercial street). The radical demolition of buildings could not prevent the deterioration of the vibrant downtown of the 1950s and early 1960s.

Before all of this wasteful and needless expansion, I left home in 1965 to attend college. My father said that he would pay for his children's college educations, as long as we went to the University of Kansas. All four siblings graduated with professional degrees from K.U. My planned medical career detoured away after graduating with a Bachelor of Arts degree in Zoology and spending three years at medical school (K.U.M.C.). In medical school, I was diagnosed with auditory aphasia, which now seems to be related to dyslexia in my case. Once for extra income, I volunteered to donate my sperm and was told that I was not perfect enough—not athletic, tall, blond, or extremely high I.Q.! After three years of frustration, the faculty and I mutually agreed that medicine was not my forte. My father was president of the State Medical Society and both the chancellor of the University and dean of the medical school at that time contacted him with the news. With this unexpected news, he told my mother that we three were going for dinner to the expensive Putsch's 210 with European continental cuisine. Mother wore an elegant, revealing, low-cut, emerald-green, raw-silk cocktail dress with her white mink stole, and my dad was in one of his best wool business suits from Wolf Brothers, which he always bought on-sale after a call from his personal salesman. Dad asked the strolling gypsy violinist to play several of his favorite tunes. I said in the restaurant at the end of evening, "I know everyone is disappointed but this is one of the finest nights of my life!" I had always enjoyed art history and told my parents that I would enroll at KU in the pioneering and excellent Art History Department. Graduating with a Master of Arts degree in the history of arts, I decided not to get a doctorate because career possibilities were limited to the academic and museum levels.

With the Vietnam War escalating, my sympathy for fighting against communism for our country was still strong! But with my raging hormones in a homosexual direction and disgust with the waste and increasing idiocy of the war, I spoke with the university psychiatrist who confirmed that I was a homosexual. Afterward, a psychiatrist of my father's choosing informed him, "Robert is bisexual." My father said, "I always suspected some of your art history friends, such as Joe Lordi, were homosexual and bad influences." Mother said, "When I was an airline hostess, several women expressed that kind of interest in me, but I ignored them." With orders from the U.S. Army, I arrived at the monumental Union Railroad Station in Kansas City, Missouri, to travel to Fort Leonard Wood in Missouri for indoctrination. I was told unsurprisingly by an army official at the station, "You have been dismissed and will shortly receive an honorable discharge." When I returned home, my shocked mother said, "You know what happens to people like you? They end up with syphilis and die in the gutter!" She angrily fled the house and drove off in her white Cadillac, as she usually did in times of conflict. After this dreadful, but predictable, event for that time in America, I went to see Dad at his nearby office. He was distantly polite and told me to sign over to him my family corporation bonds (Speer Investment Company). He informed me, "You are disinherited!"

I urgently needed to leave this mutually unhappy scene for the sake of all of us. After a three-day period of home isolation, I headed toward California in my Oldsmobile Cutlass convertible, with a few worldly possessions, in February of 1969. I took the southern route along U.S. Highway 66, which was the preferred route during the winter, and on the cold nights I slept at roadside parks. I even bought a couple of small attractively woven carpets from a Navajo reservation store in New Mexico, which was financially idiotic. The car radio played the popular French composer Jacques Brel song, newly recorded in English by the Kingston Trio, "Those were the days my friends, we thought they'd never end…." I inherently knew that settling in California was a wise choice. I had thought about going to New York City, but I was more attracted to the weather, life style, and less hectic competition in San Francisco. Everything pointed to my new home in San Francisco. On previous occasions, I had visited San Francisco and also visited my oldest paternal uncle Robert Louis and his wife Jewell, who lived in the nearby ocean-side Carmel Highlands. Their 1960s home was constructed with exterior redwood siding that aged a beautiful silvery grey. They designed for themselves a perfect contemporary Japanese style home to take in their dramatic views of Point Lobos with floor to ceiling windows. These Pacific Ocean views were constantly unfolding through the changing, surrounding, foggy, forested landscape that swept down to their own cove. My uncle died in 2002 at the age of 98, but mysteriously no one in our immediate—their favored family was notified of his death. Aunt Jewell died in 2010, at the age of 102 (being blind the last two years and tended by a nurse). They left their sizeable fortune to charities in a trust fund. As my father predicted, "The wife frequently survives the husband." My uncle and aunt would never have imagined their dream house being now greatly enlarged and much of their well-tended native two-acre landscaping being destroyed.

When I reached the California border and saw the verdant landscape of orange groves before me, I knew for sure that I had entered the "Promised Land" foretold in earlier stories by my mother. I thought, "Perhaps California will always be a state of mind!"

After staying in San Francisco briefly with a Chinese American friend from medical school and his aristocratic Xian/Shanghai family, I scouted around for an apartment. Mostly, I found many of the rental areas were bland and uninteresting. I quickly discovered I particularly liked the Fillmore District with its dynamic colorful appeal and affordability. I lived first on the north side of California Street, between Steiner and Fillmore Streets, in one of the Stick Eastlake-style row houses, circa 1880s. The earlier-mentioned five connected row houses, each consisting of a pair of Victorian flats, with servant quarters (above and below the two owner's flats), which interconnected with the corresponding flat. The eight-room, top flat had been split in half, and my apartment in the rear had a view of the large, combined backyards. To pay for my expenses and generate extra income during this period, I worked as a shop apprentice at Kotzbeck's picture-framing shop on Fillmore Street. The German American shopkeeper, Gus Drautz, owned an extensive and valuable print collection, which I helped catalogue. This enjoyable, extended education of my Art History Master's degree was an extra bonus.

Gus was a master craftsman and considered the best picture framer in the city. He had a large workshop employing six men. Bank of America was one of his clients, and he framed large photographs of their officers for the branch offices. Also, he produced exquisitely framed, original fine prints for the rooms at the exclusive Clift Hotel, located at 495 Geary Street. One day, while I was clerking in front, a withered, tiny, old lady, dressed with an ancient black lace hat and a long black dress touching her black shoes, came into the shop followed by her tall, handsome, young, male chauffeur in full livery uniform, which included a black cap and black-laced calf-length boots. Her late 1930s, black Packard town car was prominently parked in front. She showed me a metal-framed photograph with a broken face glass. I took it to Gus in the back workshop, and he had the glass immediately replaced after he saw that the order was from Mrs. Cahill. I asked him, "What shall I charge?" He said, "No charge." Later, I asked why there was no charge. He said that she was the wealthy matriarch of the locally influential Cahill Construction Company, established in 1912. He further said, "I try to keep the carriage trade happy, and I am certainly not the only one (shop owner)." He went on to explain, "Many of the (nearby) Pacific Heights extremely wealthy socialites, noted for their stinginess, would go to the prestigious I. Magnin clothing store and return haute couture gowns after the symphony and opera openings, 'as not being quite my personal style.'"

Another time at the counter, I received a call asking, "Is Gus in?" I said, "Whom should I say is calling?" The throaty voice at the end of the line said, "Tell him Sally called." When Gus returned, I told him who had called and he was thrilled. He asked me, after talking with her, whether I would like to accompany him to hang some graphics in her home. I said, "Would I ever!" Ms. Stanford, who appropriated the name of the university, was one of the most famous Madams in San Francisco history. Her magnificent four-story Classic Revival-style brick home, circa 1905, at 2324 Pacific Avenue, had been built for the president of Southern Pacific Railroad. As mentioned earlier, I was later briefly her neighbor. She possessed a witty and charming personality and a large full figure that filled out her tight dress. When I met her, I remembered she was famously quoted, as saying, "They (her male patrons) were a wonderful set of burglars, when I first came in 1923, wonderful, if they were stealing, they were doing it with class and style." San Francisco had been noted as a wild and frisky town since the Gold Rush days of 1849. Her home was decorated in a late 1890s bordello-style, with red-flocked wallpapered parlors. But the thing that I remember most was the open, huge, eight-square foot, walk-in silver vault in her kitchen that she casually showed me.

She was then operating her extremely popular Valhalla restaurant across the San Francisco Bay in Sausalito. She has been quoted, after closing her home for "cultured ladies to entertain gentlemen," that "amateurs are ruining our business." This charming Mediterranean-like town of Sausalito had been a sleepy Italian American fishing village before the opening of the Golden Gate Bridge in 1939. After she leased out her bordello at 1144 Pine Street, first as The Fallen Angel nightclub, and then as a gay bathhouse, she opened her Valhalla restaurant in 1949. She held court in the lobby in her barber chair and drank highballs. She listened to the usual inquires of wealthy ladies, "Did my husband ever visit one of your establishments?" Like the Cheshire cat, she just smiled obligingly, and the smile lingered after she left. John and I dined there many years later at her restaurant. As we entered, she said, from her front, center, barber-chair throne, "Could I buy you boys a drink?" What a wonderful memory focus! She, against the stiff, snob opposition of the "Upper Hill People of Sausalito", and many political rejections, finally became one of their most popular and pragmatic mayors.

For nightly dinner, I cooked minimally and ate nearby at cheap restaurants, such as the Chinese restaurant, that is now The Elite restaurant, which now serves expensive Creole food. The neighborhood then had dim street lights and was quite menacing, even during the daylight hours. Somehow, the street life intrigued me, and I was glad that I had moved to this most varied and vibrant Upper Fillmore neighborhood. The carriage trade, for the most part, resided and entertained privately in mansions above Washington Street in the most exclusive San Francisco district of Pacific Heights, originally part of the Western Addition. They circulated downtown with their social registry friends to their private clubs, favorite popular restaurants, such as Trader Vic's, and partied at such regal hotels as the Saint Francis, Palace, and Fairmont.

I preferred the livelier *secret* gay bars and bathhouses scattered around the city, which were becoming less vulnerable from the usual election-year police raids. I was eventually to experience what later gays would miss—those years of self-expression, independence, and the exhilarating pleasure of belonging to this special fraternity. This shadowy world was so much more interesting than my own fraternity (Phi Kappa Tau), which did adopt finally nondiscriminatory rules of membership in 1986. My earlier fascinating world on Fillmore Street has disappeared and changed for the better. Gus was a bit too autocratic, and I became restless. So I moved on to temporary jobs, and other apartments, and began writing. About this time, I met John Wong, and my deep love for him would lead to our long, domestic life together, with the usual accommodations of our similar, but individual, personality traits. I called him my Pooh-Pooh after Christopher Robin's *Winnie-the-Pooh*, but he, at first, thought that I was referring to the more generic "poop-poop." Through our individual efforts, we developed a mutual love.

MING CHUCK GEE

After many enjoyable times socializing with Ming C. Gee, he joined our household in 1979. When he introduced himself, he preferred to be called Ming, as in the Dynasty. His great sense of style, wit, helpfulness, and overall joie de vivre added an extra brightness, suggested by the meaning of his Chinese name, translated as "bright." John had known Ming's family from his early school years because his younger gay brother was a classmate and friend. Ming's parents and some of his family lived for a while in the Wong's Grant Avenue apartment building. The Gee family consisted of six boys and three girls. Ming's great-grandfather had emigrated from Canton, China to California during the Gold Rush of 1849 and did various manual jobs such as laundry work. Most Chinese then referred to San Francisco as Gim San in Taishanese i.e., Gold Mountain.

Ming's family was from the Taishan Prefecture (Guangdong Province), as were John's, in the southeast corner of China where the Pearl River flowed and produced, from silt, this exceptionally fertile area This region was conquered and consolidated in 214 BCE by the Qin Dynasty, but had been much earlier populated by his ancestors. Because of the turmoil caused by the First Opium War (1839–1842), exploration by both foreigners/regional bureaucrats, and frequent natural disasters, the men immigrated to other countries for a more prosperous situation, and their families stayed behind. They hoped to be reunited in the future back in China. It was common in the earlier Chinatown of San Francisco for these people to ask, "Do you speak Sze Yup (dialect of four counties) or Som Yup (another dialect of three counties)?" This query would closer establish the district of origin for a person. John's family spoke like Ming's, Sze Yup, but with a difference of village location. Ming jokingly called the combined areas as the seventh district. The father of modern China, Dr. Sun Yat-sen, was from the nearby Xiangshan Prefecture. He was greatly assisted financially by the Chinese in San Francisco for the revolution that created the Republic of China and the overthrow of the Ching Dynasty (Manchu) on October 10, 1911. Ming's great-grandfather immigrated to San Francisco around 1849, and John's father immigrated around 1890.The majority of Chinese in America were from the Taishan Prefecture until the 1960s. The new immigrants from this period were Chinese who had relocated to Taiwan after the Communist Revolution, as well as other overseas Chinese such as from Hong Kong. All of these Chinese immigrants arrived because of the new less-restrictive immigration laws in the United States. John and Ming were called *ABCs* or American Born Chinese.

In 1934, Ming's grandfather had taken him, as well as an older brother and two sisters, back to Taishan, when he was only four years old. His birthday is December 7, which is the date that the Japanese attacked Pearl Harbor in 1941. His sisters returned to San

Francisco in 1940. Their escape occurred as the Japanese army (there had been earlier intrusions into China in the 1920s) was invading their rural village. The family was reduced to a desperate situation to survive, even though his grandfather had built, upon his earlier arrival, two profitable commercial buildings for rental income. Both stores were burned down twice to their brick walls by the invaders, and thus hardly any rent was generated. The fields were stripped of food and their house broken into a couple of times, but with successful resistance, they had no losses. To survive, his grandmother gradually sold-off pieces of all her valuable jewelry, breaking-off pieces to sell one at a time. At this same time, Ming also suffered twice from malaria and probably had other blood ailments from the blood-sucking leeches in the rice paddies. His grandfather's business friend owned a laundry and was killed one night for not having any money. When Japanese planes bombed their market place and school, everyone would flee to the nearby mountain side for refuge. Even in his small village they heard about the distant dreadful Japanese rape of Nanking with the slaughter of 200,000 or more of their countrymen.

His grandfather died in 1943. In 1946, Ming and his older brother were sent ship passage money by their father in San Francisco; therefore, they were able to return to San Francisco just prior to the communist takeover. They were locked up for a week to be processed by the U.S. Immigration Service in the San Francisco Custom House, not the former processing center on Angel Island (the West Coast equivalent of the East Coast's Ellis Island), where he had been processed in 1934. After learning English in the public schools, he was able to adjust marginally to his new environment, which he had vaguely remembered. His earlier education was surprisingly productive despite his rural Chinese schools and the few books available in his household. He graduated in

1952 from Commerce High School, which was one of the most integrated schools in the city. It became the headquarters for the Board of Education in 1953. During these school years, he worked after school hours and Saturdays at various Chinese laundries. His schedule was six days a week with Sunday off, which he reserved for fresh-air park activities. At the laundry, he always sat near an open window for fresh air so he would not contact tuberculosis. Serving four years in the United States Air Force (three years in Frankfurt, Germany), he took the opportunity to travel extensively throughout Western Europe. With the highly valued American dollar, he received a broad cultural education. He returned home in 1956, where he enrolled with the Academy of Art through a G.I. educational grant.

After graduation, Ming could not find a job in the city as a graphic designer, because of the scarce number of jobs due to the broad popularity of San Francisco. Thus, he first went to Dallas with Neiman Marcus department store in 1960. Although he was not a party designer, early on Mrs. Edward Marcus asked him to help plan a dinner party with a hobo theme. He suggested using benches and picnic tables covered with comic newspapers as table covers. The settings included army surplus tableware, bandanas for napkins, and tin cans with flowers for table decorations. Later he was asked to design costumes for a neighbor's elaborate, summer night, "Chinese teahouse" garden party. He suggested the entire family walk up hill to the mansion wearing two-piece black outfits and conceal themselves under a Chinese carp-shaped lantern, lit up by their flashlights. Needless to say, their grand entrance was received with great delight by all. Extremely visionary ideas like this one would remain a memorable part of his oeuvre in the world of fantasy. In Dallas, he also met one of his early lovers, Murray Smither, who was five-years younger and an art dealer. He and

Ming had a comfortable living relationship together. Everything, however, changed for him with a better job offer, and he went to work from 1964 through1967 at Frost Brothers Department Store in San Antonio. There, he had another male lover, Richard, who lived in an apartment in a Victorian, divided, brick house in the King William Street (Kaiser Wilhelm Strasse, prior to World War I) District. Prosperous German American merchants had built fine homes there near their factories, such as flour mills, in the nineteenth century. In 1967, he also participated in graphic design, illustrations, and later designed uniforms for the *Hemisfair* of 1968, which was the first world's fair for Texas. He enjoyed the friendliness and generosity of many new Texan friends. He was confused about the public restrooms labeled *White* and *Colored*, so he followed his friends into the *White* restrooms. However, when the opportunity came to return to his beloved San Francisco, with an offer to become assistant art director for advertising at the avant-garde Joseph Magnin fashion store, he regretfully left for this promising career change for a dream job come true.

Then with his word-spread unique personality and talents at JM, he was lured away in 1969 to an even more rewarding position as a senior designer through much persistence of telephone calls for an interview with the company president. Finally, with introductory cocktails, in the office of the company president, he felt comfortable to accept this position. The company was Determined Productions, which was famous for their stuffed Snoopy dogs and other creatively designed items. His boss, Connie Boucher, and her accomplished graphic design partner, Jim Young, became his good friends. Connie was a self-made millionaire and a pioneer in cartoon licensing. She and Jim created a wonderful world for Ming with extended world travel at various times, from his merchandise idea assignments, to their offices in Hong Kong, Tokyo, Taipei, and Paris. These assignments, and their lavish lifestyle of limousines and fine dining, such as Maxim's restaurant in Paris, and staying at by-invitation-only country inns in Japan, helped to inspire Ming with a joyful mood to create an abundance of new products for the future. Connie was a diminutive lady and always well dressed to enhance her blonde French-roll hair style. She encouraged him to build on this world of fantasy. One memorable afternoon, over Bloody Mary cocktails at the swimming pool of their exclusive hillside apartment in Hong Kong, Connie said, "We shall call our conversations 'our think tank' for new business ventures." At the same apartment on Headland Road, she decided once, on a whim, to have a Mexican dinner party with Mexican food flown in from San Francisco, and she hired a Filipino band to entertain their guests. In California, Connie and Jim owned elegant homes, such as the Russian Hill landmarked octagon house, circa 1858, with the addition of a mansard roof, as well as a luxurious condominium on Nob Hill, and a summer home at Lake Tahoe. Her chauffeured Rolls Royce was always available for her appointments. Ming retired in 1985, shortly before the untimely death of Connie.

During this interval, Ming lived on Joice Street in the wealthy neighborhood of Nob Hill, in a comfortable 1906 working-class studio apartment, which was simple but elegantly self-decorated. In 1976, he moved to Filbert Steps on Telegraph Hill. His large ground-floor studio was located below a carpenter gothic cottage, circa 1873, in a historical and beautiful garden setting. A well-known New York City journalist, Mimi Sheraton, had visited there and purportedly said, "I was afraid to visit San Francisco for fear of seeing such a beautiful and enchanting place." After increasingly loud entertainment nightly from the tenant, with his many girlfriends in the apartment above, Ming stayed more often with us. We gladly invited Ming to move in. We three had our own individual way of helping with the management of the house. Our arrangement has created an extremely comfortable nest. We were named the *Three Monks* by a lesbian Catholic nun who lived in Western Australia and was visiting her brother, and our neighbor, Richard Wade. We each have brought our individual experiences into our home for a whole wonderful scenario. Living like quasi-monastic individuals, we each contribute to the household in a variety different ways.

OUR MUTUAL BUSINESS ENTERPRISE

In 1979, the same year that Ming moved in with us, we established a restaurant in a four-story Edwardian building (1904) that we purchased together in the *Gay Mecc*a of the Castro District. I insisted that we buy the building together, as well as the existing second-floor Japanese restaurant business opportunity. In 1980, I relocated my real estate office to the third floor. At the time, New York City and San Francisco seemed to be the focus for the opening of many successful restaurants, and in our joy we enthusiastically wanted to be part of this wildly creative scene also. So we opened a restaurant! Our restaurant, which we named Snow Peas, featured a novel fusion cuisine, blending Chinese and European food selections created from John's recipes. The stylish dining room interior was designed by Ming. The dramatic, large, dining room with a private room was painted with burgundy-colored walls and cream-colored ceiling and moldings. Accents included mirrored walls, contemporary chrome-fitted and Murano glass sconces, a luminous Lucite entrance table, and framed original, Chinese poster-girl graphics from the 1930s. The tables had white tablecloths with votive candles, and Ming carefully arranged the daily selected flowers on the tables. The waiters in their customized aprons, designed by Ming, helped complete a perfect setting, with classical music playing in the background. As a result of the raves and the compliments that John and Ming received from our dinner guests at our home dinners, we had been confident in the success of our dream operation. John managed the kitchen. In the background, I paid the bills and selected the liquor/wine list. I particularly enjoyed the wine tastings with various vintner representatives. Ming, still employed as the senior designer at Determined Productions, was the host for our evening-only service.

Ming was an enthusiastic player as maître d', and cultivated many devoted diners with his charming manner, inimitable accent, and sayings. One evening, several regular patrons complained to Ming about another nearby diner smoking a cigar. Ming went over to the offender's table and politely pointed out that the menu stated *no cigar or pipe smoking permitted*" This diner, on exiting, lectured Ming, "I will never be back and will tell all my friends not to come here!" Ming smiled and said emphatically, "Please do." He divined our diners either as slugs or butterflies, as well as the public in general. Obviously, this diner was considered a slug.

The author Armistead Maupin arrived one evening with Jamie Auchincloss, and Armistead excitedly and proudly exclaimed to Ming, "My guest is Jackie Onassis's half-brother." Ming said, "You might be interested that we have a prince tonight," pointing at Prince Egon Von Furstenberg at a central table with his male admirers. At the end of the dinner, a waiter related to us that the Prince collected money for dinner from his guests. The elegant and stylish Prince Von Furstenberg, on his second visit, invited Ming to his Carmel, California, home on the weekend to instruct his chef how to prepare the lemon chicken dish, that he so enjoyed. Ming demurely declined and stated he was needed to assist at our restaurant. That evening, the prince autographed a menu with the addition of "superlatives of love."

At his time, Ming was at his artistic height of drawing with colored pencils. He drew many male nudes. Indeed, many handsome diners offered to be his models after our waiters intimated that Ming was quite a good artist. With permission of the models, their pictures were hung on the walls of our restaurant. A nude drawing of our head English waiter was hung in the front entrance and caused comments, including being recognized by the son of one of our friends!

John managing the kitchen, as well as ordering food supplies, was the focus of the relationships between the kitchen staff and waiters. He was continuously angered by the pilfering of restaurant prime meats, expensive bottles of wine supplies, and even dinnerware by employees. The various temperamental chefs were frequently in conflict regarding the menu, but the waiters supported John and Ming. A couple of chefs dramatically quit on a busy Friday night when they theatrically threw their restaurant keys to the floor. Sometimes I would substitute as a dishwasher when our hired dishwashers did not show up.

Having moved my real estate office from downtown to the third floor in 1980, I was the accounting and general assistance partner. I also would accept the wine, liquor, and food supplies during the daytime, prior to the opening for dinner. I had planned on entertaining my business clients in our dining room, but those plans yielded few actual business transactions.

The reviews in the print media, as well as television, were excellent, and we continued to attract glamorous crowds, but mainly only on the weekends. Gradually the AIDS epidemic added a cloud over the future of success because the general public, as well as the gay community, were afraid of susceptibility of contracting AIDS in a gay district restaurant. In spite of the happy, nightly camaraderie, creative challenges, and compliments, the restaurant had never, in four years, been financially viable. We had depleted our savings and did not want to mortgage our home any further. Not having to cater to public whims or endure being robbed by our employees, I said, "Owning a restaurant proves that selling real estate is not as stressful." My father and our accountant had the foresight of the usual future financial disaster awaiting the ownership of a restaurant!

Thus, after an exciting but financially devastating four years, we sold the restaurant to a succession of restaurateurs in our building. Until 2012, I had continued to operate my own real estate brokerage on the third floor, and Ming had continued his artistic endeavors of his retirement in the fourth-floor attic's two-room studio. He shared the third floor. We now have both moved our modus operandi to our home.

6.

House History

In 1908, Dr. George J. Sweeney purchased the land on Eddy Street for his house from J. J. Sheenin, who owned a horse stable at that location. Sheenin moved the stable further west onto other land that he owned. The house was completed in 1912. His wife, Mary Sweeny, graduated from the prestigious Roman Catholic girl's school, Saint Rose Academy, with the mother of Dr. Albert Shumate.

Dr. Shumate was a physician and a major scholar in the California historical community. He lived all of his life in the original Shumate family owned pharmacy at 1901 Scott Street—an Italianate Victorian Villa, circa 1870, with a surrounding, luxuriant garden which was irrigated by its own water wells. Behind the house at 1901 Scott Street, at the rear of the lot, is a large, detached garage with six garage doors, originally used for the pharmacy trucks. John and I invited the bachelor to dinner at our home, with his neighbor and friend, Peter Minton, the talented pianist, who performed at the Fairmont Hotel and later performed at Hotel Carlisle in New York City. Dr. Shumate commented about his childhood memories, "I didn't remember the house being so small." Since he had written the excellent book, *Rincon Hill and South Park,* about the first, fashionable, bayside San Francisco residential districts, I asked him, "Why don't you write a history of the Western Addition?" He replied, "Someday." He also mentioned how attractive and charming Mrs. Sweeney was.

The young Mrs. Sweeney died suddenly during the influenza epidemic of 1918. Dr. Sweeney remarried and moved away, in 1921, to the newly fashionable district of Westwood Park, which was built on the grounds of the former Miramar horse race track. He continued to rent the house out, until his death in 1948. During this intervening time, the treasurer of a Market Street furniture company and his wife rented the home from Dr. Sweeney. A neighbor told me that that they had owned a magnificent Packard town car. At the time of his death in 1947, Dr. Sweeney's executor sold the house to Demetrio and Katherine Arboleda, who were originally from the Philippines. They divided the house up into rooms so that Filipino families and single workers could each have their own individual space. One tenant Filipino couple told me later that they and their children had lived in our formal dining room—with ropes stretched from wall to wall to hang their clothing on.

In 1973, Scott and Susan Tree bought the house and removed various artificial partitions to start bringing the house back to its original floor plan. They actively fought a take-over sale through eminent domain by the redevelopment agency. With the lot being 45 feet wide by 137.5 feet in depth, and the current zoning, our home could have been replaced by at least an eighteen-unit building. Scott was from a Jewish family background in Los Angeles, and Susan was the daughter of a career Army colonel. They were the well-educated, hippie couple, driving a 1957 Cadillac convertible and wearing outlandish tie-dyed or vintage clothing. The house was lighted with dim, amber bulbs. Irish lace curtains were hung on the windows, and their Irish wolfhound had the run of the house. Scott's master bedroom was painted a deep blue and was furnished with a large water bed. Susan's smaller bedroom was painted a deep rose, and the walls were hung with a large print collection of Roman Catholic saints in gilt frames. Since they were making a significant profit from this sale, they agreed to carry a second note and deed of trust, which allowed us to make a mere 10 percent down payment. During their residence, they procreated two children, a daughter Silver and a son Hudson. When they sold the house to us in January of 1975, the whole family moved to Sausalito, into a large two-story, idyllic, wood-frame, New Orleans-style Victorian house, with a surrounding porch and second-story balcony. The house had palm trees in front, a view of Golden Gate Bay, and a panoramic backdrop of San Francisco.

John and I decided to restore and update certain parts of the house, in November 1976, with a second Note and Deed of Trust from the redevelopment agency in the amount of $28,854 (thirty-year amortized note with a fixed five and three-quarters percent interest). The agency arranged the financing through a Japantown bank (California First Bank).

Bob Fogel, who was a talented architect and dedicated preservationist with the redevelopment agency, assisted us in planning the alterations. The modernization of the kitchen was the main focus of attention, with the servant quarters being eliminated to allow for a large, country kitchen overlooking the backyard, with floor-to-ceiling windows. Bob cleverly configured these windows to match the front living room, vertical-casement windows. John requested a built-in wok and much more cabinet and counter space. A laundry room was created out of the original kitchen. The maid's bedroom, off the new kitchen and laundry room, was converted into a cozy art gallery and TV room. The original clothes closet under the staircase had been updated by Scott Tree as a powder room. Upstairs, the original bathroom was modernized with a walk-in shower. The original claw-footed bathtub from this bathroom was moved to the former, upstairs, laundry room. The toilet room remained the same, with a new wall toilet. A second bathroom was created from the upstairs laundry room and featured a large skylight. The original tub and toilet from the toilet room were moved there, and an antique, classical-revival period, white-porcelain pedestal sink was purchased. The damaged, glass greenhouse was removed, and a new, upstairs deck above the kitchen was established. The deck is now used as an upstairs garden with cymbidium orchids and other exotic plants that do well in our Mediterranean climate. The original, ugly, and clumsy rear wooden staircase attached to the deck was removed both for aesthetic purposes as well as for the prevention of a burglar climbing the stairs. Bob Fogel would later be my first real-estate associate.

Willie Ballard, a burly, friendly, African American, who was highly recommended by the redevelopment agency, was contracted to begin the improvements with the earlier mentioned low-interest loan that we acquired from the agency. He was required by SFRA to use only African American subcontractors, who were supposed to be locally based. Our home was built of early growth Douglas fir and redwood (dry-rot and termite resistant) and had a twenty-one-inch thick, brick foundation. The supporting basement was sound, with heavy-duty piers and bracing. Therefore, only some minor termite/dry rot, corrective repairs were necessary, which is remarkable for a house of this age. We had earlier replaced the kitchen back porch, which had partially collapsed prior to the bank (Citizens Savings and Loan) approval of our loan. The recycled electrical system, updated with circuit breakers, the replacement of the old, lead-pipe, plumbing system with copper, a new roof, a new entry sidewalk, and certain interior/exterior repairs were contracted for. These agreed-upon improvements were accomplished with great personal inconvenience and discomfort to us because we decided, for financial reasons and the cost of renting elsewhere, to stay in the house during the five months of improvements. Our neighbor, Richard

Wade, was extremely accommodating by allowing us to use his bathroom facilities daily. Without the now-required lead paint disclosures, John and I probably inhaled a lot of lead paint dust during the remodeling and will expect a much-diminished life span. Under my encouragement, for practical purposes, Willie agreed to recycle most of the removed building materials, such as redwood, two by eight inch planks, into the reconstruction. Since Willie was an expert at masonry flooring, we were surprised, after arriving home from a vacation, to discover that the reddish-brown, quarry-tile flooring in the kitchen was at odd angles from not using a plumb line. Willie ungrudgingly replaced the tiles to be aligned properly to the uneven walls. In contrast, the greyish, hexagonal, porcelain tiles in both of the bathrooms worked out well.

During the remodeling, our house was broken into and several items were stolen. We decided to install a burglar alarm to protect our much-improved home. For the final touch, we hired a friend and interior designer, Robert Hamm, to repaint our home. The colors he selected were perfect for the various rooms; but the controversial color in the living room went from pea green to forest green. The new color was a result of me telling Robert, "I think the color of my pants that I am wearing is a better choice." He said, "Take off your pants, and I'll match the color at the paint store." Of course, I agreed to remove my pants, since I was wearing Jockey slim briefs in spite of an obvious big bulge. The overall results were spectacular and luxuriant from the color of my pants. After the carriage house was rehabilitated by the carriage doors being replaced with an overhead door, everything was almost perfect. Only the ugly, front cyclone fence, which I camouflaged with a black paint job, remained. We replaced it finally, in 2006, with a wrought-iron fence, which cost three times as much as the original purchase price of the house! This attractive addition brought the remodeling to a close. Only the great, magnificent, attic space, with the rafters exposed to a ridge board to twenty feet from the ceiling joists, needs to be developed—perhaps after the Great Recession.

In the summer of 1989, we had the stained, redwood wainscoting, staircase, and moldings refinished, as well as all of the golden oak floors, with a redwood, inlaid border. After the Loma Prieta earthquake on October 19, 1989, I drove home from my office, through a darkened city with the threat of civil violence. Our home, luckily, was not damaged, with the exception of a few hair line cracks in the plaster walls, and the police were on duty immediately. A latter Dexatex coating made the upstairs deck more manageable and avoided the annual leaking from winter rainstorms. The garden was my cherished, long-term project, to which I added an elongated, irregular, fish pond with Chinese-style landscaping, combined with an English, country garden, a la Gertrude Jekyll, throughout the rest of the landscaping. A one-ton limestone formation with holes, removed from a prehistoric lake in western Kansas, which I purchased in Kansas City for only $250 on one of my biannual family visits, became our Chinese scholar's rock (Tai Hu rock). Unlike the holes created by the water currents at the Chinese Lake Tai, the holes in our landscape formation were created by the roots of trees that had decomposed. As the epitome of any fine classical Chinese garden, this scholar's rock was aesthetically positioned by Ming to reflect the rising morning sun, and it provides a delight from our kitchen windows. After placing this five-foot stone sculpture on a large, concrete reinforced, iron platform at the end of the pond, the total cost of the rock was $3,000.

In the garden, I also used paving stones that once were used in the paving of the Victorian streets in San Francisco. From the ballast for nineteenth-century sailing ships, I built garden paths, flowerbed walls, and also placed them in the grassy patch down the drive way. In 1980, I paid to move fourteen grey/white Shasta granite curb stones (four feet in length), from a nearby construction site at Divisadero and Eddy Streets, to our front yard. In 1998, I added an eighteenth-century, English (Cornwall), grey granite hog tank to be used for fish on the side of the driveway, at the site where a four-foot stump was left when we removed a diseased Acacia tree. A thirty-foot Victorian boxwood tree, with its fragrant white blossoms, is a constant remainder of the original garden. My job profile includes being the chauffeur and general handyman, besides being the gardener. John is the chef, and Ming is the sous chef, as well as the official Ikebana arranger.

The garden has been a lovely sylvan and tranquilizing atmosphere for us in the middle of the city. The grass lawn, between a dense, perennial fern bed next to the house, extended to the pond. In garden beds around the lawn, I filled in these areas with baby tears. All of which adds a year-round, verdant, green background. I planted all the flora in mostly shades of pink, lavender, and white to take advantage of our mild climate and to have something blooming each season. Our kitchen floor-to-ceiling windows look out on an ever-changing scene. Many different seasonal species of birds can be seen, but the star species is the year-round Anna humming birds, with the male having spectacular iridescent-green plumage and scarlet-red throats. The crows appear much more frequently nowadays to build nests in trees around our yard. Every so often, a forty-pound raccoon, sometimes with family, roams into the backyard at night looking for snails, and they fish in our pond. We are surprised that they are not at all intimidated by our flood lights that filter through the blackness.

During the winter season, we experience herons, egrets, and peregrine falcons (even, once-in-a-while, a brilliant turquoise kingfisher), attempting also to feed on our fish. The winter rainstorms usually warm the air to a comfortable level in the high sixties and provide more economical irrigation for the garden than during the dry seasons of spring, summer, and fall. This very welcomed moisture also produces oxalis, with its green clover leaves and yellow flowers. I tried, without success, to eliminate this awful bulbous plant of South African origin from expanding. But, finally, I have decided to try to enjoy the colorful show at Ming's suggestion. The beautiful, perennial, purple-shaded cineraria and white calla lilies follow. February offers a spectacular white cloud from the Santa Rosa plum tree, followed by its delicious plums. Spring brings blooming rhododendrons, lilacs, camellias (japonica), hydrangeas of various hues, and azaleas. Many migrating birds, such as robins, finches, wrens, juncos, stellar blue jays, mourning doves, and mocking birds come to nest in the garden again. The bird-song is wonderful, and at night the mocking birds sing as beautifully as nightingales. Unfortunately, pesky crows also nest in nearby trees, and all the other birds disappear when the crows fly through the yard.

The summer, with irrigation, produces roses, and the fog cover at night brings forth blossoms on the many, multicolored fuchsia, both climbing and bushes, and the pink amaryllis (Amaryllis Belladonna) in the front flower bed explode in color. Fall is the warmest time of the year in San Francisco, and everything in the garden continues to be luxuriant, but with some coloring of ornamentals and the foliage. In the front of the house, the now three-story high, vibrant magenta bougainvillea—planted by the previous owner, Scott Tree—the quince bush, and the large magnolia grand flora tree provide spectacular displays from spring until fall. I have often thought, "The beauty of our garden, and my personal gardening, provide me with a mentally healthy, wholesome attitude toward society."

7.

Upper Eddy Street

Many of our original, surrounding, African American neighbors still live across the street, on both sides, and behind our back yard. We were friends with our neighbors from the beginning. My particular favorites were Lonnie and Frankie Herndon, at that time in their mid-50s, who were our next-door neighbors to the west. Frankie was a tall, stout woman with a beaming countenance, and Lonnie was rail thin and clean shaven. They built their dream home in 1954. Their idea of respectability was a two-story, white, stucco house of modern design on the site of an old, neighborhood stable. The upstairs consists of a living room with a fireplace, a kitchen/dining area combination in the front, and two bedrooms in the rear overlooking their large backyard that has a vegetable and flower garden. Downstairs is a large studio apartment, with a kitchen and a bathroom, along with a two-car garage. In the garage, Frankie kept her prized collection of salt and pepper shakers in three glass display cabinets. They could not believe that we would buy such a decrepit old house—particularly with bad plumbing. But they politely never mentioned their opinions. Lonnie was a plumber who had met Frankie (a welder) in the shipyards during World War II. One day Lonnie came over to help fix some leaky faucets in our home. He kept muttering about the poor condition of the plumbing and advised me that Vaseline was the best lubricant for any plumbing job. Frankie once mentioned to me that one of the former owners of our home, "Mrs. Arboleta was a Negro and perhaps the second wife of her Filipino husband."

Frankie, being an enterprising person, had established a popular catering business. With peaches from our trees, and some of our donated sugar, she made delicious peach sauce for both households. She hung her clothing on the backyard clothes lines to dry. Although they both came from large families in Texas, they never had children. With their frugality and combined income, they were able to acquire other properties. They were extremely positive about our neighborhood and were able to coax the city into providing modern arc-shaped streetlight fixtures and to be instrumental in designating perpendicular parking on our steep, wide street. Frankie told me that she would hose down the prostitutes that circulated from the newly built, public housing projects of the 1950s as they walked on the sidewalk in front of her home! Lonnie and Frankie were like many other African American neighbors, who considered our neighborhood just as desirable as the Sugar Hill in Harlem (New York City). Like me, Lonnie was always interested in improving and tending to his garden. But when he died, Frankie lost interest in maintaining their garden. During the summer, Frankie kept her full-length mink coat in storage in the fur vaults at the elegant, downtown I. Magnin Department Store. That coat became available during the mild winter season to wear to their Baptist church, along with her fabulous hats. Lonnie and Frankie were both teetotalers and disapproved of the jazz nightclub life.

Old age seemed to creep up suddenly on Frankie after her sweetheart Lonnie died. She became confused and disoriented. I remember stopping her one day on Divisadero Street, and I asked her, "Where do you live?" She had no idea. At this point, I contacted her niece Bernice, who kindly took over Frankie's affairs. Some strange man had moved in earlier with Frankie, and her niece evicted him. Eventually, Frankie moved to the home of her niece. Her grand-niece Jo, with her granddaughter, now lives next door. The handsome husband of the grand-niece disappeared shortly after they moved in. Over the years, we have had a comfortable, neighborly relationship, and have watched her daughter, Aurielle, who has a parochial school education, grow into a fine young adult.

Essie Collins, an African American from Alabama, was another neighbor to the west of the Herndons. She was already a major mover and shaker in the Western Addition. She gradually accumulated many real estate investments. Her five-unit apartment building was on the rest of the site of the former livery stable. The 1920s, stucco-covered, wooden-frame building was odd because it consisted of two, identical buildings that the SFRA had relocated by repositioning the façade of one building to face the rear yard on this 137-foot-deep lot. Supposedly, Essie had come to San Francisco with her husband, who was assigned to the Army at The Presidio. As a single woman, she was one of the founders of our neighborhood group and became extremely well connected with the redevelopment agency. She rarely missed any public meeting. In 1978, she fought against most of her neighbors in the 1900 block of Eddy Street when she supported the building of public housing on a vacated lot there. The irony was that the criminally impacted, large Yerba Buena West public housing was only a block away. Curiously, with the "blessing" of the redevelopment agency, she was eventually chosen as the developer of a market-rate condominium complex of fifteen units at this site. She was a fervent member of the Third Baptist Church. She was as controversial in the Caucasian community, as well as the African American community, for her many redevelopment agency development projects. Her accomplishments are a strong and impressive statement for black enterprise, and persistence by any individual.

Across the street was a duplex with the same type of construction as next door to us, and it was also built by Lonnie Herndon in the 1960s. The owner, Bertha, is a sophisticated, attractive, African American lady who worked, before her retirement as a grocery check-out clerk at Petrini's grocery. She was proud of her extensive doll collection. Two of her elderly, female tenants, in their late nineties, were related to Lonnie. Once an elderly African American friend of theirs, who was on the staff at the White House, came to visit them, and she became a local celebrity after speaking of her experiences at the White House. She informed us, "Mamie Eisenhower was not an alcoholic but had dizzy spells." Bertha dated a banker by the name of Ernest King, who was a brother to Leroy King, a longshoreman leader and probably the longest-serving reappointed Redevelopment Commissioner (still a commissioner in 2011). The elegant Bertha and outgoing Ernest owned matching 1957 Thunderbird cars, with one being coral colored and the other turquoise, which were parked in her garages. They were as devoted as any two people could be. And when Ernest's wife died, after a lengthy, devastating illness, Ernest and Bertha married, and she moved out of the neighborhood to a building that Ernest owned. We were invited to a delightful party there. She lost Ernest and has remarried. She continues to own the pair of flats and collects the rent payments. When she arrives in her Cadillac, she is always graciously cordial.

Behind us, in a two-flat Stick Eastlake Victorian building lived the African Americans, Earl and Ruby Alford and their family. They had, with the same financial assistance from the redevelopment agency as us, earlier completed a beautiful restoration of their perfectly intact, original facade and modernized the interior. The light-skinned Earl was called the "Mayor of Ellis Street" by his neighbors. In appreciation, a bronze plaque in his honor was affixed to the balustrade on the front stairs of his home. He had the most beautiful, light-blue eyes that I have ever seen in an African American man. The ebony-skinned Ruby was the first treasurer of our neighborhood group.

Next door, to the east of us, was a three-flat building that had been built in 1912, and the two top flats were later split in half. The owner, from the World War II-period onward, was a Canadian American woman. After she died, her daughter, a physician, hired a property manager to maintain the building. The lower flat was occupied by a single African American woman who ran a day-care center but did not do a good job of managing the toddlers. They were often playing on the sidewalk without supervision and had dirty diapers. Her flat was filled with cockroaches. The tall, distinguished-looking African American gay, John Cole, lived on the top floor and has been in the neighborhood ever since. He now lives across the street in Bertha's building. He has always been a great and friendly neighbor. He worked for Chevron Oil Company and is now retired. In 1977, a Jewish New Yorker, Judy Brown, who was quite pregnant, bought the building that I had listed with a Canadian American woman's estate. Judy moved into the lower flat. She had divorced her extremely handsome African American husband when he became threatening her about their pregnancy. They had owned a four-story, magnificent, Queen Anne Victorian house with a ground-floor ballroom, circa 1895, a few blocks away near Alamo Square, which they sold. An associate of mine, and a later owner of the house, sold it many years later for over $1 million and now worth $3 million.

Benjamin (Ben), Judy's son, was cute and popular in the neighborhood, particularly with Frankie Herndon, who spoiled him. She became particularly distressed as he grew older that he spoke

Spanish because of their Mexican housekeeper. As Frankie lowered candy suckers on a string from her second floor, she always said to him, "Speak American." Judy was an executive director with a nonprofit foundation and was beautiful, lively, and intelligent. She became a close friend and we enjoyed the frequent visits by her Jewish parents, who owned nursing homes in upper New York State. We regretted when she moved to a house on Twin Peaks, that I sold her, and then later moved to Miami, Florida. She remarried a Chinese/Portuguese/Jamaican. I had also listed her property for sale on Eddy Street, and she made a significant profit. The Larkin family, who are well respected African Americans in the community, bought the property in 1989, and Marion Larkin (the mother) lives in one of the apartments. Marion was originally from Kansas City, Missouri. Her son, who was a San Francisco fireman, keeps upgrading the building. We continue to have good relationship. Her other son is an investment broker and lives with his family in an outstanding Queen Anne Victorian near Alamo Square. Her former husband, a music group promoter, married a white woman and they have children. Her grandchildren are cute, smart, and a delight to watch. The backyard has been mostly tended by interested tenants in recent years, and then neglected in between tenants.

8.

Neighborhood Organizations

Beideman Area Neighborhood Group

At the time that John and I moved to the neighborhood, various neighbors were organizing groups to fight many of the decisions that were being made by the SFRA for the existing vacant lots, which the redevelopment agency had created through the demolition of housing by the use of eminent domain. Also, there was concern about the negative quality of life that the housing projects produced. The area needed much infrastructure upgrading.

In 1975, the Beideman Area Neighborhood Group, or BANG, was founded. I had suggested that we focus our name on the Beideman Historical District that was created in the early 1970s, with the few remaining Stick Eastlake Victorian buildings in-place in our neighborhood, as well as twenty other Victorian houses that were relocated there from other locations in the Western Addition. The relocated houses were financially sponsored by the newly organized Foundation for San Francisco Architectural Heritage. This positive relationship will be elaborated on later. In the early 1960s, through the efforts of the A-2 Project Area director, Enid Sales, there was a new effort to preserve these buildings, as well as some intact, surrounding historical blocks, such as the south side of the 1900 block of Ellis Street. The SFRA headquarters for the historical architectural preservation staff was established in a Victorian building on O'Farrell Street between Webster and Buchanan Streets. The historical district was to be specifically created around Beideman Street, with the boundaries of Divisadero, Scott, O'Farrell, and Eddy Streets. BANG established our boundaries as Geary Boulevard on the north, Pierce Street on the east, Saint Josephs Avenue on the west, and Turk Street on the south. This was essentially the entire residential district in the San Francisco Redevelopment Agency A-2 Project Area south of Geary Boulevard, but did not include the commercial strips along Geary Boulevard, which were in the A-1 Project Area.

Our first president was Jim Gibbs, who owned a detached 1920s, brown-shingled house on the hillside on Ellis Street two blocks above Divisadero Street. He was a congenial middle-aged, African American, gay man who worked in the pharmacy at the nearby Kaiser Permanente Hospital. Our vice-president was Dr. Jim Delameter, who was an emergency-room doctor at Kaiser Permanente Hospital and owned a pair of flats on the 1900 block of Eddy Street. I was a second vice-president. My neighbor, Ruby Alford, was treasurer.

Most of the members of the group were home owners, but a few were tenants. The most active of the members were a diverse group with a common uniting factor of monitoring the SFRA and preventing them from doing any more destruction and poor planning in our neighborhood. Sometimes the cooperation from the agency was quite good, but other times our development proposals were rejected. Gene Suttle, who, in 1974, had become the A-2 Project director, was generally as conciliatory as he was allowed to be. He was a handsome, light-skinned, tall, and well-educated

African American. We became good friends at a distance through political necessity, and I would often see him in the Castro District with his various, younger, white boyfriends.

Within the Beideman Historical District, several political active couples with younger children moved into the SFRA rehabilitated Victorian pairs of flats. These families included the Richens and Cancinos, and would later include the Millers and Tostas. A long time existing resident was Essie Sutton, the sister of the New York City Assemblyman, Percy Sutton. Essie was elegant, light-skinned African American lady, with her grey hair tied in a bun, and was originally from San Antonio, Texas. She forcibly worked toward African American children having a good education, as well as a safe neighborhood to live.

During the following years, such condominium and cooperative developments as Divisadero Heights, Elizabeth Terrace, The Sun Houses, Ermancio Ergina Village, and Endicott Court resulted, with his assistance, for a much more attractive and livable neighborhood. These developments will be explored in a later chapter. The effect of the requested city tree planting made for a more sylvan environment. Some neighbors, such as Frankie Herndon, were afraid that her sidewalks would be damaged, or that thieves would hide behind them. But she and others reluctantly agreed to have trees planted in front of their homes anyway. Zoned permit parking was much more popular because of the excessive parking by patients and staff from Kaiser Permanente Hospital. Eventually, the hospital built a large parking garage adjacent to their hospital facilities. The expansion of the Kaiser Permanente Medical Center and the consolidation of their physical presence greatly enhanced our neighborhood and will be explored in a later chapter.

Western Addition Neighborhood Association

The property owners and tenants living in the A-2 Project Area on the north side of Geary Boulevard had organized the Western Addition Neighborhood Association (WANA) in 1973, with the same purposes as our group. We often joined forces to help one another with our prospective neighborhood approved development, as well as for nearby SFRA proposed large-scale commercial and residential developments in the whole A-2 Project Area. The whole redevelopment plan for the A-2 Project Area was approved in 1964 but did not get underway until 1966 with funding from the U.S. Department of Housing and Urban Development (HUD). The total Western Addition approved A-2 Project Area (as mentioned earlier) approximately 277 acres of land, which included 106 acres of streets. The boundaries for WANA were Baker Street on the west, Laguna Street on the east, Post Street on the south, and Bush Street on the north. The adjacent A-1 Project Area (the commercial strip on both the south and north sides of Geary Boulevard) was established earlier in the 1956 and had progressed rapidly. This development near WANA was the commercial strip that extended along the north side of Geary Boulevard from Van Ness Avenue to Masonic Street. WANA focused primarily on the Japantown center.

WANA's Historical District was Cottage Row, which is a row of small 1870s two-story servant cottages, with no yards, and the surrounding, intact, elegant Italianate Victorian houses between Sutter and Bush Streets that were concentrated around Webster Street. In the early 1970s, certain designated historical buildings were moved from other obliterated locations to this A-2 Project Area. One important house moved here from 773 Turk Street to 1737 Webster Street in 1975, and was restored by the wealthy gay, George Stewart, a scion of an early pioneer family. His outstanding Stick Eastlake house was built in 1885 by the prodigious brothers, Samuel Newsom and Joseph Cather Newsom.

In this neighborhood along Fillmore Street, between Geary Boulevard and Sutter Street, with an extension halfway to Webster

Street, were existing Victorian commercial buildings with residential flats above. One of these buildings was owned by our neighbor Essie Collins. Similar Victorian buildings were relocated by the SFRA to complete a commercial district with residential housing above. Bob Vogel, our gay SFRA architect, was, as always, extremely affirmatively instrumental in this major restoration project with his associates, Susan Bragstad and Jane Duncome, who were both purportedly lesbians. Their creative 1970s efforts can be much appreciated today. One Stick Eastlake building, circa 1885, which had previously been located on 1970 Post Street at Buchanan Street (now the Nihonmachi Mall); was moved to 1712 Fillmore Street. In the 1950s, this building had been the location of Jimbo's Bop City, the famous after-hours jazz club. This relocated building was raised one story to provide a commercial space at street level. The commercial space became in 1981 the site of Marcus (Garvey) Books, which is an important resource center for African American literature. The owners, Raye Richardson and her husband Julian, established the business in 1960. During the late 1960s, the store became an unofficial headquarters for the Black Panthers, a radical, anarchist group with mostly African American members. The store continues to be family owned and is now the oldest African American bookseller in the United States. Other Victorian buildings were similarly moved and raised for commercial space on this block. If one looks above Bush Street on Fillmore Street, there is a more integrated and unplanned urban renewal in existence—unaffected by the rehabilitation costs associated with the redevelopment agency!

The early, moving forces in WANA were Mary Jane (M.J.) and her husband Blair Staymetz, who owned an Italianate house on the 1900 block of Sutter Street. George Stewart was the owner of a SFRA-relocated, landmarked Italianate mansion on Webster Street,

Palmer Sessel bought an Italianate flat-fronted house, circa 1870s, with a large, rear, carriage house on Bush Street. Many of these houses, along with the other nearby row houses, were financed and marketed by The Real Estate Associates. The early president, M. J., from Texas, was a particularly interesting and dynamic individual. A strawberry blond with a short haircut and a wiry body, she was a joy to watch at redevelopment agency or housing authority commission meetings. She always had her facts straight and could be expected to intellectually counter any commissioner. She was comfortable physically with the solid backdrop of her gentle Blair, who was employed by Southern Pacific Railroad. They had met when she was doing business accounting there. Palmer was of the old, southern-school, gentlemen background and projected a smooth approach to city matters. George was always dramatic and effective, as a member of the exclusive Bohemian Club. Sadly, George contracted AIDS. Many other competent members of WANA, such as Calvin Lau, Charles Bush, Jan Bolaffi, and others carried on the tradition of improving their community.

FULTON

Alamo Square Neighborhood Association

The earliest neighborhood group opposing the SFRA was the Alamo Square Neighborhood Association (ASNA). This neighborhood group was founded in 1966 and consists of a radius of two blocks around the famous 12.7 acre Alamo Square (city Historical Landmarked District), which had been a wealthy, Victorian residential district and an important refuge for the 1906 earthquake victims. Today, this district is one of the most photographed places in San Francisco! The boundaries of this neighborhood have been expanded to Baker Street on the west, Buchanan Street on the east, Turk Street on the north, and Page Street on the south. The park is surrounded by many magnificent Victorian mansions that were saved from SFRA demolition in the designated A-3 Project Area. Some of the most notable houses are the large spectacular Stick Eastlake Westerfeld house with a square tower at the corner of Scott and Fulton Streets, circa 1889, designed by Henry Geilfuss; the charming Arts and Crafts-style cottage, circa 1895, designed by A. Page Brown; and the row of houses called "seven sisters" in the Queen Anne-style, circa 1895, developed by Matthew Kavanaugh on the 700 Block of Steiner Street. His family resided at 722 Steiner Street. These particular multicolored-painted sisters are now the most photographed Victorian houses in the United States for commercial advertisements and feature the modern city, which arises in the background. In addition, there is the impressive Beaux Arts former Roman Catholic Archbishop's mansion, circa 1895, with a mansard roof surrounded by unusual wrought iron balconies. It later became an exquisite bed-and-breakfast at the northeast corner of Fulton and Steiner Streets. In 2012, the mansion was sold for $7 M and became again a single family home.

There are many other outstanding well-preserved homes on the square, as well as in the surrounding blocks. This protected historical district reveals an idea of the residential districts that previously existed in the Western Addition before redevelopment. The founders were a brave lot and resourceful. Some of the notable neighbors included: Peter Witmer (1928–2011), a preservation architect (whose father was the chief architect for the Pentagon in Washington D.C.), who bought, with his partner Don Nehls in 1957, a Queen Anne Victorian pair of flats with a witch cap tower on Alamo Square, which had been converted to a boarding house for shipyard workers in World War II. They converted this dilapidated structure to its original state; Marvin Edwards, an African American property owner and first president of ASNA; Greg and Kathy Calegari, who reared their family on the world-famous 700 block of Steiner; Barney Kearney owned a large Queen Anne house, also on Alamo Square; Richard Reutlinger owns a much-beloved Italianate Victorian house at 924 Grove Street and is an important figure in the Victorian Alliance; and the late Bruce McNair. Later, the important house historian, Joe Pecora, and Jim Siegel, who owns the Westerfeld House added additional energy and support. Their main stalling effort for a takeover of their neighborhood by the SFRA as the A-3 Project Area was the Federal Assistance Code Enforcement (FACE) program. This program assisted property owners with loans to rehabilitate their homes and buildings to upgrade them to current building code requirements. Thus, this area was able to escape the notorious destruction and wanton demolition that had occurred in other Western Addition neighborhoods. As with many of the neighborhood associations, this group continues to grow and attract new talent and energy. With their Internet connection, monthly meetings, and personal interactions, the Alamo Square Historical District, expanded to a three bock radius, is particularly well organized to meet the demands of the twenty-first century.

Anza Vista Neighborhood Association

This neighborhood was developed, beginning in 1947, on the forty-nine acre site of the Roman Catholic Calvary Cemetery (established in 1860), after the bodies were relocated to Colma (the nearby city of cemeteries). This development was not included in the A-2 Project Area. The original name for the neighborhood association was the Anza Vista Civic Improvement Club, and it was founded in 1960. There were exclusion restrictions for certain ethnicities, which were later eliminated. The exclusive San Francisco suburb of Saint Francis Wood (earlier home of Shirley Temple) had tried to exclude the great African American baseball player Willie Mays in 1957 but was rebuffed in a court lawsuit!

Later this neighborhood group changed their name to the Anza Vista Neighborhood Association (AVNA). The neighborhood boundaries are Saint Josephs Avenue on the east, Masonic Avenue on the west, Geary Boulevard on the north, and Turk Street on the south. The late Fred Wagner, a gay Pan-American steward, formerly a Mormon from Idaho and companion to a Japanese boyfriend, was a long-time president of AVNA. He actively participated with other neighborhood groups in protesting against the crime in the nearby public housing projects and the activities in the adjacent SFRA A-2 Project Area. This new, closer relationship of the AVNA, started in 1970s, was advantageous to all, as opposed to their earlier self-imposed isolationism on the top of the heights. The early community residents were mostly Italian American families with a few Chinese American and Japanese American families. There were few African American households.

9.

Western Addition Project Action Committee

The U.S. presidential creation of the cabinet status of the Department of Housing and Urban Development in 1965 was primarily to coordinate the dispersal of large amounts of funding to the local agencies. The SFRA formed, in accordance within HUD guide lines, an advisory neighborhood group called the Western Addition Community Organization (WACO) in 1966. Several African American ministers were members. Reverend Hannibal Williams, the minister for the New Liberation Presbyterian Church, and who later became a redevelopment commissioner, was a notable member. One consequence of their political actions was to get one of their own members, Reverend Wilbur Hamilton, appointed the A-2 Project director. He would become the executive director of the SFRA upon the resignation of Robert Rumsey in 1974. Rumsey had been appointed by Mayor Joseph Alioto in 1971 upon the death of the earlier-mentioned, infamous Executive Director M. Justin Herman. During Rumsey's tenure, the new policies of Mayor Alioto were to reverse the former trend of demolishing buildings and to replace with new housing on the vacant land for a more compact modern city, with African American input. However, he did defend the earlier demolition of housing stock to make a newer, vibrant city. He was more focused on the SFRA developments of the Golden Gateway Project and the Yerba Buena Center.

After the Watts riots in 1965, and the tumultuous civil rights movement for African American equality, he was acutely aware of forming a close-working relationship with that community. Thereby, the African American churches were given carte blanche to erect new churches and to build subsidized, cooperative housing, as well as senior housing for their congregation members. Reverend Wilbur Hamilton was to have a long-standing tenure and was usually realistic about it appearing to be a "good balancing act" for everyone in the Western Addition. This committee, for all practical purposes, came to be seen by all of the other impacted neighborhood groups as a rubber stamp for whatever the agency wanted.

Later, this group was reorganized as the Western Addition Project Action Committee (WAPAC). Leona Robertson, an elegant, elderly, African American property owner in the BANG district and a member of St. Cyprian's Episcopal Church, and I visited one of their meetings in 1979 and were told, in no uncertain terms, that we were not welcome, meaning both of us. One of the members pulled out a handgun to emphasize his point. He said, "Your kinds aren't wanted here." We were glad to escape alive without any police protection being present! Their headquarters were in a dilapidated building with a former ground-floor commercial space and two upper floors of rental units, which were occupied by a constantly changing group of tenants. The building was located on Sutter Street, between Fillmore and Webster Streets, next to Mary Jane and Blair Staymetz, who were constantly harassed. They coped with a lot of loud noise at night. The building was eventually demolished and the vacant lot next door became part of the attractive The Amelia, with condominiums above commercial stores. The self-styled "hell raiser," Mary Rogers, who was a fifty-seven-year-old African American, and a one-time Board of Supervisors candidate, was chairman from 1977 and was replaced in

1982 by thirty-nine-year-old Don Bryant, an architectural draftsman, photographer, and talk-show interviewer for the African American public interest FM radio station KPOO.

Rogers acted in her capacity as a paid staff employee of the SFRA for this publicly funded watchdog organization in spite of the implied collusion. At SFRA Commission meetings in February of 1982, the *San Francisco Examiner* staff writer, Gerald Adams, quoted remarks by Ms. Rogers saying "...different strokes for different folks." She also said, "...especially in making it easier for white developers than for black developers to obtain options on agency-owned land." Another outburst from her was "Black folks are always left to fight....You put us in a bucket like a damn bunch of crabs." She was always demonic, dramatic, and racist toward white people. I did admire her for saying that government interference in the Western Addition was unwarranted, but she consequently made everything seem a travesty with her narrow vision and payback from her special interests, including the SFRA and SFHA. The actions of this short, stout, mean-faced woman, in traditional African headdress and flowing gowns, often caused embarrassment to the ever-dignified Executive Director Wilbur Hamilton. At this time, she indicated that her opponents in the WAPAC election were merely racist Black Muslims and former ambitious San Francisco State College activists who were prominent during Black Student Union (BSU) protests after the Watts riots of 1965. These students began a protest strike from 1968 to 1969 on the campus. A college of Ethnic Studies would evolve in 1970 from this strike and was the first, and still the only, academic department of its kind in the United States.

In 1968, as the president of San Francisco State College, which became a University in 1973, the Japanese American S. I. Hayakawa was able to effectively moderate all factions during these trying times. A photograph of him wearing a tam -o'-shanter, jumping upon a stage of striking students, and pulling out the wiring of their sound-amplifying system received immediate national attention in the press. This expert in linguistics and semantics was elected as a conservative Republican from California to the U.S. Senate from 1977 to 1983. Another WAPAC board member, a prominent member of the Japanese American community, and a University of California Board of Regent, Yori Wada, was involved with WAPAC at this time. As members of BANG, Essie Collins and Rodolfo Cancino (secretary) were later on the board of directors.

WAPAC eventually disbanded as a formal organization in the late 1980s but returned again in 2005. This reappearance followed my suggestion at a commission meeting, that the SFRA no longer had a citizen's advisory board. I was, of course excluded. The results were the formation of the mayor's Western Addition A-2 Citizens Advisory Committee (WACAC) with Reverend Arnold Townsend (an early BSU member) as their chairperson and Barbara Meskunas as vice-chairperson. The general membership included an interesting, diverse mixture of personalities: Estelle Crawford, Richard Hashimoto (former site manager of the Japantown garage), Paul Hyams, Sandy Mori (Japantown activist), Dr. Raye Richardson (Marcus Books), Noni Richen (member of BANG and president of The Small Properties Owners Assoc.), Palmer Sessel (WANA), George Smith, Charles Spencer, and Rev. Floyd Trammell (African American minister).

10.

Historical Architectual Groups

A renewed interest in architectural preservation started a new impulse to reassess anything old. The milestone book, *Here Today* (perhaps gone tomorrow) was written by authors Richard Olmsted and T. H. Watkins with photographs furnished by Morley Baer. The book was sponsored by the Junior League of San Francisco, Inc., in 1968, and was instrumental in summing up the interest in and importance of preservation of historical buildings. Also, the demolition of the historic City of Paris department store building on Union Square (earlier established in 1850 on a sailing ship of the same name in the San Francisco Bay) was important. The fashionable French store was designed originally by Clinton Day, in1896, and rebuilt after the 1906 earthquake by Blakewell and Brown, and Louis Bourgeois in the Renaissance /Baroque-style was an important catalyst. Although there was some restoration after the Loma Prieta earthquake of 1989, the earlier earthquake-remodeled interior, with an incredible, giant, stained-glass dome picturing a square-rigged sailing ship located in an interior court yard. The middle floor was still intact, as well as the original lower floors, which were constructed of cast iron.

The original owner, a Frenchman named Paul Verdier, had created an incredible interior with counters for perfume, gloves, etc., on the main floor, which was serviced by an impeccably well-dressed female staff. The cellars below created a quaint Parisian street setting with wine shops, exclusive imported food shops, and bistro dining. At Christmas, a four-story, live, evergreen fir tree, with imported antique tree ornaments, was placed on the ground floor beneath the glass dome.

The preservation of this elegant, much loved, and historically important building became a cause célèbre in the early 1970s, much like the earlier Stonewall protests in1969 for gays, and civil rights protests for African Americans after the Watts riots of 1965. It was a major rallying point for the preservation community. Philip Johnson, a member of the gay fraternity and a world-renowned architect, proposed a bland, granite, checker-board design as the future site of a Neiman Marcus department store in place of the City of Paris building. The newly organized Foundation for San Francisco Architectural Heritage, dating from 1972, and the Victorian Alliance, dating from 1973, emerged to fight this destruction. As a volunteer, I sat at a table at the southeast corner of Geary and Stockton Streets to collect signatures on a petition to stop the demolition. The result was that only the interior was preserved, and two vital and quite important historical-preservation groups were established. The two organizations were, however, contrastingly different in orientation. Heritage and the Victorian Alliance would early compete on the primordial basis of *Privilege vs. Home Ownership*. I have been, from the beginning, a member of both organizations. Both are important and symbolize the desire for preserving the best of the past but living with the future. San Francisco has become a city that is recognized for its unique and noble architectural heritage, as important as that of New York City, Boston, Chicago, New Orleans, Santa Fe, and Seattle. Los Angeles seems to be on a different planet.

11.

San Francisco Redevelopment Agency Residential Development In The Western Addition A-2 Project Area

A Galvanizing Moment

In 1978, the neighborhood groups of BANG, WANA, and ASNA joined together to organize a coalition to stop the redevelopment agency from giving the housing authority exclusive negotiating rights to build forty-two large, family housing units on four scattered sites in the A-2 Project Area. The coalition formed was called the Concerned Citizens for Better Housing (CCBH). This energized coalition of mostly lower-income and middle-class property owners of various ethnic backgrounds were outraged that these units would be built close to the already existing 1,130 public family housing units. The steering committee consisted of myself and Jim Delameter from BANG; Peter Witmer, Alan Hall, and Bruce McNair from ASNA; and M. J. Staymetz, George Stewart, and Steven Richards from WANA. The committee consisted only of Whites because African Americans in the Project Area were either intimidated, complacent, or allies of the politically powerful SFRA Executive Director Wilbur Hamilton. We were the only major players in this war against the powerful forces at all levels of city politics. John was not pleased and asked me not to get involved. I replied, "How can I honestly ignore the graft and corruption that's involved?" In retrospect, I learned that the SFHA could only sponsor new public housing throughout SFRA-designated redevelopment areas.

This whole drama was played out with a beginning backdrop of Guyana, in November 1978, amidst the ghastly mass suicide of many ethnicities, which included 918 African Americans, including 305 children in all, from San Francisco and Oakland. The crazed demagogue Reverend Jim Jones had persuaded members of his church to commit suicide with potassium cyanide-laced grape-flavored Kool Aid, either voluntarily or involuntarily! The children were brought first by security guards to drink the poisoned liquid. They died in the newly built rural commune of Jonestown in Guyana. Some of the congregation escaped into the surrounding jungles. Their many grieving congregation members, who had not relocated with friends and relatives, remained safe in the San Francisco Bay Area. In 1972, Reverend Jones had established the Peoples Temple in San Francisco at the old Albert Pike Masonic Temple, next to the vacant Temple Beth Israel on Geary Boulevard, between Fillmore and Steiner Streets. The synagogue had relocated in 1969. Even though he was a white man preaching an outreach to all ethnic groups, he appealed mostly to the African American community, which was located in the nearby public-housing projects and the equally nearby church congregations. Many of my neighbors and I were quite suspicious of his motivations. The Pentecostal preacher, who practiced faith healing, called Jesus Christ the first communist. He asked his congregation to practice communal sharing of their personal material resources. The church flyers that were stuck in our front gates or doors, offering "paradise on earth" with his rainbow family, as well as paradise in heaven, were outrageous!

Amazingly, Jones had been enabled by major politicians who sponsored his political and religious aspirations. He returned the favor by getting his congregation members to vote, canvass. And thereby help their favored candidates win on election days. U.S. Representative Phillip Burton (1964–1983) and his powerful, emerging coalition of assorted politicians benefited primarily by being elected to political offices. His brother, John Burton, also became a U.S. Representative. The now U.S. Senator Barbara Boxer was on his staff earlier and became his replacement as the U.S. Congress. John Burton would become later a long-time California state legislator. John Burton famously proposed, at one point, floating an Alaskan iceberg to San Francisco for fresh water. Another major player was Willie Brown Jr., who became a state assemblyman and later the extremely influential Speaker of the Assembly. He was eventually to become mayor of San Francisco. Other beneficiaries of Phillip Burton were George Moscone, Harvey Milk, and Art Agnos! Many of these political personages appeared at Jones's church meetings but, noticeably, not the powerful "Boss" Congressman Phillip Burton. Phillip Burton (both he and John were the sons of a local physician) had challenged the well-established Irish political machine and the heterogeneous coalition of then Mayor Joseph Alioto. Many San Franciscans considered that the ultra-liberal ("progressive") Mayor George Moscone and the openly gay Supervisor Harvey Milk were elected in 1975 due in large part through the efforts of these church members.

Reverend Jones's success provided him with an appointment by Mayor Moscone to the presidency of the SFHA commission! This appointment, along with many introductions, would provide him numerous telephone calls to First Lady Rosalyn Carter. They had dinner together in San Francisco. The locally reared Governor of California Jerry Brown (1975–1983), former Jesuit priest and son of a former governor (Edmond "Pat" Brown) seemed also to have been embroiled in the whole morass, even sleeping one evening in a SFHA public-housing unit (Yerba Buena Annex), with guards around him. He was elected again in 2010 as governor. The majority of the legal documents, with regard to the People's Temple, remain classified to this day in spite of various U.S. Freedom of Information Act requests!

Reverend Jones's personal physician, Dr. Carleton B. Goodlett, was the owner of the influential African American *the Sun-Reporter* newspaper. Dr. Goodlett visited Jonestown in August of 1978. He was a much-respected member of the community. Dr. Goodlett was also a close friend of Phillip Burton's wife, Sala Burton, who became our U. S. Representative when her husband died in 1983 of a cerebral aneurism, at the age of fifty-six. Sala Burton later died from colon cancer. From her deathbed, she had purportedly given her blessing for her congressional seat to go to Nancy Pelosi in 1987. Pelosi, an attractive Pacific Heights housewife, was a very successful fundraiser for the Democratic Party. She had never held public office. But, as the politically talented and intelligent daughter of former U.S. Representative Thomas D'Alesandro, Jr. from Maryland (1939–1947) and Mayor of Baltimore (1947–1959), she easily won over the gay Supervisor Harry Britt. In 2006, she would become the first female speaker of the U.S. House of Representatives.

Dr. Goodlett lived near the People's Temple in an apartment building constructed in the 1960s at the southeast corner of Divisadero Street and Geary Boulevard, which was designed by the well-respected architectural firm, Skidmore, Owings, and Merrill. This building is a redevelopment-subsidized building in the BANG area. The initially low-cost rental apartments are now cooperative units. He was later immortalized by the naming of the block of Polk Street in front of City Hall as # 1 Dr. Carlton B. Goodlett Place. The renaming of Fillmore Street had been first suggested but was rejected after much negative public input.

More shock and horror followed on November 27, 1978, when Supervisor Dan White used a handgun to assassinate Mayor George Moscone and Supervisor Harvey Milk, the first openly gay public official in the United States! The politically independent and wealthy Democrat Dianne Feinstein, as the president of Board of Supervisors, became an important stabilizing factor as our calm, intelligent, and extremely effective new mayor.

Now our coalition (CCBH) was dealing with a completely changed political scene. But the mechanics of the inherent city bureaucracy continued. In August 1979, the redevelopment agency, under the directorship of Reverend Wilbur Hamilton, gave approval to this outrageous agreement to build SFHA "scattered site" housing, in spite of more than thirty speakers being against the proposal at the redevelopment commission meeting. I was quoted in the *San Francisco Chronicle*, "We all know the disastrous track record of the housing authority." The commissioners voted unanimously in favor of approving the six scattered sites, which included our block. Reverend Hamilton had been appointed the executive director, as noted earlier, on the death of M. Justin Herman in 1974. An African American named Gene Suttle replaced him as the A-2 Project director. The support for the "scattered site," forty units of public family housing was sparse. But the funding from the California Housing Financing Agency of $2,354,000, used as "bait," made this quite attractive to the supporters of this housing.

Our opponents were the housing authority employees, the redevelopment agency employees and a small, extremist segment of the African American community. The members of the African American community consisted of Cleo Wallace, who was president of the SFHA Tenants Association, Mary Rogers, who was a paid SFHA employee, and Assistant Reverend Arnold Townsend, who was a student leader at San Francisco State College during the race riots of 1967. Carl Williams, the African American director of the housing authority had the temerity to say that the authority would employ more effective screening techniques so as to weed out undesirable people prone to vandalism or other anti-social behavior. He was jeered by the audience and the mood was very ugly. Carl Williams's legacy of inaction at the SFHA has continued to the present day with his successors of all ethnic backgrounds.

Curiously, these bureaucrats seem to be recycled to every racially challenged city in the United States and always cause more grief and graft! Kansas City, Missouri, is a good example, but the worst case is Detroit. These same, misplaced, government policies seem to extend to even the politically popular relocation of disgraced, crooked, and incompetent school superintendents to other large major American cities.

Our new mayor, Dianne Feinstein, had earlier visited one of the existing housing projects and was appalled by what she saw. After the Redevelopment Commission meeting, we (CCBH) privately pointed out to her that the issue was not housing for low income families, but the issue was the corruption of public housing. We had naively hoped that both elected and appointed officials would have the will and the wisdom to see this difference. We approached our Supervisor Ella Hill Hutch, who was the first

African American female San Francisco supervisor, and a jovial personality, but a militant labor official. She was not willing to consider helping us. The Fourth Supervisorial District, where we lived, had the highest concentration of public housing and also the highest concentration of robbery, rape, assault, burglary, theft, purse snatching, and arson in the city! The five proposed units to be constructed on the 1900 block of Eddy Street were only one block from the highest concentration of public housing in the city—the Yerba Buena West Plaza projects. With great consternation at being ignored, the CCBH steering committee was forced to contract with the law firm of Paul and Baker in Oakland to pursue a lawsuit against the redevelopment agency and housing authority to prevent the building of these scattered public-housing sites.

Our attorney, Richard Carrington, filed our law suit on September 28, 1979. The main thrust was the validation of our claims through federal regulation code §880.122 that was established by HUD with regard to redevelopment areas.

> ***An overriding need may not serve if the only reason the need cannot otherwise feasibly be met is that discrimination on the basis of race, color, religion, creed, sex or national origin renders sites outside areas of minority concentration unavailable. The site shall avoid undue concentration of low-income persons. The neighborhood must not be one which is detrimental to family life or in which substandard dwelling or other undesirable elements predominate, unless there is actively in progress a concerted program to remedy the undesirable conditions.***

Also cited was California Health and Safety Code §33039. ".... It is further declared to be the public policy of this State that such rehabilitation or redevelopment programs shall not be undertaken and operated in such a manner as to exchange new slums or to congest individuals from one slum to another slum."

By June 1980, our attorney notified us that the redevelopment agency was rethinking their position and would make the parcels available for alternative development proposals. Our attorney said that we should not dismiss our lawsuit. But we decided, after what was becoming extremely expensive litigation fighting the public-funded agency legal counsel, not to pursue further legal action.

New Developments in the BANG A-2 Project Area

Our immediate neighborhood part of the BANG was on the west side of Divisadero (Devisadero) Street, which had been part of the original Spanish-era (high view) road in 1776, from the Mission Dolores founded by Padre Junipero Serra, to the Presidio (a Spanish fort with adobe walls, which was located near essential year-round water springs). Later, the American army occupied the Presidio, located at the Golden Gate of San Francisco Bay, and immediately became the major army base for the West Coast until becoming part of the enormous Golden Gate National Park in 1994, through the powerful influence of our local U.S. Representative Phillip Burton, and later his wife Sala. They are both buried there. Because Divisadero is a wide, major street, I have, for convenience sake, divided the neighborhood into two districts. The west side slopes steeply uphill to Saint Josephs Avenue, where the original cemeteries, circa 1860, began. The east side is level and stretches to Pierce Street. It is two blocks from the Fillmore Street business district. The east side has suffered completely, with the extensive new HUD, section-8, cooperative-housing development and the nearby SFHA Yerba Buena West public-housing project. Somehow, climbing our hill seemed to deter the same amount of crime.

Elizabeth Terrace

Essie Collins, who was not a plaintiff in our lawsuit but was an early important BANG member, was awarded a SFRA contract, in 1982, to develop that earlier-mentioned contested parcel on our block. Thus, she added to her inventory of four other buildings. Her contractor was Chinese American, and many of the residents of the A-2 Project Area were hired as construction workers to create her three-story building over an enclosed garage. During construction of the concrete foundation, the city building inspector was not present to inspect the placement of the iron rebar before the concrete was poured in place and required the whole foundation to be demolished and rebuilt with his inspections. Essie built an attractive market-rate condominium complex of fifteen units (one to three bedrooms) with an interior, landscaped, entry court and a surrounding garden space. A healthy one-hundred-year-old eucalyptus tree (Eucalyptus Globulus), which was one-hundred-feet tall with a bole of eighty-six inches that was at the back of the parcel was, unfortunately, cut down. I had hired a professional arborist (Arbor Vitae), in 1985, to report on the health status of the tree and how to mitigate possible damage. His report gave a specific plan to protect the tree, which would not impact the design of the building. Ed Brennan stated, "In conclusion, I find that the eucalyptus tree in question is a large, healthy specimen, which is well balanced and has no sign of disease or significant decay. If construction activities are limited, as I have suggested, the tree will continue to thrive, I believe these statements reflect proper practices and principles of arbor-culture." The president of the redevelopment agency, Walter Newman (son-in-law to Cyril Magnin), who was a fellow member of the Stybring Arboretum (San Francisco Botanical Garden) and one of my favorite, local, social celebrities, particularly disappointed me when he voted with the other commissioners in favor of destroying this noble tree.

Newman had the decency to send me a personal letter that stated, "As you may recall, there is and continues to be disagreement on the condition of the tree, and whether this species of eucalyptus is compatible with structures and urban setting." I personally believed, "Early San Franciscans/Californians had seen benefit of the Australian tree as an asset for lumber and its drought resistant quality." Typical of the current thinking, we have the local, native plant extremists who would try to remove my Bougainvillea and Magnolia tree as not being native flora.

The Elizabeth Terrace condominium complex was completed in 1986 and named in honor of Essie's mother. The building certainly is an asset to the neighborhood. The small, yellow roses on a trellis around the entryway are a particularly touching memory of her mother and her.

Sun Houses

In 1972, Jim Delamater, a plaintiff in our lawsuit and one of the founders of BANG, had purchased with his wife, Pat, a pair of Victorian flats at 1980-1982 Eddy Street. He had offered to buy that same contested parcel and to build market-rate housing. His proposal was rejected by the SFRA in favor of Essie. Jim was a popular, young, and enterprising emergency-room physician at the nearby Kaiser Permanente Hospital. His 1870s, two-story, peaked-roof, flat-front, farm house with clapboard siding had been converted into two flats and a garage in the early 1900s. Jim was very much into hands-on improvement, as well as subcontracting work that he was personally not able to do. With the redevelopment agency demolishing houses a block away, he rescued a Queen Anne Victorian porch to give the flats a more imposing entrance. One evening, Jim and Pat invited me up the block to have some wine and soak in their hot tub in the enclosed building in back yard. Under my clothes, I wore an emerald-green swimming bikini that I had purchased in Greece that summer. John was on duty at the hospital. Stripped to my bikini, I soaked with them in the warm water and had several glasses of wine. All of sudden, the nude Jim and his curvaceous blonde wife began to be very sexually suggestive. I said coyly, "I think that I've had too much wine and better go home to John."

In January 1978, Jim Delameter bought through my real estate firm, another house on the corner of Eddy and Broderick Streets from the Fillmore Fell Corporation (Essie Collins was a board member). This striking Dutch Colonial house with a corner cupola had probably been covered over with brown, wooden, shake shingles at a later date. This large, eight-room house, with a finished basement room, had previously been used as a shelter for pregnant African American girls. During this period as a shelter, there was a lot of outside noise as their boyfriends surrounded the house at all hours.

After his former wife Pat sold their original flats in September 1979 through my company, in November 1979, Jim bought an original Edwardian three-flat building, circa 1914, from a real estate broker who had greatly neglected the building. Two of the flats were divided in half, and Jim converted them back to the original flats. The proposed contested parcel for public housing was adjacent to the east of this building at 1942-1946 Eddy Street. Two of the apartments were in such neglect, even though tenant occupied, that they needed to be almost completely gutted. The flats were updated with as much of the original detailing as possible kept intact. Jim's brother, Bill, and his wife, Carol, moved into the original, unaltered, middle flat. This building was converted by Jim into condominiums several years later. Afterward, a series of accomplished owners made significant, attractive, interior improvements over the years.

Jim and his new wife, Margaret, completed a stunning, major remodeling and restoration of their corner house at the same time. The side yard had been created by the redevelopment agency by condemning a small Victorian cottage, through eminent domain, that was owned by a Japanese American couple. This cottage was demolished and the rear yard added to the next-door building on Broderick Street, owned by the delightfully intelligent Renee Renouf Hall. The Delameters landscaped this barren sandy yard with a palm tree, other exotic plantings, and a lap swimming pool. Jim owned an old, faded, red pickup truck and was always busy loading and unloading building supplies.

In the late 1970s, the redevelopment agency put a corner lot out to bid, which was combined from five demolished houses across from the Delameter's home. Most of the neighborhood responded favorably to Jim's plans over several less desirable designs. He created a condominium complex of the first solar townhouses in the city, located from 1965-97 Eddy Street. They were completed in 1981. These five rhythmically composed, shingled condominiums feature south-facing, solar greenhouses, and were an immediate success. The ground-floor level consists of a garage, storage area, and the large, solar-storage unit. On the main floor is a large living room with views and a fireplace, and a kitchen/dining area is connected to the two-story solarium by sliding doors. There is a communal garden behind. A rear staircase from the dining area connects the second floor, consisting of two bedrooms, two bathrooms, an upstairs laundry, and access to the roof top for a possible deck. During the early construction, someone stole the copper plumbing out of two of the units. The Sun Houses development is a stellar and visionary accomplishment. This fact is amplified by the knowledge that most of the original couples who bought there still live in their townhomes. Also, this building anticipated the energy conservation (Green) movement of the twenty-first century.

Divisadero Heights

We moved to Eddy Street in 1975, and on the northwest corner of Divisadero Street and Eddy Street was a large, unsightly, steep vacant lot. Before their demolition by the redevelopment agency in the 1960s, this space had originally consisted of a corner building with ground-floor stores, surrounded by large mansions on both the nearby blocks. There were still some old Monterey cypress trees at the top of the hill. A large cut-down eucalyptus tree had been dragged to the corner, and the top of the tree trunk had been carved into the likeness of the head of an African American man by some unknown local artist. The trunk, missing the stolen carved head, was moved to the southeast corner of Turk and Webster Streets and is currently there. Active springs gushed water even during the summer. Some of the homes that were condemned were on the lots that were 85 feet wide by 137.5 feet, which would indicate wealthy owners. Also, within two blocks there are still some exceedingly grand, surviving Queen Anne Victorian homes that provide examples. With several of these houses, the large side gardens were subdivided and new condominium buildings were built. All of the names on the 1900 Block Directory were people of Western European ancestry.

The development of this site caused egregious public Redevelopment Commission hearings. Arguments from the usual neighborhood activists (Mary Rogers, etc.) wanted their favored subsidized low-income housing for this site. In fact, at one SFRA meeting, Mary screamed, her customary phrase at me after I had finished speaking: "We don't want your kind in our neighborhood." She proceeded to grab me and throw me to the floor! The police pulled her large, bulky body off me. She was escorted to a corner of the room and glared at me like the cat that ate the canary. Everybody watched! I was grateful that she had not broken any bones or my eyeglasses. I remained in a highly disturbed mood at the meeting. I thought nobody could change my convictions that I was correct. In spite of her opprobrious behavior, I knew I was one of the people attending the meeting who could not be bought.

Eventually a developer, Nicholas Sapunar of Sapunar Realty, was selected with the approval of the BANG. On this assemblage was built a market-rate condominium complex starting in 1980. There are six buildings (five buildings with six-units, and one building with three units above corner, commercial condominiums). All are nestled in an *L* shape around a lovely, secluded garden fed by the earlier-mentioned natural springs. The Victorian/ Contemporary units with bay windows have elegant, semicircular staircases leading to the three front doors, one for each flat. On the front sidewalks and front yards, trees are planted, and the beautiful landscaping created around the staircases, which BANG had requested from the architects, Bulkley and Descamps, flourish. This change of the plans gives the buildings an integrated and neighborly feeling with the rest of the block. The units themselves are a reverse floor plan, with the living room and dining room leading to a rear deck facing the garden, and most of them had good city views. The flats vary from two bedrooms to three bedrooms, and all had two full bathrooms. There is assigned parking in the garages at ground level. One evening during the building construction, we were shocked to see a red glow in our backyard. An arsonist had torched the partially completed new building!

All of the neighbors, who had enthusiastically approved this attractive design over the fortress, drive-in building of other developers, held our collective breath as to whether the fifty-percent-destroyed construction would ever be finished. Fortunately, the insurance company and the developer quickly provided money to complete the complex. Thus, in 1982, the beautiful multicolored buildings with stunning roof designs provide a grand entrance to our neighborhood, and the block is known as Divisadero Heights, after the name of the condominium association. Previously, we had designated the block as upper Eddy Street to differentiate from the poverty and crime associated with the much more depressing Eddy Street in the Tenderloin district, which was a favored spot for the homeless immigrants who favored our mild winters and bountiful welfare benefits.

Magland Arms Apartment Building

On the opposite northeast corner from the Divisadero Heights development, another developer, Ed West, was a prominent figure in the gay leather community, which is patronized secretly by many of the elite of San Francisco society. He was the son of the owners of a Mediterranean-style apartment building, the Maglands. Together they borrowed money from the redevelopment agency to rehabilitate and upgrade their three-story building after the completion of

Divisadero Heights. The Maglans, an elderly Jewish couple, lived in a safer San Francisco neighborhood and had maximized their income by doing a minimum of maintenance. They even placed an obnoxious, large, outdoor billboard on the Eddy Street wall for additional income! Ed removed the sign and did a remarkably good upgrading of the 1920s, stucco, twelve-unit building, with the exception of the existing corner grocery store. This corner store, operated by a series of Middle Eastern immigrants, continued to attract the public-housing residents for liquor, expired food, and snack foods. The corner was always congested by the public-housing tenants, who were particularly noisy in the evening. The store hours are from eleven o'clock in the morning to two o'clock in the morning the next day! We, like most of our neighbors shopped, in protest, outside of our neighborhood for groceries, even for last-minute needs. Later, Ed, now afflicted with AIDS, sold his building to another gay man, Walter Palmer, who did an elegant upgrade on the two units that Ed had combined for himself. Walter removed, with neighborhood influence, the three, sidewalk, coin-operated, public telephones that the drug dealers used frequently. Later, cameras were used as a security system. However, cellular telephones used by the drug dealers negated the usefulness of the cameras. Walter, the new owner, would also die of AIDS.

During the AIDS epidemic in the 1980s, many gay former property owners and new property owners from our block of Eddy Street, as well as the other block on the east side of Divisadero Street, died. The death of Jim Foster, on the east side, was a particularly notable loss. His funeral service in Grace Cathedral was a spectacularly major political affair. He was the first national figure in the gay movement within the Democratic Party and gave a speech at the Democratic Convention in 1984. The loss of these many, varied, talented individuals created a large gap of those property owners who had done the excellent restorations of their properties. The "gay movement" in San Francisco was generally decimated by these losses, but, like the city, is now a gay phoenix arisen. It must not be underestimated!

Anza Vista Condominiums

Nolan Frank, an African American from North Carolina, married to a Japanese American wife, was also an active local developer. As a licensed contractor, he negotiated the right, from the SFRA, to rehabilitate and execute a major expansion of the building on the northwest corner of Divisadero and Turk Streets. He already owned a twelve-unit Marina-style apartment building halfway up the block on Turk Street. Beginning in the 1980s, through a long, convoluted, construction project, he converted this wood-frame building with a basement, and small corner store with two flats and an attic floor above, into an essentially modern condominium building. The resulting elevator now services a five-story building consisting of four stories over a fully enclosed parking garage. The sixteen condominium units consist of two bedroom units with one or two bathrooms. The sales prices ranged from $475,000-$625,000. Most are view-oriented units and are available with a variety of elegant finish options chosen by the buyer. I always admired Nolan's determination and thought, "I only wished he had given me the listing to sell the condominiums." Interestingly, many of the units were purchased by overseas Chinese, perhaps with the idea of having a haven should the economy of China collapse.

In the 1990s, Nolan obtained the rights from the SFRA to rehabilitate a large outstanding single family Italianate Victorian house, circa 1870s, on the south side of the 1900 block of Eddy Street. The house originally had a large side yard, which is now occupied by the

Divisadero Heights Condominiums. The house had been converted into a rooming house in the 1940s, which was needed during the World War II years to help create income from the new workers in the shipyards and for wives to be closer to their husbands in the Pacific Theater of World War II. The greedy owner/property management company/real estate company had allowed the building to deteriorate and had added an ugly fire escape to the front of the building.

When we first moved to Eddy Street, a large, bulky, mentally disturbed African American man, who was a tenant, would wake up the whole neighborhood in the middle of the night with his Bible reading and the shooting of his revolver for attention! After a couple of years, he suddenly disappeared, to the relief of everyone. Nolan partially converted the property into four condominiums of unequal size. The remainder of the expansion was completed by Essie Collins, who was his good friend and had helped finance his rehabilitation. The rear of the building was expanded, a penthouse was added through a second floor access, and a three-car, side-by-side garage was built into the front yard hillside with interior access to the upstairs deck and rear garden. Essie's nephew and his wife live in the luxurious penthouse rear condominium with sweeping views of the city.

As mentioned earlier, the BANG A-2 Project Area has been artificially divided by the major thoroughfare of Divisadero Street. The developments on the east side were more impacted by the more extensive demolition of existing building and the nearby public housing, which were all on the same level ground.

Divisadero/O'Farrell Cooperatives

One of our first disappointments in a SFRA development project was at the southeast corner of Divisadero Street and

O'Farrell Streets. A nondescript, wooden-frame building with a strange, false, triangular, wood, roof projection was built in the supposed Beideman Historical District. Although, this building is composed of market-rate condominiums, it was quite out of place with the many already-relocated historic buildings and the surrounding original historic buildings. Perhaps adding further insult, Gigi Platt, a landmark board member; oddly and strongly supported this poorly integrated development in a historical district. This condominium complex would signal to many of us the rather false commitment by the SFRA to historical preservation. Many additional developments would prove us visionary.

Amancio Ergina Village

Another large, cleared-block assemblage between Scott, Pierce, O'Farrell, and Ellis Streets was designated as a development site and attracted the usual controversy concerning the use and design. BANG, under the capable leadership of our then president Nonie Richen lobbied very hard for market-rate cooperatives and a neighborhood-friendly design in 1980. She dutifully pursued many possible angles and balanced the rearing of three children with her husband in their top flat of an original Stick Eastlake pair of flats. The original design for this parcel of 1.72 acres was a cheap, ugly, shingled, suburban strip-like motel with no relationship to the neighboring buildings, visually or aesthetically. Several historical houses had, however, been preserved earlier at this site and were assembled with other relocated historical buildings into a charming condominium collective called Endicott Court. Also at the northeast corner of Scott and O'Farrell Streets were two pairs of flats connected by a common wall, with the more ornate mirror image being the corner building. This building, which we were to buy, was moved a block away in the late 1970s, to a Scott Street site between Ellis and Eddy Streets.

The sponsor of this SFRA-approved, new, cooperative development was a nonprofit cooperative with James San Jule as chairman and Amancio Ergina as vice-chairman. Dr. Ergina had immigrated to San Francisco in 1951 and later opened one of the first healthcare facilities in the Mission District (Bataan Memorial Pharmacy). He was politically well connected as a leader in the Filipino community and was appointed as the first member of his community to the SFHA Commission by Mayor Joseph Alioto in 1971. The construction financing was funded by the International Longshoremen's and Warehousemen's, Pacific Maritime Association Pension Fund. The board consisted of several labor leaders, such as James San Jule, as well as local leaders, such as Essie Collins, on the Board of Directors. The mortgage financing was funded by City and County of San Francisco Mortgage Revenue bonds and serviced by First Nationwide Savings and Loan Association. The housing development team was sponsored by this non-profit corporation, which is dedicated to the principal of well-designed, affordable housing for individuals and families of lower and moderate income. Each of the cooperative owners was in a partnership ownership with the city.

The resulting open-occupancy development is called the Amancio Ergina Village and consists of seventy-two cooperative units of subsidized, moderate-income housing. The development was completed in 1985. The Ellis Street elevation is particularly exciting and faces the later Jewish Community High School of the Bay. The architects, Daniel Solomon and Associates, accomplished a thoughtful, contemporary/Arts and Crafts design, with row townhouses and flats, entrances to the street, and surface parking for cars in an inner, landscaped, garden courtyard. The units are compact one/two bedroom units and two-story townhouses, with a roof deck opening from the townhouses of three bedrooms. The complex was originally managed by the John Stewart Company, who also managed the newly constructed redevelopment-originated cooperatives on Cathedral Hill in the A-1 Project Area. At the present time, the company is responsible for the leasing, management, and restoration or remodeling of buildings at the former United States Army fort, The Presidio (now a national park). John Stewart had previously been an administrator with HUD.

Over the years much of the original building construction has been replaced because of the use of cheap materials and inferior construction. The cooperatives were converted into condominiums and gradually upgraded, which occurred under the able administration of the association president Barbara Meskunas, who is an original owner with her husband. She has been the longtime president of BANG and was president of the San Francisco Housing Authority during the administration of Mayor Frank Jordan. This was a real eye opener for her with regard to the entrenched administration of the SFHA. Like the earlier-mentioned Divisadero Heights Condominium Association, both condominium groups have contributed a better quality and stability to our neighborhood.

Endicott Court

Endicott Court is surrounded by this village and has a quiet-enclave quality about it. The O'Farrell Street-facing Victorian houses were already in place. A series of similar Italianate, flat-fronted Victorian buildings were moved to this location in the 1960s and placed at the rear of the cleared parcel. An enchanting, beautiful, luxuriant, garden mews was created in the middle. Each of the two-story, detached, Victorian houses was jacked-up and a charming studio was created on the ground floor. The whole complex strongly emphasizes the value of good design and the durability of the old-growth redwood construction of these nineteenth-century homes. This design was largely laid out by the redevelopment architects, Bob Fogel, Susan Bragstad, and Jane Duncombe. Enid Sales, the A-2 Project director, was most interested in preservation and promoted the Beideman Historical District through the relocation of historic buildings after the ubiquitous wrecking ball arrived.

Beideman Place Townhouses

In 1989, Daniel Solomon, Inc., in collaboration with John Goldman, designed eleven market-rate townhouses—similarly combining townhouses at the rear with a courtyard and townhouses in the front. Garages occupy the ground floor of each townhouse, and the rear-building garages are reached from the courtyard through a majestic, arched entryway. The basic architectural style is much more successful than Amancio Ergina Village. The structural engineer was Raj Desai and Associates. Although this complex violates the historical district designation of moving historical buildings slated to be demolished, the overall sensitivity to the historical district is remarkable in relating to this relocated grouping of original, historically important Victorian buildings. These condominiums have been popular on the resale market.

As compared to the SFRA-sanctioned Section-8 housing, this condominium complex has withstood age remarkably well.

Bell Mews Condominiums

In November 1995, the SFRA put out a notice for the biding of ten affordable townhomes for Parcel 1100-T at the northeast corner of Ellis and Divisadero Streets. This parcel is in the historical Beideman District, and several of us argued that buildings should blend with the historical fabric of the previously relocated Victorian housing. Several historical buildings were available to be relocated to this site. We had earlier lost the district to the undistinguished Divisadero/ O' Farrell Cooperatives. The team that won the competitive bidding was the formidable, well-connected, San Francisco Housing Development Corporation, with the noted architectural firm of David Baker+Partners Architects. The developer, SFHDC, was an African American firm, founded in 1988, and a nonprofit, community-based organization. Michael Simmons was the president, and on his board he had leaders from the Western Addition and Bayview/Hunter's Point neighborhoods. SFHDC had purchased the 10,200 square-foot lot from the SFRA for $5,000. The construction firm was Nibbi Brothers, who obtained many contracts for new construction through the SFRA and SFHA. The architect, David Baker, an opinionated and arrogant individual, carried around his Lhasa apso dog at our meetings. His artistic style was avant garde with the use of common materials, such as corrugated metal and plywood. I said, "Your bland and uninteresting design is a perfect match for the garish Union 76 gasoline station across the street." His response was a distant stare. Although I have always valued architecturally new styles, I feel that he compromised the neighborhood.

As the BANG president, I negotiated for other board members/neighbors to obtain a few compromises in the exterior of the complex of two and three-story townhouse designs around a dead-end mews to allow access to the garages. David Baker, however, said after the completion of the building in 1997 that he would not compromise on the exterior color palette of mustard and olive tones. He said, "My feeling is that as the building ages, and the landscape grows in, the colors will become a more acceptable family of hues for the surrounding area." Sales prices were based on income, which was in the range of mid-to-high one-hundred-thousand dollars. The sales prices would be in the mid-two-hundred-thousand-dollar range. A scandal later erupted on a resale of one of the townhouses by an SFRA employee, who sold with a large profit and refused to rebate the profit back to the mayor's fund for affordable housing. She stated that she needed to sell to cover the cost of taking care of her handicapped son. Of course, unlike most other owners with comparable, affordable-housing units, she was allowed to keep the money!

Basilica Lofts

In 2001, across the street from the newly built Robert B. Pitts Plaza (sarcastically called "The Pitts" by the neighbors from the beginning) on Eddy Street, a Chinese (Taiwan) Buddhist temple was created with a renovation and rehabilitation of the existing limestone masonry Holy Cross Roman Catholic Church, which is in the Italian Baroque-style with twin bell towers. The church was constructed from 1893 to 1898. Next door is the Holy Cross parish hall in a plain-front, classical revival-style and is a simple one-story, wood-frame building above an elevated basement and connected by front stairs. This city, historically landmarked, 1854 structure is the old Saint Patrick's Church, which was moved several times from the original Market Street site of the Palace Hotel. Moved to this location in 1921, this oldest, wooden, religious structure in San Francisco became a social hall next to Holy Cross. BANG, with my strong reinforcement, had been able to force the Archdiocese to sell, rather than demolish the church, and to sell it to a developer who would preserve it. I argued, "These buildings are an important

historical architectural focus for our neighborhood." The property was eventually sold, with vacant lots on both sides, to a developer who agreed to preserve the buildings. The Archdiocese, in revenge, stripped the church of its magnificent life-sized Carrara Italian marble angels at the sides of the high altar, the agate and brass prayer rail, and the magnificent organ in its loft. The bells in the towers were left behind.

The architect for the temple, Mark Topetcher, sensitively restored the church with the geometrical rose windows kept in place, and also the parish hall, which now is a museum, with a rear addition for the monastery. Rental-housing units for visitors are planned for the vacant lots east of this complex. The monks in their cinnabar robes and shaved heads; the huge, colorful, fiberglass bodhisattvas inside; the large, bronze, incense burners in front of the temple; and the cloth banners strung around the buildings create an almost surrealistic atmosphere of other worldliness. The Macang Monastery and the Temple of Good Fortune and Wisdom, I hope, will bring a peaceful and tranquil energy to our neighborhood.

On the west side of the temple, on the vacant lots of former Victorian housing, two buildings with market-rate condominiums above a garage space were constructed and marketed in 2000. The condominiums ranged from $420,000 to $560,000. The sixteen units in the stucco-covered buildings with pitched roofs are open-floor, two-story lofts, with 1.5 or 2 bathrooms. The seventeen-foot, ground-floor space is connected by spiral staircases to the mezzanine floor level. The units were wired with the then-new, Cat-5, high-tech, enhanced cable. The overall Tuscan tan-colored appearance gives a calming effect, and the maturing plantings add a wonderful terrace-garden appearance.

Jewish Community High School of the Bay

The Jewish Community High School of the Bay was constructed in 2001 from the remnants of the former California College of Podiatric Medicine. The new structure, in a handsome, new, campus setting, features an extensive library, classrooms equipped with the latest in technology, an auditorium, an informal gathering area in the middle, a courtyard with palm trees, and a garage for parking. Transit buses are used to transport the students from all over the Bay area. The students are hardly noticeable, and certain calmness emanates from the school. Enclosing the school are high fences and electric gates that are monitored with additional patrolling by security guards. In 2005, a lot that had been excluded by the redevelopment agency from the purchase of the original podiatry school parcel hotly contested in our neighborhood between a new gymnasium for the high school or low-cost housing, which would be squeezed on the lot with no green-belt area. BANG organized again to reinforce the position of the school. And, after a long nervous battle, the vacant lot was purchased by the high school. A generous settlement by the high school to the redevelopment agency was to be used for low-cost housing at other locations. Most probably, the funds went into the general fund, which may unfortunately end up in the pockets of various, favored, "respectable" politicians, as well as those neighborhood activists connected with the politicians.

New Developments in the WANA A-2 Project Area

The neighborhood group that existed on the north side of Geary Boulevard had not been as negatively impacted by the SFRA and SFHA as our neighborhood (BANG). There was only one low-level public housing project, which was called West Side Court, at their western border, as compared to our neighborhood, with numerous, massive, public-housing projects. The site had originally been a commercial vegetable nursery and West Side court was the first public housing project in San Francisco. Allegedly, Willie Brown Jr. had purportedly lived at the West Side Court, when he came to San Francisco in the late 1940s from Mineola, Texas. The main affluent commercial development nearby was on upper Fillmore Street and the east to west streets, such as Post, Sutter, Bush, Pine, and California Streets. Other than the remaining, earlier, residential, Victorian row houses, the existing commercial buildings were mostly churches, a synagogue, auditoriums, and pre-World War II apartment buildings.

Interestingly, these commercial buildings had unusual adaptations in the 1960s. The rock music impresario, Bill Graham, converted a roller-skating rink into Fillmore West Auditorium on the other side of Geary Boulevard at Fillmore Street and an ice-skating rink into Winterland at Post and Steiner Streets—both concert halls. In the early 1970s, John and I attended several memorable concerts at Winterland, featuring Janice Joplin with her penetrating, raw, husky voice. Another 1910s massive building on Sutter Street was the Jacobean Phase of Medieval Revival-style steel-reinforced structure with brick exterior walls (Golden Gate Commander #16 Knights Templar), with stone, decorative, tracery elements and Tudor arches and escutcheons topped by winged faces. In the 1950s, the building had become the Macedonian Missionary Baptist Church. This African American church sponsored a group who marched from Selma to Montgomery, Alabama; two sermons by Dr. Martin Luther King, Jr.; speeches by Congressman Adam Clayton Powell, Jr. and Rev. Jessie Jackson; and gospel concerts by such famous people as Mahalia Jackson. Many in this congregation joined the nearby Peoples Temple and died in Jonestown. But perhaps fortunately for important African American historical sites, a small, intimidated congregation and the preservation community, including me, were able to stop the destruction of this supposed *seismically unstable* church masonry after the 1989 earthquake.

In contrast to the Macedonian Missionary Baptist Church, an equally early, 1900s, architecturally handsome brick church, with Tudor stone detailing, a square central tower, and handsome stained-glass windows, owned by the Jones Memorial United Methodist Church (Hamilton Square Baptist), that occupied the southeast corner of Post and Steiner Streets has been demolished. The saving grace was that an attractively designed contemporary church was built in its place. Former Mayor Willie Brown is a member of this congregation. The California Assembly Speaker Brown had introduced and passed legislation, in 1994, that stated houses of worship were exempted from all local landmark status! Curiously, all of the African American churches in SF are allowed to double-park cars in the street for church services and funerals. Around the church is their supported senior housing that the SFRA had subsidized. The SFRA would be responsible for subsidizing the erection of many new churches and many church-supported low- and high-rise senior centers for the African American community.

2000 Post Street Apartment Building

This development was on the land previously occupied by the Sutter Theater and Iceland Pavilion. This project completely engulfed the Macedonian Missionary Baptist Church. This massive, four-story, wooden-shingled, rental apartment complex occupies 10,332 square feet and was constructed in 1987. There are 328 units, consisting of two bedrooms/two baths, one bedroom/ one bath, and studios. The units vary from four hundred to one thousand square feet, and the present rents are from one thousand to four thousand dollars per month. The building is serviced by a two-level, underground parking garage and a popular corner restaurant at Sutter and Steiner Streets.

As mentioned previously, this Macedonian Missionary Baptist Church is an important historical focus for the Western Addition. In 1992, Patricia Vaughey and I, with the endorsement of the historical preservation community, had been able to elevate this church to the list of historically and architecturally distinguished buildings, through the City Landmarks Board, prior to the state legislation. This landmark status was based on the architecture of the building, circa 1907, and the history of the Knights Templar, that became a Masonic order and had its origins in the Christian Knights (Crusaders) from Europe who went to the Holy Land in the twelfth century. The knights claimed to protect Christian pilgrims from being attacked by Mohammedan soldiers. In Jerusalem, the congregated Jews were burned alive in the main synagogue, the now called Muslims were completely eliminated, and the Christians paid money for their lives!

This African American church has been an important civil rights historical site since 1950. Several members of the church were purported proxies for the 2000 Post Street developers, who hired Alice Suet Yee Barkley, the powerful and well-connected land-rights attorney, to overturn this landmark status. Quoted in the *San Francisco Examiner*, she called it a "useless white elephant." The Planning Commission recommendation of landmark status was ratified by the Board of Supervisors. The church still exists but has been neglected by the city, the African American community, and the parishioners, in spite of its important historical connections, spectacular large auditorium, and the magnificent theater with its oilcloth backdrop canvases depicting pastoral and other scenes.

The Amelia Condominiums

This building at the corner of Sutter and Fillmore Streets is particularly refined and was developed in1984 by the mysterious Joe (Joseph) Skiffer, a handsome, young African American. Several Irish American developers were quite agitated that they had been given wrong and misleading information in the pre-bid SFRA development packages. But, in an executive session, the SFRA commissioners decided they would not put the parcel out for development again and voted in favor of Skiffer's proposal. The ground-floor shops and condominiums make this complex particularly attractive. There are on three floors: thirty-one condominiums with a mix of two bedroom and one bedroom units, each with one bathroom, above the exclusive shops and enclosed parking. The units sold originally in the price range of $215,000 to $300,000 and now sell for double this amount.

In 2001, the adjoining vacant lot on Sutter Street was developed with a masonry facade and floor plans that became townhouses with a post-modern brick and concrete-block facade. Purportedly, the SFRA commissioners awarded development rights to Skiffer in a secret executive session. Part of this lot had been occupied by the infamous WAPC headquarters, where my neighbor, Leona Robertson, and I had been warned by a member, with a handgun pointed at us, never to return! They did not want "our kind" interfering with their plans for redevelopment in the Western Addition. The neighbors of this development, Palmer Sessell and M. J. Staymetz were able to protect a one hundred-year-old Magnolia Grandfloria, which had branches arching over the back of the vacated lot, from being severely trimmed back to the point of destruction. The nineteen units of the 1970 Sutter Street Condominiums reflect the then-popular two-story loft developments popularized by Joe O'Donoghue and the Residential Builders Association in the South of Market Street area (SOMA). The nineteen townhouses are approximately 1,100 square feet, one bedroom and two bathroom units, and are luxurious with, among other upgrades, Brazilian mahogany floors. The units originally sold for approximately $550,000 and are now selling for over $750,000. There is a private, rooftop deck and enclosed parking at the ground-floor level.

Speer Investment Company Property

My father, in Kansas City, decided after we bought our home in 1975 that perhaps I might just have some positive insight about San Francisco real estate. As a result, he bought a Victorian store-front building at 1928 Fillmore Street in 1976. It was a block away from where, later, The Amelia Condominiums were built. The African American congregation of Little Zion Baptist Church, who owned the building, used the purchase price of $56,000 toward constructing a new church on an SFRA-owned lot at the southwest corner of Ellis and Divisadero Streets, near our home. As a result of this purchase, Speer Investment Company (family held investment trust) helped by support with purchase money for the building of their new church. The vacant land was granted as a free subsidy by the SFRA. In our communications, I was rather surprised when the congenial pastor, Reverend Drummer, mentioned to me, "I have never eaten Japanese or Chinese food, and know I wouldn't like it."

Our first tenants on Fillmore Street, in 1977, converted the premises into a series of steam baths and massage rooms. They called their business Miracle Baths. We had a congenial relationship with Penny and Kathy, who were lesbians (Kathy being a particularly stunning brunette). When my mother and father came to visit John and me in 1978, I set up an appointment for my mother to get a massage and facial. She went for the appointment but afterward proclaimed, "I'm not particularly fond of strangers touching my body." This session was obviously not particularly successful. My mother did not visit San Francisco again. She liked John but was uncomfortable about us sleeping together in a queen-sized bed. However, she would become completely reconciled with us over the years and enjoys our visits to Kansas City.

Later, after Ming joined our household, he would accompany us and became a great favorite of hers. She would frequently say to me on the telephone, "How are the boys?" and, "You take care of one-another." One interesting event on this visit was when mother came home by bus from Union Square, with its nearby flower stands and fashionable stores. An African American gentleman commented favorably on her newly purchased lapel gardenia, her favorite flower since The Treasure Island Fair days. He asked, "Have you been to church?"

In 1984, my father sold the Fillmore Street property for $390,000 and carried a note and deed of trust in the amount of $330,000, at an interest rate of 12 percent, with payments of interest-only for ten years. He was pleased that I had been able to get him such a good return on his investment of $56,000, with only $70,000 in improvements.

Dad came to San Francisco many times afterward to buy other desirable properties. I would assist with private subcontractors to rehabilitate his buildings in the Western Addition. I was able to obtain an incredibly good return on his investment, which made him happy. However, as the frugal Warren Buffett might have said to his children, Dad said, "You will receive the benefits later from

Speer Investment Company." I told him, "I need the money to pay expenses now with my much-deserved commissions, and I have other viable clients." He relented and paid me a rightly earned commission.

He bought a twelve -unit, Mediterranean, 1920s building with a water fountain in the back garden, from a Jewish owner, in the 1600 block of Golden Gate Avenue, which I managed. My resident manager was the older Robert Lyles, who was an African American with Cherokee American Indian ancestry. He and his attractive wife, Rosie, were delightful and managed the ethnically mixed tenant building quite efficiently. I told Mr. Lyles, "If you ever decide to sell your Chrysler Imperial, please call me." Another tenant was an elderly African American lady named Alice Levine. She had a tall, slender body and wore large, silver hoop earrings. She had been in the U.S. Army previously and loved her Scotch whiskey. Somehow, the subject of a house-cleaning job came up in our conversations, and I hired her to clean our home. She was thorough, but I had to leave my business during the week to carry the vacuum cleaner up to the second floor of our house. When she said she could no longer clean the house, we were disappointed because we had come to treasure her dry sense of humor.

Another African American tenant owned a bar on Third Street and asked me to sell his building. I will never forget the expression on the title officer's face when the buyer, who was a short, plump, African American attorney, increased the down payment with cash from an attaché case. Each finger was encased with a jeweled ring as he laid the bundles of cash on the desk of the title officer. Another African American tenant was the attractive and intelligent Francee Covington. I had persuaded her that the residents of the building were top-drawer. Reluctantly, she moved in, even though she was a politically savvy African American from New York City. I admired her abilities and later asked her to be on the WAPC board. I also sold her and her husband their home. She was a long-time SFRA commissioner. She is presently a SF Fire commissioner. I have great respect for her.

Much of Dad's profits (Speer Investment Company) from San Francisco properties were lost with his purchase in Kansas City, Kansas, of the enormous Armour Packing House Company in the *bottoms* which is the river valley at the conjunction of the Missouri and Kansas Rivers. It consisted of ten acres of buildings, holding pens, wooden ramps for the animals, and a railroad spur. The main building had been previously converted into a private, petroleum-oil packing business, which he improved with the manufacturing of plastic bottling onsite to contain the oil. In the beginning, he had cautiously contracted verbally with Phillips Petroleum Oil Company to furnish them the bottled petroleum oil. Then, after his considerable investment, the company deceived him by not providing the agreed upon oil. A judge, without a jury trial, ruled against his lawsuit. The same judge later shot his wife and then committed suicide! My father always said, "Education is expensive." Although Dad was well focused, perhaps by genes, he was often naïve in estimating the brutality of many business negotiations. He, as a solo-practicing, popular pediatrician, had made his own personal investments (subject to the risks of the market place). He had not hidden behind the corporate veil or used public financing. Because his investments were not funded by the SFHA or SFRA, he took chances, unlike some politically connected, local San Franciscans or Kansas City personages. Realistically, those individuals, who are connected to lobbyists or directly connected to congressional, state, and city legislators, are obviously closer to the mother lode of a financial reward in this less-than-perfect world.

When my mother was asked by anyone if she was wealthy, she says, "We have many mortgages." She shrewdly would not let my father sell our 140-acre family farm. He bought it with his inheritance from his father and had contracted to build prefab, two-bedroom homes, financed with GI subsidies in the early 1950s. This proposed San Marcos Village was supposed to be a large subdivision but only some twenty houses were built. The contractor was crooked, and most returning GIs did not want to move that far from the city. Thus, most of the land remained undeveloped. In the 1980s, Dad invited a quite-wealthy, next-door couple to dinner at our townhome to convince my mother to sell the farm. She sensed the situation immediately and politely disagreed. The neighbor's wife confided to me much later, "Frances was very smart in not selling." The farm today is worth much more money because it is close to major commercial and residential development. The farm house has collapsed, but the magnificent setting still exists. The future commercial-urbanization development will be a misuse of the valuable fertile soil, unfortunately, while the downtown remains abandoned. In the meantime, a tenant farmer raises crops within the city limits. At least our family has the memory of those idyllic summers at the farm, which it was so called in the Kansas City Social Registry—"The Farm" at (Cyprus) (CY-9-4444).

Sutter Street Condominiums

These condominiums reinforce the fact that larger numbers of the market-rate housing were built in the WANA district. Also, they highlight the difference between the moderate-rate to higher-income condominiums developed on the north side of Geary Boulevard, with some lower-income, subsidized housing in the Japantown area. In contrast, the south side of Geary Boulevard was developed with lower-income, subsidized housing near concentrated, existing public housing, and remains predominately African American. In 1984, the 2040 and 2060 Sutter Street buildings added two units with thirty-two condominiums each to the housing stock. These units are luxurious and appeal to the younger, Silicon Valley employees who want to live in San Francisco. The four-story, wooden structures over a ground-floor garage are a combination of two bedrooms with two bathrooms, and one bedroom with one bathroom. The condominium units sold originally in the range of $225,000 to $270,000 and are nearly double that value in 2010. Only a few of these units have been resold.

Westwood Condominiums

This condominium complex that is across the street is a mirror image of the other Sutter Street developments. This wood-frame, four-story building above ground-floor parking was built later, in 1992. This development consists of forty-five units of two bedrooms with two bathrooms, and one bedroom with one bathroom, units, and reinforces the exclusivity of this neighborhood. The original units sold from $193,000 to $347,000. They now sell for $325,000 to $650,000. This development was one of the last projects constructed in the WANA A-2 Project Area. This condominium development further completes the concentrated market-rate housing and the professional-class owner/tenant profile. These residents have made the Upper Fillmore shopping area into a highly desirable and lively destination point for tourists as well the residents themselves. The area between California Street and Geary Boulevard is now designated by the San Francisco Board of Realtors as the Lower Pacific Heights subdistrict. What a dramatic difference in the area from experiences with my first rental apartment, in 1969, on the north side of California Street, which is now the most exclusive Pacific Heights district!

Saint Dominic's Church

In the center of this new, upper-income district, Saint Dominic's Church (Roman Catholic) is the prominent and stabilizing major historical landmark. The original church parcel was a city block bounded by Steiner Street on the east, Bush Street on the south, Pine Street on the north, and Pierce Street on the west.

On Bush Street, in the next block west, was Saint Rose Academy, which Mary Sweeney had attended with Mrs. Shumate. The church is the center for the Dominican Order in San Francisco and is owned exclusively by the Dominicans, not the Archbishop of San Francisco. The original church was consecrated in 1873 and was described in church documents as "pure Tudor Gothic in the style of Henry VIII." A second church, designed by T. J. Welsh, began construction in 1883 and was completed in 1903, in the Gothic revival-style, with a high, Baroque altar. In the 1906 earthquake and fire, this church was badly damaged.

A new church was designed by the architect Arnold Constable, with the firm Breezer Brothers of Seattle. The new Gothic cathedral-style church of gray granite, with a lofty tower, was under construction for ten years and dedicated in 1928. The majestic interior of the sanctuary is made of cast stone, which was fabricated at the construction site. The handsome, interior-carved wood detailing, marble altars, and stained-glass windows, by Charles J. Connick Studios in Boston, contribute to an old-world European atmosphere. No expense was spared to make both the exterior and interior exquisite and grand. Today, the church is known for its outstanding choir and shrines of St. Jude and of the Holy Rosary. The congregation is quite diverse and has changed according to the times.

John belongs to this parish, and we have contributed funds for restorations and structural repairs after the 1989 Loma Prieta earthquake. He also has donated his time generously to the church Lima Center to serve to breakfast and some lunches. He also attended to other needs for the homeless who circulated nearby. Dr. Albert Shumate, among other generous parishioners, donated money for the construction of new supporting buttresses to strengthen the exterior. One day, I noticed that some of the tower finials, of terra cotta with a gray granite glaze, that had been replaced were scattered in a passageway next to the church. John asked whether we could purchase some of these fragments toppled by the earthquake with a donation to the church. These architectural artifacts now reside splendidly in our garden.

My personal church of preference is Grace Cathedral (Episcopalian) on Nob Hill, which replaced the French, Second Empire, Crocker family mansion that was destroyed in the 1906 earthquake and fire. This massive Gothic styled church, constructed of steel reinforced concrete, designed by Lewis Hobart, is the third-largest Episcopal Cathedral in the United States. The existing footprint was not completed until 1964, with the consecration by Bishop Pike. Many style changes evolved but the original elements, such as the bronze-gilded reproduction of Lorenzo Ghiberti's doors (called "The Gates of Paradise" by Michelangelo) for the baptistery in front of the cathedral in Florence, the north tower with a carillon of forty-four bells, and the elegant Chapel of Grace are awe inspiring. These elements contrast well with the more-contemporary additions to the later-expanded sanctuary. These include the unfinished fill in of the vaulted ceilings, the more contemporary stained-glass windows (Willett of Philadelphia vs. the biblical earlier ones by Charles Connick of Boston) and the AIDS Chapel with a Keith Haring metal wall sculpture. There will always be poverty, illness, wars, earthquakes and political turmoil, but the physical edifices of all ecclesiastical buildings, built as spiritual bridges to Heaven by generous people of all economic classes and all faiths, will always exist. This architectural prominence everywhere gives one hope for the life after death, in contrast to nonsectarian buildings, such as the 2010 CE one-half-mile skyscraper in Dubai (Tower of Babel?).

In 2012, John and I mutually agreed to have our cremated remains placed in a niche of the to-be-constructed new columbarium wall behind the altar of Saint Dominic's Church. This part of the columbarium faces the exquisite Lady Chapel. At a future date Ming's name will be on a plaque across from our niche. He has requested that his cremated ashes be scattered in the Pacific Ocean. Upon the completion of the columbarium, the church was completely restored and earthquake retrofitted. We contributed financially to this outstanding effort.

New Developments in the Van Ness Avenue Corridor

The focus of this development was essentially the high-rise buildings on the west side of Van Ness Avenue, with a back fill of subsidized housing surrounding them. This portion of the SFRA Project Area A-2 is bordered by Bush Street on the north to an uneven southern border, which is from McAllister Street to Grove Street. Many property owners refused to sell their commercial and apartment buildings to the SFRA on this famous, automobile-showcase row. A preservation movement to make historical landmarks of these grand buildings is presently underway.

The result of the SFRA efforts was a persistent movement to in-fill construction with a southern anchor of the most successful Opera Plaza complex of condominiums in 1985, with commercial, as well as such popular restaurants as Max's, with New York City Jewish deli food on the ground floor and underground parking. The nearby, magnificent-landmarked Beaux Arts Civic Center, post-1906 earthquake, enhances the whole revitalized area. In the civic center, the City Hall (1915), with a partially gilded dome, is the crown jewel.

The City Hall was designed by the architectural firm of Blakewell and Brown. Later buildings that surrounded it are the Opera House (1932), Veterans Building (1932), a much-later Davies Symphony Hall (1981), state office building (1926), the Bill Graham Auditorium (1915), a contemporary public library designed in 1996 by Pei, Cobb, Fried & Partners, and the magnificent Asian Art Museum, Chong-Moon Lee Center for Asian Art and Culture. The exquisite and significant Asian Art Museum is a restructuring and restoration, in 2002, of the original 1916 public library building (George Kelham); by the world-renowned architect Gae Allante. John, Ming, and I are active in supporting the AAM. I served on the board of directors of the Society of Asian Art (travel chairperson 2005–2011).

The nearby, earlier popular McAllister Street flea market area, pre-SFRA, with its Victorian buildings, was obliterated and replaced by low-rise, subsidized housing of varying degrees of architectural mediocrity. A visit to the nearby Hayes Street business district, or the lower Haight Street business district, gives an idea of what this once-vibrant Victorian shopping area looked like. These districts, which were not afflicted by the SFRA, demonstrate the historical value of preserving Victorian architecture.

On the east side of Van Ness Avenue, on Sutter Street in the block to Polk Street, was the Avalon Ballroom, next to the original Butterfield Auction House. The second-floor space was a popular venue for rock music, such as the *Family Dog* in the 1960s and 1970s. Chet Helms, almost as well-known as Bill Graham, attracted large crowds of young people and added to the frolicking of the hippie *Summer of Love.*

The now-important anchor for the north end is the Daniel Burnham Court (1989) on Post Street, designed by Wurster, Bernardi, and Emmons, which is a condominium development with two floors of commercial sheathed in red granite, an underground garage, and a high-rise condominium tower. This postmodern building is definitely a tribute to a visionary American architect.

In juxtaposition, at the same end of Van Ness Avenue, are two major disasters of construction. The twelve-story, reinforced-concrete Jack Tar Hotel, with a professional building (a full block) between Geary and Post Streets, consisting of 416,333 sq. ft., was constructed in 1959. The facade was a metal Mondrian patterning of turquoise and white square panels and provided the somewhat then-contemporary Las Vegas-style. Nearby, M. Justin Herman constructed a concrete fortress building at 939 Ellis Street in 1961, which was his headquarters for the SFRA. This brutally abstract, seven-story building, with small, oddly spaced windows and a ground-floor parking garage is certainly an oddity in architecture.

The brilliant journalist Herb Caen (a walkway along the Embarcadero is named for him in front of iconic M. Justin Herman Plaza) called the Cathedral Hill Hotel, with it's now uniformly-painted beige panels, as well as the SFRA headquarters, as both being "abortions of architecture." He and I were both transplants, who love our adopted city. He was born in Sacramento, California. The late Herb Caen was the foremost promoter of San Francisco then and even now in the form of quotes. The Cathedral Hill Hotel is presently slated to be razed and replaced by a major medical complex under the auspices of California Pacific Medical Center. The controversial, formerly proposed future fifteen-story building will consolidate a variety of healthcare services and will be seismically protected. The hospital complex will house 555 hospital rooms, as well as a variety of hospital services, and have underground parking. Medical office buildings are planned on two surrounding blocks. The projected cost is $2.5 billion. In 2012, Mayor Edwin Lee and the Board of Supervisors required many concessions and changes to the original plans. The previous SFRA headquarters is now the Bay Area Air Quality Management District headquarters, named after Milton Feldstein, one of the early directors.

A few examples of the once-grand Victorian Italianate mansions that were built here can still be seen in the 800 and 900 blocks of Eddy Street. George Stewart's home (the Samuel Newsom- and Joseph Cather Newsom-designed Stick Eastlake style masterpiece) was moved by the SFRA, under the auspices of the Foundation for San Francisco Architectural Heritage, from 773 Turk Street to 1737 Webster Street in 1975. This same sponsorship of other residences occurred in the BANG neighborhood.

The SFRA architects, as opposed to the bureaucrats, were located in a more sympathetic Victorian building on O'Farrell Street between Webster and Buchanan Streets. The nearby public elementary school at 1501 O' Farrell Street was originally named for the wealthy Jewish merchant and philanthropist Raphael Weill. He owned the White House Department Store, which is today the flagship store for the Banana Republic clothing store, a division of the locally owned GAP clothing empire. The school was renamed later for the famous civil-rights leader Rosa Parks, who would not give up her seat on a bus in the segregated southern United States.

12.

Our Socializing

As mentioned earlier, John, Ming, and I frequently socialized with neighbors in the Western Addition. We were able to develop a kinship to counteract the SFRA and SFHA, as well as enjoying one another's company. We also socialized with many other friends and acquaintances in San Francisco and the greater Bay Area. Surprisingly, the more recently arrived, young property owners/tenants seem to be more inward and unaware, or do not seem to care about our pioneer struggles to better this neighborhood. We do not have much interaction for better or worse. Perhaps, this has to do with our noninterest in the technological revolution of communicating through Twitter and Facebook or computer-age chat in general. From our early residence, most of our neighbors entertained one another. There was much good comradeship, plus a warm sense of a comfortable improvement of our neighborhood. As mentioned previously, the now luxuriant city street trees were planted, and permit parking was realized to discourage the overwhelming parking problems from the people at Kaiser Permanente Hospital. For example, Frankie Herndon was sure that the street tree would uproot her sidewalk, but she supported us, as well as other neighbors, in a goodwill gesture by allowing an iron-bark eucalyptus tree to be planted in front of her home. There were many other neighborhood-supported activities. This book is dedicated to the earlier civic-oriented neighbors, as a historical document to our neighbors, in appreciation and a welcome to a better neighborhood. We hope that we all will continue to build on this camaraderie.

During, the late 1970s, we had many lively parties and entertained constantly, inviting neighbors and good friends, both straight and gay, to holiday parties and dinner parties in our formal dining room. There was always a good feeling of friendship, with fine food and plenty of wine and liquor. John, who is an excellent chef, could efficiently manage large parties. Ming and I added backup assistance. Our Christmas parties were particularly memorable, with Ming's spectacularly decorated tree in the main center hallway and a blazing fire in the living room fireplace. We hired a musician to play flute music, and another year we hired a musical group called the *Pointless Sisters*. On these occasions, we usually suspected there just might be some romantic activity in the bedrooms. This activity would be occasionally interrupted. Unfortunately, John discovered me on one of those occasions in the guest bedroom with a cute guy (one of my multiple mini flings of this free-love period). Several years later, John announced that he was visiting Toronto, Canada, to see his new boyfriend, Paul, who was of Scotch Irish ancestry. John did not stay long, and Paul is presently living happily with his Jewish-attorney lover of many years. John forgave me for my many indiscretions by making believe they did not happen. Sometimes, I did endure several days of icy-cold silences from him. Although we never verbally lashed out at each other, I am sure he had his anguish, and I often felt heavily guilty.

On Easter Sundays, we invited John's family every year, consisting of many nephews and nieces, plus some other close friends, and the children would hunt for hidden Easter eggs. The eggs had been tucked away in the garden. We served a buffet in our dining room. The children were lively and excited by the whole festive affair. This buffet always featured my mother's famous glazed ham loaf, scalloped potatoes, fresh asparagus, and delicious, rich, lemon-meringue pies, made by John's sister-in-law. Easter chocolates were given in silver bowls for the children. The dining table glistened with polished silver serving pieces; linen napkins; and was lighted with a pair of Italian baroque candlesticks. The garden was always in full bloom at that time, with lilacs, calla lilies, camellias, and roses. Typical of San Francisco, the garden was beautiful and colorful during the whole year. Near the end of our Easter parties, we hung a huge colorful piñata on a large branch of the Victorian boxwood tree in the driveway. The children had exuberant fun batting the piñata to release all of the sweets inside.

At our various, private dinners, guests enjoyed delicious, bountiful cuisine, served on fine chinaware. There were always animated, as well as intellectually lively conversations. Classical music drifted throughout the house. A log fire on colder days crackled in the living room fireplace. Both Jim and his second wife Margaret were frequent guests, as were Bill and Carol Delameter, Richard Wade, and Judy Brown. I particularly remember one early Christmas holiday season, when Frankie, who was wearing a beautiful frock, and Bertha, wearing a gold lamé black-wool sheath. They were both the height of sophistication. Essie Collins came once and was also elegantly dressed. She coolly reminded me that she could have bought our house. She came a second time after that Christmas party and was mellower. Later, she asked me to sell a nearby lot that she owned on Divisadero Street but then crazily tried to stop the escrow from continuing because of black community pressure. After the close of the escrow, I took her nephew, Bob, and his wife, Rose, to then-popular Jeremy Tower's Stars restaurant to celebrate.

After we sold our restaurant in 1984, we began socializing again but at a much slower pace. We realized even more fully that San Francisco is the perfect place to meet new and interesting people from all walks of life and sexual persuasions. We also had more time to appreciate the weather, which, with its few extremes, is delightful. The summer fog was a welcome air conditioning, and the generally mild, winter rainstorms were comforting. Our neighborhood is in one of the less-foggy areas during the summer. The fog disappears in the afternoon, and returns in the evening, accompanied by the sound of foghorns.

At this time, I became involved with Republican politics and was elected president of the oldest gay Republican club (August, 1997 Concerned Republicans for Individual Rights–CRIR) in the country in 1991. I held board meetings for then renamed Log Cabin Republicans of San Francisco (LCCSF) in my office. The earlier presidents, Christopher Bowman and Ron Kershaw (a pioneer for Mormon gay rights) were my mentors. Leonard Matlovich (July 6, 1943-June 22, 1988) was earlier involved with our club. He had been dishonorably discharged in 1975 from the U.S. Army for stating that he was a homosexual. He famously said, "When I was in the military, they gave me a medal for killing two men and a discharge for loving one." That year of my presidency was particularly devastating because our supposed friend, Republican Governor Pete Wilson vetoed landmark legislation (AB101) for gay rights and our club lost many members. The reality of the inherent manipulation within the various Republican clubs through the county central committee and the vanity/venality of most politicians became quickly apparent to me and influenced me to be less politically active. However, I did continue to support, for several years, a Bay-Area local nonpartisan political group of affluent gays and lesbians. In 1993, I send my Republican father a copy of Randy Shilts *Conduct Unbecoming* and he was quite receptive to the content.

My real estate firm continued on at our commercial building in the Castro District, to prosper and to increase by five associates. The synergy from my enlarged, vibrant company was quite satisfying to me. At that location, Ming would continue into his retirement to be quite productive artistically in his loft attic studio

Daily, from our kitchen dining area, we could again admire even more our ever-changing and maturing luscious enclosed garden, which was flood-lighted at night. The fish pond would reflect the glowing, electric, bright light from Japanese-styled light wooden posts. There were a few more private dinners, and we began to entertain guests at various restaurants—particularly for the intricately, freshly prepared, and delicious Chinese food from various regions. The sterling-silver flat ware, linen napkins, and a variety of porcelain dinnerware remained in the side China cabinet for the occasional dinner party or for group socializing. John, Ming, and I could still walk daily through our magnificently wooden-paneled, side dining room, with classical music playing from hidden speakers and remember the many former grand dinner parties.

As Johann Wolfgang Goethe said, "*Musik ist Die Brucke zwischen Himmel und Erde* (music is the bridge between Heaven and Earth!)" Our long-time dedication to the excellent San Francisco Opera, San Francisco Symphony, and Philharmonia Baroque Orchestra added a special meaning for us. Our annual season subscriptions, along with the excellent San Francisco Ballet (the oldest ballet company in the United States) performances at the nearby civic center reinforce this grand experience. We have experienced the joy of survival and enjoy our consoling camaraderie.

Richard Augustus Wade

One of the most superb party hosts was Richard Augustus Wade (Gus or Richard), who was our affable neighbor on the block. He was an immigrant from County Mayo, Ireland. When his mother died, he took care of his seven siblings. Upon his father remarrying a woman that he disliked, he left school at the age of twelve and worked in a village butcher shop that was located in one of several buildings owned by his prosperous father. When he was in his early 20s, he moved to New York City to be a butcher in a shop owned by his brother, and then moved to San Francisco. In 1976, he bought a beautiful pair of flats that were in the Classic Revival-style, circa 1902, and had been built for the daughters of the wealthy Tobin banking family, who owned Hibernia Bank. A mutual friend had convinced him that the neighborhood was not a poverty-ridden ghetto. When he visited us with his friend, he was impressed with us and our home. He was pleased to purchase something affordable, with significant architecture, in a good weather zone without a summer blanket of fog or the cold winds from the Pacific Ocean.

The flats he bought were particularly well laid out in a telescopic manner so every room had sunlight. For the façade, he chose a background color of ox-blood red with cream-colored trim and a bottle-green-colored accent to the window sashes and scattered decorative panels. He had a masterful way of restoring the flats that reflected an elegant eighteenth-century Dublin townhouse, with the beautiful interior palate of Robert Adam, and furnishings to match. Everything down to the last detail of lace and Victorian light fixtures with colored, glass accents was precious. His city views were fabulous. He looked from his front parlor windows directly onto our master bedroom and made several snide comments about seeing me coming nude out of the shower room. I said, "Richard, I didn't know you were a voyeur!" Richard and I often compared gardening notes. He personally landscaped the barren front-terrace yard of the former rest home into a luxuriant paradise. He gradually started calling me *Squire Speer*. He did, however, indicate that John and Ming were certainly the more engaging and approachable individuals. His Sunday parties were memorable for his candlelit dinners and two wood-burning fires, one in the dining room and the other in the front parlor.

He would invite certain guests for cocktails and the more favored were invited for the following dinner. Happily John, Ming, and I were in the latter category!

His parties were a mixed bag of pretentious, rich, old gay *queens* good-looking young men, and straight women of a certain age with worldly knowledge. Richard was a butcher at Petrini's Market; thus, the sirloin beef steaks at his dinner parties were always first rate. One time, I brought him a house gift of a bottle of Gates barbecue sauce from Kansas City. As we left for home, he gave the bottle back to me at the top of the staircase. He then said, indignantly, "You should never disguise a piece of meat." Although the meals were carefully proportioned in size, there was plenty wine and liquor. With his limited education, he preferred social intercourse and entertaining, as opposed to reading. His cultivation of friendships with his neighbors was magnanimous. He was also extremely popular with his loyal customers. He oozed charm and perhaps had kissed the Blarney Stone and loved his Irish whisky. He was a popular society figure in the gay community, as well as being a wonderfully amusing neighbor. Once, while he was walking his silver-grey, wire-haired terrier, Pepper, he was attacked from behind. With the great strength of his lanky, muscular body, he threw the punk over his head. The punk ran off terrified! Later, someone robbed his top-floor flat and placed Pepper in the washing machine. Luckily, Pepper was unharmed. And Richard was extremely grateful for that. He also owned a large, white cat named Salt that was fond of Pepper and followed him everywhere.

He insisted that once you are at his dinner table that only rude people arrive tardy by emptying their bladders first. Once, he saw John's watch while he was seating guests for dinner and indignantly said, "Gentlemen do not wear watches to the dinner table!"

Being much aggravated by his tenants in a four-unit building at 1855 Golden Gate Avenue, Richard asked me to sell it in 1980 I was able to get him an extremely good profit. Over the years, we would continue socializing at his home on a regular basis, usually on the weekends, particularly on Sundays.

In the late 1990s, at one Sunday evening dinner party consisting of the three of us and two gay friends (one younger computer programmer and a retired internist from Kaiser Permanente Hospital), I commented, "Chuck is particularly well endowed." Richard furiously said, "I don't allow that kind of talk at my dinner table." We continued to be friendly but ceased to invite each other to our respective homes. Richard died in 2009, at the age of seventy-four, and he was given a deeply moving memorial service, which included an Irish tenor singing, at the graceful Lady Chapel of Saint Dominic's Church. At the reception that followed in his flat, with wine flowing and good food, each invited friend had a memorable experience to relate about their contact with Richard. He is buried back in County Mayo, Ireland, next to his mother. He was lovable, gracious, and cantankerous, as only the Irish can be!

Jim and Margaret Delameter

Jim and Margaret Delameter were the most fabulous party givers on the block. They had remodeled their corner home, through the interior design firm of Charles Pfister and Jeffery Wiseman, to entertain with a spacious ground floor plan, which was perfect for parties. The kitchen overlooked their side yard with a lap pool and a large palm tree. Margaret, of Irish American ancestry, was an excellent chef and had taken professional lessons. She knew the best purveyors of food, which included even Costco Wholesale and Trader Joe's. Dr. Jim, who had been an army brat, was always amusing and perceptive about the foibles of human nature. Their private dinner parties or large social gatherings were well prepared, and the cuisine was always delicious. A well-equipped private bar in a side room, with a bartender, made the parties even more festive in the distinctive San Francisco manner. They were both extroverts. Their diverse groups of guests provided interesting conversations. One festive evening, Margaret bid us good-bye at the interior front door, wearing a slinky, sheath black dress with a plunging neckline. Ming asked, "How far do the freckles go down?" She laughed and pushed us out the front door. They had enclosed their front porch so the outside door faced the Pacific Heights side on Broderick Street, versus the less-acceptable Tenderloin side at the Eddy Street address. Thus, this rearrangement provided for a more sociably acceptable address on Broderick Street.

They commuted up to their wine-country ranch in Healdsburg between Jim's emergency shifts at Kaiser Permanente Hospital or for weekly vacations. One night in 1982, while they were in the country, John and I, returning from the opera, dressed in our tuxedos, saw someone coming out of their front door. We noticed that their rounded corner window was open. I yelled to a tall, dark stranger, "Just who are you visiting?" Then he and another person started to run quickly down the hill. We pursued them in our 1978 Cadillac Seville—right into the courtyard of the nearby public housing project (Yerba Buena West Plaza). Our car was instantly surrounded by a couple dozen menacing juveniles. Suddenly, a police car with flashing red lights sped into the courtyard, and the crowd dispersed. The policemen shook their heads and said, "You know you should stay out of this dangerous neighborhood." I explained that we lived a block away, and they looked at us in amazement. Most of the city policemen live in outlying counties, such as San Mateo, or in districts in the city which do not have public housing, such as the Sunset and Richmond Districts.

Bill and Carol Delameter

Bill and Carol Delameter were our neighbors. Bill was Jim's brother and lived in a condominium flat two doors down. We became close friends and often got together. Bill and I compared notes about our gardens and their antique collecting. Carol, who was a second-generation Irish American from Massachusetts, was always entertaining us with her wit and considerable knowledge of literature. After over ten years of marriage, they separated. After their divorce, Carol returned to her maiden name of Pardridge, and then she increased her household by two cats (Rumple and Hilda). She and Ming often commiserated over her *children*. Ming, who is a cat person, unlike me who is allergic to them, said diplomatically, "I like both of them but prefer (the older, amiable, fat cat) Rumple to (the younger, skittish, abandoned, and smaller cat) Hilda." One evening, she had a dinner party, and we three were invited with Richard Wade and an older, English decorator "queen" of a wealthy, mercantile-class family, who was Carol's neighbor in the flat below. Because we were having roast beef for dinner, the interior decorator said to Richard, "Do you know only the English eat roast beef and leave the pork for the Irish?" The Englishman's American lover was terribly embarrassed. (They later moved to Palm Springs). Needless to say the evening became a little bit tense. But Carol, always the gracious hostess, smoothed things over by never inviting them together again.

Another time, she invited an elderly, African American lady, who was visiting Bertha's old tenant sisters. She had been an employee on the White House staff. The friend said, "Mamie Eisenhower was often accused of being drunk, but she actually had a vertigo problem." We enjoyed many spontaneous visits with Carol, as well as other neighbors. Carol moved back to Newbury Port, Massachusetts in 2000. At present, she is residing in an adult condominium community in New Hampshire, but we still keep in touch by telephone, occasional visits, and holiday cards. We miss her!

Giovanni Camajani and Margaret Chase

Another neighbor who lived in the Sun Houses, Margaret Chase, had been in the Red Cross in World War II and served on the staff of General Dwight Eisenhower in the North-African Theater. She said over dinner at her home, "The rumor that Ike had an affair with his female, English chauffeur is definitely incorrect." Her husband, Giovanni Camijani, conducted the first performance of Carl Orff's entrancing and hypnotic *Carmina Burana* in North America, in 1954, at the San Francisco War Memorial Opera House during a concert of the University of San Francisco Schola Cantorum (consisting largely of San Francisco Symphony players). Carl Orff (1895–1982 in Munich) composed the musical score between 1935 and 1936, which was based on poems that came from the preserved archives of a Bavarian Benedictine monastery founded in 733 CE. The poet, Michael Hofmann, organized twenty-four of the poems into a libretto. After a riotously successful, staged, premier production at the Frankfurt Opera in 1937, Orff told the house of Schott, his only publisher since 1927, "Everything I have written to date, and which you have, unfortunately, printed, can be destroyed. With *Carmina Burana* my collected works begin." Margaret, who married late in life, was a deeply dedicated art instructor at the elite Lowell Public High School, and she was extremely cultured. Both of them were dining with us one evening, and I surprised them by showing Federico Fellini's iconic *The Ship Sails On* on our VCR, which was about great opera stars in the early 1900s, who were aboard a ship to celebrate the cremated remains of another great soprano, who was to be committed to the sea. They both were delighted. And, we enjoyed Giovanni's introducing to us a delicious gift of arugula that he had tended from his garden. Although we met them late in their lives, our memories together are treasured. Next-door neighbors of theirs, in a relocated Victorian cottage, were the talented actor Peter Donat and his beautiful Swedish wife Marika. Peter was one of the early mainstays of the American Conservatory Theater (ACT) in San Francisco, as well as a favorite in various film roles.

John Horton Cooper and Iris

On the northeast corner of Eddy and Divisadero Streets was a redevelopment-relocated Stick Lake Victorian house (circa 1878), which was occupied in the early 1970s by good friends of Jim and Margaret Delameter, John Horton Cooper (another highly creative artist) and his partner Iris (the former wife of a Houston cardiac surgeon). They were a lively couple with whom we occasionally socialized. John was a popular, light-skinned African American jazz pianist. This handsome man, with his distinguished Ivy League appearance, perfect down to his gold signet ring, was a commanding and popular figure as a high-class jazz pianist in the 1950s and 1960s at the El Matador Club (with bullfight movies and owned by the notable author, Barnaby Conrad) on Broadway.

The equally popular bassist, Vernon Alley, his long-time friend, and John were a dynamic duo and popular with both the jazz fans and the social elite of San Francisco.

An article in the *San Francisco Chronicle*, in October of 1986, memorializes his retirement from a Friday- and Saturday-night gig at the Washington Square Bar and Grill—dubbed the *Wash Bag* and popular with journalists and politicians. The article mentions that, although his father, a candy maker in San Jose, California, died when he was two-years old, his mother wanted him to have a good education, including music, and to be a gentleman. She preferred that he be a physician, but she did introduce him to show business because she was an assistant manager for a vaudeville theater in San Jose. The article states, "One of eleven blacks in a high school of more than thirty-five hundred [students], he was elected head of the student body." John is further quoted as saying, "I never sat around and waited for someone to give me anything."

He supplemented his income with daytime jobs at Robert Kirk, a fashionable, men's, English clothing store, and also at Wells Fargo Bank. As a member of the Bohemian Club, he was a popular bon vivant. His charming blond Iris, who was an I. Magnin fashion-store buyer, made them an ideal couple.

They contracted with the earlier-mentioned, well-known, interior-designer (interior of Davies Symphony Hall) and neighbor, Charles Pfister, to create for them a stunning interior. Among one of the most-striking rooms was the cream-colored front parlor, with a large, U-shaped, neutral, raw-silk-covered sofa, which surrounded John's prominent, black-lacquered grand piano, which was once, supposedly, owned by George Gershwin. The effect was dramatic. John's daytime drink was gin, and the evening drink was Scotch whisky.

In 1982, Jonathan Benjamin and Pat Ban bought the house, did their own unique remodeling, and completely modernized the kitchen. Jonathan was from a wealthy, Jewish, textile-manufacturing family in North Carolina, and Pat was a native of Oregon. They were both quite politically astute and helped, as members of BANG, to effect concessions from the redevelopment agency to revive the neighborhood through their knowledgeable grasp of political manipulation. Their (Pat's) daughter would be associated with my firm for several years.

Richard Reutlinger

In the Alamo Square area, at 824 Grove Street (Italianate Victorian Mansion, circa 1886), Richard Reutlinger entertained with his much-anticipated, annual, breathtaking, Halloween parties. Some people were already preparing afterward for the party next year. His extensive collection of Eastlake Victorian furniture was covered with sheets, and his other-period antiques, including large, period chandeliers, offered a glittering and exciting backdrop. His columned, double parlor led to a majestic dining room, with an ample table buffet lit with florid, silver candelabra. The original kitchen, with a large, old-fashioned, steel stove, brought forth deliciously prepared dishes. In the background, talented pianists played and vocalists sang. With lights dimmed, the same guests had the option of visiting the amazing, originally decorated, Victorian rooms, as well as a garden room on the main floor and four large bedrooms upstairs. The Turkish room was the site of many amorous scenes. But the most spectacular and fun room was the basement ballroom, where his large collection of player pianos were playing, and a well-staffed bar was set up. The invitation for his party specified, "For you, and your guests as well, bringing a bottle of champagne per person." Thus, it became a bubbly, colorful and boisterous evening. Although the crowd was predominately gay, many neighbors of diverse backgrounds participated. The costumes were an assortment of skimpy, full leather, full drag, and the frivolously unusual.

The tall, commanding, husky figure of Richard would dramatically appear at the top of the stairs early in the evening and gracefully descend to meet his guests. Whether he was a southern belle or a flapper, this Nebraska small-town native would graciously greet all guests in a coquettish manner. The vivacious, red-headed Cathy Furniss, a child actress in Hollywood, a music publicist, and neighborhood historical activist, was dressed in a full, black gown with stars, and with a pointed hat, as a seer with a crystal ball in her hand. Her companion, an attorney and writer, Michel Lipman, would come as the physician *Dr. Quackenbush*, with a stethoscope and a laboratory coat with attached fake one hundred dollar bills and bearing the sign "VISA cards accepted." Peter Witmer always came as a pirate. And his beefy partner, Don Nehls, in drag, wore black orthopedic, laced-up shoes, a black and white polka-dot dress, several dead minks attached together around his neck, and a black felt hat with lace, which was perched on a horrid gray wig. John liked to be mysterious and went one Halloween wearing black-white-red theatrical makeup (Chinese theatrical mask) and an Egyptian black and white striped caftan. Sedately, Ming liked wearing carefully selected Asian clothing. I preferred to wear exotic Asian or Middle Eastern clothing. We always wore masks. The guests in the skimpiest costumes always had clusters of masked figures around them. Sometimes, the guests mysteriously disappeared into the nooks and crannies of this grand Victorian house. On various New Year's Eves, Richard would rent out his home to a group of gay nudists and disappear for the evening. Prior to his purchase in 1958, the previously derelict house was used as an African American Baptist church. Now, it has been "blessed" many times by intoxication and joy!

Richard has been restoring and adding exotic collections to his home since he purchased it fifty years ago. As an early member and the former long-serving treasurer of the Victorian Alliance, he has been a solid presence for the historical-preservation community. He was also an early member, and is a long-time active participant, in ASNA. For both groups, he has been extremely generous in opening the doors of his home for numerous events. His Christmas parties for the Victorian Alliance are another highlight of the year. Many accomplished cooks turn out old and proven recipes for a sumptuous feast, and good cheer is everywhere. In addition, his neighbor, another important preservationist, Joe Pecora, entertains grandly in his equally sumptuous home. His Victorian afternoon Christmas party is complete with a towering Christmas tree, which Joe decorated with one of the largest collections of antique Christmas ornaments and memorabilia in the United States. Guests provided their favorite cuisine dishes to add the perfect touch to an anticipated, enjoyable, afternoon party.

James Oliver Siegel III

In the towering Stick Eastlake Victorian Westerfield House (circa 1889), of 8,500 square feet (National Landmark) on Alamo Square, Jimmy Siegel (James O. Siegel III), who bought the house in 1985, is also extremely generous with his home for fund-raising events for preservation groups. He and his prior partner lavishly decorated the large, spacious, ground-floor rooms, which have thirteen-foot ceilings in high Victorian fashion, including a room under the stairs, which is off the dramatic entrance hall containing a large cage with a large parrot. We all suspect the squawking was somewhat, salty language. The second floor contains four bedrooms, including one filled with taxidermy animals, which the vegetarian Barbara Meskunas called, "The meat room." There is a sixteen-foot tower-room on the third floor, which has high ceilings and dramatic views in every direction. He and Richard Reutlinger would often compete, in a friendly manner, at auctions for Eastlake furniture, etc. Jim, who is tall, thin (vegetarian), and blond-headed, arrived from the East Coast, in 1965, as a hippie in his late teens. He opened on Haight Street business, Distractions, a successful head shop with merchandise, such as tie-dyed clothing, glass smoking pipes, and psychedelic-themed posters. He has now switched the merchandise to new/vintage clothing only. The walls of one room in his home are covered with the priceless, original, rock/psychedelic concert posters from Bill Graham's presentations, as well as independent operators. He jokingly said one of his distant relatives was the infamous gangster Bugsy Siegel, who went west to develop gambling in Las Vegas. Jim's immediate East Coast family consists of quite respectable, prosperous, and public-spirited citizens. Jim has more energy than anyone that I have ever met. As he calls me his official real estate broker, we purchased our earlier mentioned historical-landmarked building together on Scott Street, connected by common wall.

In 1996, the Lesbian Gay Bisexual Transgender (LGBT) Community Center Project purchased a parcel of land that included the Fallon Building, circa 1894. This Stick Eastlake-style commercial/residential building had survived the fire and earthquake of 1906, which had destroyed all of the Market Street buildings east of it. When Jim heard that the board of directors planned to demolish the building, he protested, "The queer movement has done the most to preserve the architectural history in San Francisco." With his adrenaline pumping, he asked me to draw up a Contract to Purchase the property, stating that he would fund the restoration. The result was that a group called The Friends of 1800 Market Street was formed, in 1997, to fund the preservation of the building. The San Francisco Landmarks Preservation Board, through the able direction of Vincent Marsh, voted unanimously to designate the building as a San Francisco landmark. The San Francisco Planning Commission, the Board of Supervisors, and Mayor Willie Brown Jr. approved the designation. The Community Center Board withdrew its opposition and the California State Legislation later awarded $1 million for the restoration of the National Landmarked Fallon Building, through the efforts of the Heritage Foundation for San Francisco Architectural Heritage. John and I made contributions to the center, which was completed in 2001. Today, the building reflects the important contribution of then-united LGBT and the sweat equity of Jim Siegel.

In 2002, Jim decided to seek elective office as a city supervisor. I was his treasurer and Barbara Meskunas was his campaign manager. Although he got many important endorsements, I kept thinking, "Jim, you should not be so up front and direct in this city of complicated politics. You are running on the progressive ideas of Teddy Roosevelt in a tightly controlled political city." He lost to Ross Mirkarimi, who he endorsed before the election when he saw that he probably would not win. Ross, who is of Persian and Russian ancestry, proved to be a more community based Supervisor in District 5, as opposed to the former Supervisor Matt Gonzalez (Green Party), who ran later for U.S. vice-president, with Ron Paul, as a Libertarian. San Franciscans have always had a love-hate relationship with supervisorial districts and resurrected them in 2000 after the first district elections were abandoned for a brief moment in the late 1970s. Jim finished restoring a Victorian house that he moved from Ohio in 2004 to his country property in Russian River. He regularly attends the annual *Burning Man* camp-outs in Idaho. He recently repainted his huge mansion completely by himself on rented scaffolding. I said earlier, "Jim, I think that it is dangerous, and I don't want to attend your funeral." He said, "I can't afford a painting contractor, and tell my father that you are my real estate broker."

Richard and Cher Zillman

Richard and Cher Zillman purchased a National Landmark, Italianate French Second Empire-style Victorian house, circa 1885, at 280 Divisadero Street, through my firm. The house was built by Charles Hinkel, whose five brothers were all prolific builders. The Zillmans' ornate, vivid, multi-colored (certainly not the original colors) villa has a striking Mansard roof with dormers; square bays, a classical, portico entrance with a pair of solid, exterior, wooden doors; with an interior pair of stained-glass doors; as well as a side drive to a two-story carriage house. The mostly original interior contains an elegant double parlor with the original ceiling, which is painted with birds, and floral swags. The house supposedly has a resident ghost that lurks near the front interior staircase, and many guests have felt its presence. The Zillmans are actively involved with the Victorian Alliance. They have generously opened their home often for many fundraising events for the preservation movement.

The Zillmans have been battling for ten years with the Department of Building Inspection (DPI.) about their redesign for the plain, dilapidated, carriage house that has a hay loft at the rear of their lot, which leads into a well-researched Victorian fantasy building. No photographs exist of the original design, which has obviously undergone many physical alterations. The carriage house is hidden from public view by the house and a high, wooden, driveway fence. They have much support from their neighbors, friends as well as fellow preservationists. Even with this support and their great expense for architectural plans, the newly elected two-year-old San Francisco Historical Preservation Commission would idiotically side with the DBI and reject their researched and enlightened redesign plans. Many of us were disappointed that we had supported the establishment of this commission over the more-pragmatic San Francisco Landmarks Preservation Board.

On March 9, 2011, forty of their fellow preservations and friends attended the Zillmans' appeal hearing at the Board of Appeals in City Hall (One Dr. Carlton B. Goodlett Place). After spending ten years arguing for their remodel, they both were physically exhausted. In fact, Richard had been seriously ill for two years but has recovered. We were in Room 416 at 5:00 p.m. and waited until 10:45 p.m. to hear their appeal of the San Francisco Preservation Commission ruling. The president, a plump Caucasian woman named Kendall Goh asked for members of the audience favoring the Zillmans to stand, and although 30 percent of the supporters had left, it was still a significant presence. She said that, unlike the usual procedure, we would be limited to one minute, not three minutes, and we were to choose only a few speakers. A few of us, including the president of the ASNA, vice-president of Victorian Alliance, Jim Siegel, John Barbey, several others, and I made quickly revised editing to our speeches. After our glowing support, the board members began the usual pontificating, with long dialogues among themselves, and asked for information from Richard Zillman and his attorney Brett Gladstone (our attorney for lawsuit against the Pitts Plaza), as well as the DBI civil servants. The pompous and odious President Goh said, "I wouldn't mind living in this building in its present state." The board members finally decided to give the Zillmans two months to mutually agree with the DBI on an alternative remodel and reappear before them.

The Board of Appeals overall approach was that the new design did not reflect the "original" design.

We all gave a collective, anguished groan! Jim Siegal went up to the board gallery and yelled, "You are all a bunch of a– holes!"

John Barbey followed by saying, "I am shocked that you allowed us to stay here to 11:30 at night with a one-minute speech."

Later, I learned that the nearby Civic Center Garage, where I was parked, closed at twelve midnight. I shouted, "There is no way that I would landmark our home and restore the impractical, original, carriage-house doors." In passing, I said to Tim, the preservation representative of DBI, "That performance of yours was rather shabby and unsupportable."

His immediate superior said, "You can't talk to my staff like that."

I almost said, "Please remember you are public servants." Then, I remembered why I hated these many personal, supposed forums of public discussion so much, with their prejudices and pre-decisions.

Joseph O'Donoghue and Sherrie Matza

Joe O'Donoghue and Sherrie Matza reside in an Arts and Crafts house, circa 1914, which had been owned originally by a physician who had his office on the second floor of this four-story house in the Alamo Square area. They bought their home through my firm at a very reasonable price. This house has a similar, original, intact interior, much like our home. An African American family had owned the house since the 1940s, and the heirs sold when their grandmother died. Joe and I had been acquainted since a real estate transaction in the late 1970s. His wife at that time, Beverly, was an African American physician and was extremely attractive, much like Michelle Obama. I have always admired his ability to connect people together. In fact, one year he was selected as the Grand Marshall for the Saint Patrick's Day parade. Through his sponsorship of the Residential Builders Association, which was mostly Irish immigrant contractors, he was responsible for the major transformation of the South of Market housing.

This transformation in the 1990s consisted of constructing work-live loft condominiums (euphemistically called artist lofts) and rental complexes to replace the pre-existing light industrial buildings. This private development created a great new source of housing for the city but was highly controversial, for diverse reasons. These well-designed, modern buildings are quite a contrast to the ugly, bland buildings in the Richmond District, which were constructed by Irish contractors in the 1950s and 1960s. I had mentioned to Joe that he should encourage the builders to hire better architects and be respectful to the historical preservationists, if they were to be more successful. These changes did occur, with additional criticism from the general public and a more intensive plan review at the Department of Building Inspection.

Their home social parties were the ultimate political soiree, where Joe held court. Nancy Ho, attorney Melvin Belli's (King of Torts) widow, was present there "protecting" her Belli investments in the historic Jackson Street Square district. (The famous, brilliant, trial attorney, Melvin Belli, had been quite flamboyant, with his white, Rolls Royce convertible with red upholstery, his many wives, and the winning of famous lawsuits, such as for the woman who became a nymphomaniac after being hit by a city cable car.)

Alice Suet Barkley, who was the most formidable property-rights attorney in the city, sulked in the background and made future contacts. Julie Lee, who was the ever-smiling Chinese American and a politically powerful real estate broker, made the rounds. She would later to be jailed for fraudulent behavior in a political transaction. Barbara Meskunas was the ace political operative, who quietly surveyed the scene. The handsome blond, tall, and accomplished Irish American architect, Ted Eden, with his beautiful wife, added a special flair to the evening. His late identical twin brother and he were both yachtsmen and designed the new St. Francis Yacht Club after a disastrous fire. They both had the perfect features and aristocratic manners.

The journalist, Warren Hinckle, was present in suit and tie, wearing his black eye patch and accompanied by his formidable basset hound Bentley. His always absent wife was the daughter of the novelist John Cheever. As a self-confessed alcoholic and fallen-away Roman Catholic, his colorful presence was much anticipated. Jack Davis, the shrewd political consultant, originally from Texas, had helped elect Frank Jordan and Willie Brown Jr. as mayors. Jack was infamous at that time for staging his birthday party, at which he sat on a bourbon bottle, according to the local newspapers.

But perhaps the most anticipated appearance was the "Lord Mayor," Willie L. Brown Jr., who governed the city with his *noblesse oblige*. Purportedly almost blind, Willie was definitely the most worldly and charming person in the room. He had grown up in the small town of Mineola, Texas, and progressed politically in San Francisco at the speed of a rocket. Joe had allegedly one daily lunch with the mayor on a regular, weekly basis. Filling out the party, there were always a large number of Irish contractors (sometimes with their wives) who had made fortunes with the new, booming, construction developments in San Francisco.

Although Joe never drank alcohol, his bar was always well stocked and active. In 1997, Joe presented me with an Irish crystal vase at the Residential Builders Association annual meeting. The wooden base was inscribed with my name and the phrase "For outstanding contribution and commitment to the Construction Industry in San Francisco." Joe bought a two-story Victorian building through my firm, in the Castro District near my office. He reconstructed the building into essentially a new building consisting of two townhouse condominiums above a one-flat condominium and a parking garage. After I sold the two townhouses in 2002, Joe refused to extend the listing period for the unsold unit. At that time, I was to see a particularly violent side of him that I had not previously seen. I realized, perhaps, that I did not know him as well as I thought.

Wayne Corn and Klaus May

Wayne Corn and Klaus May were the owners of the bed and breakfast, Alamo Square Inn, which was located at 719 Scott Street on the west side of Alamo Square. The main building was a late Queen Anne Victorian connected by a large, covered, central deck, with an Ernest Coxhead designed house on the corner and three flats that fronted on Fulton Street. The whole complex was furnished with early twentieth-century, updated copies of Victorian furniture, such as overstuffed sofas, lamps with fringed light shades, and a lot of dark wood furniture. The inn was comfortable and popular with out-of-town visitors. Since they served breakfast and catered special-occasion events, they generously offered their inn for many community fundraising events. Wayne, a native of North Carolina, had an innate political sense of every situation. He and Klaus, who was from Germany, had met when they both were airline stewards on the same Pan American flights. I met Wayne because we were both always involved in many of the same political causes in the Western Addition. He was quite active in ASNA, the Victorian Alliance, and the Planning Association for Divisadero Street (PADS). He personally created a coalition organization called the Western Addition Society to promote awareness to visitors, as well as San Franciscans, of the historical architectural magnificence of the Western Addition through a published brochure, distributed by the City Convention and Visitors Bureau. Beginning in the late 1980s, he and I would meet on a regular basis, once a week, in the morning, at the inn.

When I became president of Planning Association for Divisadero Street PADS in 1992, Wayne and I formulated a new street-improvement plan. And I am proud of what we, and other board members, were able to accomplish during this period. Wayne had profile-scale city planning drawings of the present improvements on Divisadero Street, and we viewed them together to upgrade this important corridor street linking the upper Market Area to Pacific Heights. We both knew that Divisadero had the potential to be as important as any of the grand boulevard streets in San Francisco. We first proposed to the city the placing of planter boxes on the median concrete-divider strip on Divisadero Street, from Duboce Avenue to California Street, but were informed by the San Francisco Planning Department that the local utilities company, Pacific Gas and Electric, had utility lines located there. Thus, we were told that nothing could be done with our landscaping idea. Our visionary plan would become a reality in 2009! Also, we suggested placing banners on the double-cantilevered street lights but were told that we would have to provide liability insurance at our expense. Another idea from a gay member of PADS was to plant the prehistoric Ginkgo Bulbous trees along the sidewalk. Male trees were to be planted because the female trees drop fruit. We were able to obtain some private grant money to plant forty trees. The city, through the urban forest division of the Public Works Department, added some extra saplings and planted them. These slow-growing, ancient trees provided beautiful golden foliage each fall. Unfortunately, some vandals broke off limbs or pushed the saplings over.

In 1985, Wayne and Klaus purchased a large Italianate house with a huge, south, side yard at Buchanan and Bush Streets, in the now designated Lower Pacific Heights district. As dedicated historical preservationists, they were thrilled. This probated purchased house, through my firm, was mainly in its original condition except for broken windows and a leaking roof. The house had been occupied by an elderly Japanese American man, who had survived the interment camps and was obviously delusional and/or poverty stricken. A dumpster in front made me nostalgic, seeing the photographs that were, unfortunately, being thrown out. One particular photograph I remember showed a formal reception, in the pre-war Japantown, of men in long-frocked formal wear. Their dream home was to be renovated and a large garage built under the side yard.

A neighbor, Judge J. Anthony Kline did not want this wilderness site changed. He was one of two attorneys who, in the 1960s, represented many tenants and some property owners in contesting the SFRA construction of a convention center and a sports arena in the South of Market. A group called Tenants and Owners in Opposition to Redevelopment (TOOR) was formed to protest M. Justin Herman's aggressive plans for the Yerba Buena Center. This battle was to pit the economically disadvantaged pensioners against the formidable, well-vested, downtown business interests. An opposing group was then formed to promote this development, called the San Francisco

Planning and Urban Renewal Association (SPUR). The politically astute and distinguished Mayor Joseph Alioto became busy balancing the corporate business interests, the large-property owners, hotels, Chamber of Commerce, and the labor unions. The various labor unions wanted more construction jobs in spite of their retired unionist members living there. The activist tenants, and also some small property owners, wanted nothing to do with the redevelopment project. Today, this area is an enormous convention center surrounded by an expansive, rolling green lawn, with a two-level waterfall dedicated to Martin Luther King, Jr., retail operations, museums, theaters, and hotels. The displaced tenants were given a small concession of subsidized housing in scattered, high-rise buildings nearby.

Wayne was furious with the opposition from Judge Kline and some other neighbors. In revenge and as a refusal to live near them, he decided to build two townhouses on the legal side-yard lot and combine them, with the rehabilitated house, as condominiums. With great determination against his hated San Francisco Department of Building Inspection and Planning Department, he was able to get his plans approved. During a particularly brutal winter of heavy rainstorms, an earthen wall of the newly excavated lot began to collapse, and the Victorian house started sliding into the excavated side yard. He hired crews to stabilize the house. One day, he went out to the site and slipped and fell. With his already-weakened AIDS condition, he had become much feebler. He and Klaus called me to sell their property with the approved architectural plans. They made some profit from the sale, but nothing approached their disappointment of their hoped-for restoration of a grand home and the grief that followed.

In the late 1990s, Klaus, always the exacting and the precise one, climbed three stories on some exterior scaffolding to inspect the new paint job at the inn. A stiff wind blowing that day caused him to trip, and he fell to the sidewalk, suffering a fatal, cerebral brain concussion! Klaus was buried in Germany in the family plot. Wayne, not in good health, became worse after Klaus's accident. He eventually moved to Hawaii and died April 9, 2011, at the age of seventy.

IN RETROSPECT

This period of neighborhood socializing was exhilarating! Like so many periods in one's life, this will be particularly remembered as a golden age. Further wine/cocktails, fine dining, music, and new friendships reverberate with a hope for the future. As *Carmina Burana* stated in a translated form, *Made of matter rose from dust, I am like a leaf tossed in play to the winds.*

13.

San Francisco Housing Authority

The SFHA was established earlier than the SFRA. The U.S. Housing Act of 1937 established housing authorities to provide low-rent housing for the American urban poor during the Great Depression. In April of 1938, the U.S. Housing Authority announced that they had set aside $15 million for the first California authority, the SFHA, to build five housing projects. The first was Holly Courts in 1939, followed by Poterero Terrace, Sunnydale, Valencia Gardens, and North Beach Place. Some of the best San Franciscan contemporary architects, such as William Wurster, Harry Thomsen, Jr., Frederick Meyer, John Blakewell, and Warren Perry were hired to design workers' housing that would provide human living conditions in park-like settings. The highly acknowledged landscape architect, Thomas Church, designed the gardens at Valencia Gardens (demolished 2005). These utopian centers would contain laundry rooms, social halls, and hobby/craft rooms. The four-story and ten-story concrete complexes were built in the modern International-style. After 1941, the only other project to be completed was the Westside Courts, which was the first in the Western Addition. Other planned public-housing projects were put on hold until the end of World War II. In the interim, the SFHA concentrated on building temporary wartime housing for 35,000 workers and their families at Hunters Point.

With termination of World War II, as mentioned previously, the newly created SFRA and SFHA were both funded by a combination of Federal Financial Aid under Title I of the Housing Act of 1949, through Urban Renewal Administration Housing, and bonds issued by the Home Finance Agency and the city.

Although the SFHA had earlier constructed Westside Courts near the SFRA A-1 Project Area north of Geary Boulevard, the most concentrated project public housing was south of Geary Boulevard and was contingent to both the A-1 and A-2 Project Areas. The Yerba Buena West Plaza was the only project within the borders of BANG. The SFRA had no jurisdiction over those buildings, but could make vacated land available for development about the 1900 block of Eddy Street, which was discussed earlier. Only the SFHA had jurisdiction over their properties. Curiously, these properties, unlike all properties throughout the city, are not listed on any property-ownership records with the office of the city assessor to this day!

In 1984, the housing authority sought government funding from the Department of Housing and Urban Development (HUD) to tear down the Yerba Buena West Plaza high-rise buildings and replace them with family oriented housing. This public-housing complex occupied two, large, city blocks, with two monolithic towers and a total combination of 332 units (one and two bedrooms). The specific boundaries were Divisadero Street on the west, Pierce Street on the east, Eddy Street on the north, and Turk Street on the south. This proposed development would consist of detached two-story townhouses over ground-floor flats with off-street parking to replace the existing eleven-story, reinforced-concrete buildings that were built in the mid-1950s. The new public housing was to provide three and four bedrooms, so the units would be more viable for families than the one and two bedroom apartments. The plans included landscaping and proposed lower-rise units, which would blend more into the surrounding neighborhood architectural profile.

The neighbors from a variety of ethnic backgrounds were not enthusiastic and protested that the public housing would promote more of the same neighborhood crime that presently existed. Of course, the housing authority, their commission, and some city officials said that the neighbors were all NIMBYS (Not-in-My-Back-Yard). They belittled our attempts to protest. Our main concerns were realistically with the incompetence and graft inherent in the housing authority and the obvious bad idea of warehousing disadvantaged residents of the city. These eleven-story buildings with elevators were essentially structurally well-constructed and seismically stable.

For example, a similar public-housing building survived the 1989 earthquake and was only three-blocks away. This Yerba Buena Annex building had been converted in 1985, without any seismic upgrading, into the Rosa Parks Senior Apartments by the architectural firms of Marquis Associates and Young & Associates. We neighbors argued that, even as a vacant parcel, this land would bring a splendid return from purchase by private developers, as evidenced by the nearby new construction and the renovations of the now much-desired Victorian buildings. The excessive, realized funds could be then used to subsidize scattered, small-site, disbursed housing. The only problem was that no other San Franciscan neighborhood wanted the blight of a housing project built in their neighborhood. Vacant land was still available, and the SFRA had the right of eminent domain in industrial areas. Also, we mentioned the well-documented, stop-light robberies in our neighborhood. Local commuters in their cars stopped for red street lights and would be held-up at gunpoint and robbed by male juveniles from the projects!

In the intervening time, the Yerba Buena Plaza West Plaza was closed, in 1985, after a city grand jury denounced the living conditions in the project as being uninhabitable. We were thereby spared the nightly gunshots, the constant mugging of tourists and unsuspecting local citizens, as well as the roar of speeding cars. The hold-up of the drivers of the cars at the nearby traffic stoplights disappeared, and the police reports showed a dramatic decrease in crime. Previously, the police had been ambivalent about the crime scene. They usually said, "What do you think public housing is all about?" Many of the police admitted they would never live near public housing. Most lived in the surrounding suburban cities, or the Sunset/Richmond Districts of the city. Not surprising to us, we all felt safer now to walk in our newly invigorated neighborhood. The quality of life increased, and the area became a new source of pride. Crime dropped dramatically by 600 percent, and downtown commuters once again felt secure stopping for red lights in our district. We hoped that the buildings would be turned into something better than public housing!

We faced incredible opposition. However, the heroic Mayor Diane Feinstein was somewhat sympathetic to our arguments but was being forcibly lobbied by a largely African American activist community. We were collectively called white racists. In 1985, she had been confronted with a HUD-ordered audit from Touche, Ross & Co. and Ferguson, Moorhead & Co. They were able to balance the accounting records of the SFRA to date except for $14 million. The audit cost the SFRA about $400,000. Mayor Feinstein fired the African American SFHA Executive Director Carl Williams from a seven-year directorship, and hired James E. Clay, another African American, who had been a professional manager in Washington, D. C. He was to reorganize the dysfunctional SFHA. In addition, he was asked to pay such debtors as Pacific Gas and Electric Company (PG&E) and the San Francisco Water

Department. The agency was put on the HUD list of financially troubled housing authorities. In 1986, the unanimous SFHA Commission decided to write off the debt because the agency could not reconcile the differences that dated back to the late 1970s. The irony is that Mayor Feinstein's office of Housing and Economic Development was able to appropriate $2.9 million for demolition and construction costs for the Yerba Buena West site!

HUD would come up with the other projected $14 million for development costs. The demolition cost of the 322 reinforced-concrete units would be $1.2 million. As a member, and later president in 1991, of the gay Republican Log Cabin Club of San Francisco (the oldest in the USA), I was shocked that the Reagan administration, like the Eisenhower administration, would fund these wasteful, dinosaur-like, concentrated, housing projects. Reagan's Secretary of HUD Jack Kemp, was much more in favor of homeownership and scattered-site public housing. A worse situation for the neighborhood was to follow, with the election of the grossly incompetent, one-term Mayor Art Agnos, in 1988. A symbol of his administration was the concentrated gathering of the homeless in the Civic Center Plaza. The assemblage was referred to by many San Franciscans as *Camp Agnos*. A notable, devastating, campaign pamphlet, written by Warren Hinkle, with vivid urban photographs of a declining city, *The Agnos Years (1988–1991)*, would lambast his misguided and socially inept administration. The gay Jack Davis was the campaign manager for Frank Jordan, a former police chief. Mayor Jordan, elected in 1992, was a level-headed administrator.

In retrospect, I felt that the only good thing that developed from Art Agnos' administration was the destruction of the Embarcadero and Central Freeways in the Loma Prieta earthquake, on October

17, 1989, and his support for the complete demolishment of them. Ironically, a fellow Greek American, Mayor George Christopher, had been responsible for the freeway construction. Mr. Clay, the Executive Director of the SFHA, who had been appointed by Mayor Feinstein, had the audacity to comment that the Yerba Buena West buildings were not earthquake proof!

The projected new development of the Yerba Buena West building site would consist of 203 units of wooden-framed construction: 67 two-bedroom units of 730 sq. ft., 11 two-bedroom units equipped for the handicapped of 725 sq. ft., 108 three-bedroom units of 925 sq. ft., and 17 four-bedroom units of 1200 sq. ft. Mr. Clay had "admirably" estimated in a newspaper article in 1986, "It will cost $23,227,000 to correct deferred maintenance and other problems of the existing Yerba Buena West through a rehabilitation project." In addition, he further projected that the HUD-funded Comprehensive Improvement Assistance Program would not support this cost. Although a reduction to 129 (one to two bedrooms) units of the proposed new 203 family units into a low-rise apartment complex would be feasible." As a Realtor, rehabilitation subcontractor, and property manager, I was amazed at this outrageous exaggeration of the costs! I increasingly became indignant at the distortions presented by the staffs of the SFRA and SFHA.

The opposition was vicious and spiteful against us neighbors, who opposed this construction at many SFHA commission meetings at their new headquarters building at 440 Turk Street. The president was Reverend. James Goode, who was an African American Roman Catholic priest, and administered a parish in the Bayview district (largely African American after World War II). Goode was arrogant and extremely condescending to our multiethnic coalition. Margaret Verges of BANG commented, "I think we should start calling him Reverend no-good." Commissioner Lewis Lillian was the CEO of a company that was involved in much of the advertising that was allowed on public property. Commissioner Reverend Harry Chuck was a well-connected Chinese American minister with the Presbyterian Church in Chinatown. I commented to him at one of the always contentious meetings, "One of my relatives, Reverend William Speer (a physician who had been a Presbyterian missionary to China for five years previously), started the first protestant mission to the Chinese in North America here in 1853." Rev. Chuck acknowledged my ancestor's involvement in his church but sloughed off any compromise on our current issue. I wondered what the Christian missions had accomplished. I doubt that their purpose would be to promote a bloated bureaucracy devoted to self-promotion!

Commissioner Bill (William) Drypolcher, who was the broker at Zephyr Real Estate and president of the San Francisco Association of Realtors in1987, was equally distant. I had been chairman of the SFAR investment committee in1987 and a long-time member of the political-action committee of the SFAR. I obviously was well acquainted with him. I asked him, "Bill would you want public housing near your new, contemporary home in Clarendon Heights?" He looked at me blankly. After his vote in favor of the project housing, I realized that this seemingly intelligent and radiant person was not the fair and honest person that I had imagined. Years later, I would point out to him how the new public housing had again impacted our neighborhood. He shrugged his shoulders and walked away. His company is greatly expanded today and is heavily invested in the miracle of loft/condominium housing in the South of Market area. His prominence in that market perhaps owes its origins to political connections. The other three commissioners, Robert Boileau, Albert Reem, and Carlene Williams were so well programmed they seemed like robots. The smarmy Executive Director James Clay was replaced, by the morose Mayor Agnos, with an even worse choice—David Gilmore, who was a *spin-off* from the Boston Housing Authority. This well-paid executive director of the SFHA, David Gilmore was a short, fat, and arrogant white man who preened and directed churlish behavior to any opponents at these meetings. He refused to give any consideration to the reality of the situation. Upon his retirement, he received a major appointment to the national office of HUD!

At this time, Art Agnos and I had a long, intimate, controversial conversation at a gay, political fundraiser at the home of Dr. Jerry Goldstein (a noted neurologist) and his lover Tom Taylor. Their Victorian Dolores Heights home had been expanded to include astonishing, expansive, city views. Every Christmas season, with the colorful and extravagantly decorated house as a backdrop, Jerry, wearing a Santa Claus costume, would wave to passing passenger cars. That particular evening, after listening to my complaints about the proposed housing project, Art suggested that I was a NIMBY, which was the typical bureaucratic response. I then mentioned that the three recent sales that I had transacted in his Graystone Terrace neighborhood would never accept public housing. He laughed and said again, "You're a NIMBY." I walked away. Later, a now deceased friend, Dr. Seth Charney, a psychiatrist, had said that Jerry related to him, "I was poisonous to the whole gay community, and he would attempt to steer away anyone from retaining me for any future real estate transactions." As a footnote, Jerry had, for years, made extremely aggressive sexual advances toward me.

Jim Foster who owned an Italianate Victorian row house at1830 Eddy Street, across the street from the proposed development, actively protested the renewed public housing in our neighborhood. He was a co-founder of Society for Individual Rights (SIR), an early homophile organization in 1964. In 1971, he, along with early lesbian leaders Del Martin and Phyllis Lyon, transformed SIR into the Alice B. Toklas Memorial Democratic Club. He was a very influential politico in the city. As a delegate, he and fellow delegate Madeline Davis were the first openly LGBT people to address a Democratic National Convention in Chicago in 1972. He called upon the Democratic Party to add a gay-rights plank to the party platform. He had a good rapport with both Mayors Feinstein and Agnos. Mayor Agnos refused to acquiesce to his opinions on the new public housing but did have a street tree planted in front of his home in his honor. Jim died of the age of fifty-six from an AIDS-related illness at his home in 1990, before the housing project was completed. An overflowing audience attended his memorial service at the Episcopal Grace Cathedral.

With the assistance of neighborhood hirelings and the current SFHA tenant leaders; these SFHA commissioners reinforced their surrealistic authority in regard to the proposed housing project. Mayor Art Agnos had appointed most of these commissioners and reinforced them with latter appointments, saying quite vocally that he would force us to yield to his wishes. His hostile attitude was completely different from the intelligent mediations of former Mayor Feinstein. He would later become the local regional director of HUD and continue to promote that same unrealistic, hostile attitude, which would reestablish the same blight on our neighborhood.

The president of the Yerba Buena Plaza West Tenant Association, Ms. Eva Mae Williams (an African American) claimed, "You whites don't want our kind livin' as good as you and you're afraid of our families." The irony was that many of the protesting neighbors of different social and ethnic backgrounds had families and were not prejudiced at all. Ms. Williams reiterated, "My children and I have always lived in public housing, and I expect that my grandchildren will live there." Several of the tenant leaders physically attacked my neighbors and me at various SFHA meetings. Two police officers were present to prevent the violence that was prevalent in the commission meeting room. Unfortunately, our neighbors, who were African American supporters, were very early intimidated by the actions of their radical, ethnic supporters of the new public-housing project and just stopped coming to the SFHA commission meetings.

Mary Rogers, who did not live in public housing, was always present wearing her African headdresses and long robes. Because of her racial hatred of whites, she and I would become so emotional that she became incoherent. She was the first president of the Western Addition Project Committee, which monitored community input to the SFRA. She rented, at an extremely low monthly rent, a redevelopment agency-owned, large house in the same block as ours on Turk Street. The house was only one block away from our home. Several of her 13 children by different absentee fathers were arrested after robbing their adjacent neighbors and dealing openly in drugs. The police set up a camera in an apartment across the street and were eventually able to present evidence of drug dealing to the courts. The SFRA finally evicted her, and she went to live with a daughter in HUD Section-8 subsidized housing. Since 1975, the Housing Choice Voucher program—better known as Section 8 vouchers—was established; the total number of households receiving certificate and vouchers has risen from 162,000 to 2 million in 2010 nationally. She died from a progressive cancer.

Geraldine Johnson, an African American labor leader, was particularly vicious in her attacks. I could not help noting she resembled her two Doberman Pincher dogs when I saw her walking them in the Panhandle part of Golden Gate Park in the Haight-Ashbury. A portrait of her is now "enshrined" in a wall photograph behind the Martin Luther King Jr. waterfall monument in the Yerba Buena Center. She was visited at the hospital by some neighbors who observed that she would take off her oxygen mask and smoke a few cigarettes. She died of lung cancer.

Randall Evans, an African American, appeared in army camouflage fatigues and paraded around the commission hearing room. He fondled something that looked suspiciously like a revolver in a holster. He gave all of the opposition menacing stares. We believed him capable of any violence. However, he turned out to be somewhat of a *pussy cat* and was only there to get his fair share of money for his advocacy of the SFHA, as well as appearing at SFRA commission meetings.

The SFHA bused their tenants into the commission meetings to further confuse and disrupt these meetings. In fact, some of them came to one of our BANG meetings and disrupted it. Judge Wheatley's daughter, who was an African American neighbor and property owner on our same block but on Ellis Street, hit me in the face and broke my eyeglasses at the same meeting. I was shocked and speechless. Being a gentleman, I did not strike back at her. Although physically not injured, but mentally injured, I was able to get reimbursed for the repair of my eyeglasses from the courts. I thought, "How could a judge's daughter resort to such obviously unruly, racist behavior?"

During this period, the SFHA, HUD, and the city bureaucracy briefly considered several other options, but eventually, with such political pressure, they decided to build the 203 family units. We neighbors were horrified and extremely angry with the SFHA commission approval and betrayal. We appealed to the San Francisco Planning Commission. Their meetings yielded more of the same angst to the neighbors. And, as expected, the unanimous planning commission approved this public housing project.

Rationally, the impacted neighborhood groups had appealed to the planning commission to reject the development on the basis of environment grounds. These issues were based on the facts: only eighty parking spaces for a projected twelve-hundred residents, ignored evidence of toxic chemicals and life-threatening substances at the project site and fuel tanks for the steam boilers, as well as the future airborne particles from the future demolition of these buildings. Ironically, the planning commission granted a conditional-use permit, finding the project "compatible" with the neighborhood, promoting "health, safety, convenience, and general welfare of persons working in the vicinity." The Board of Supervisors, which was still elected at large, voted seven to four in June, 1988, to uphold these same illogical conclusions. Supervisor Hsieh stated the city is "blindly chasing after the 'Federal buck,' which was an unknown cost to itself." Supervisor Molinari said, "It's going to be the same sociological problem. I'm not going to vote for another project that's going to be a graffiti-ridden ghetto." These quotations are from a *San Francisco Chronicle* article, dated June 14, 1988. Voting for the project were Supervisors Harry Britt (gay), Bill Maher (brother of the founder of the Delancy Street drug rehabilitation nonprofit), Carol Ruth Silver (real estate agent and self-promoter), Willie Kennedy (African American), Doris Ward (African American), Jim Gonzales (first Hispanic), and Nancy Walker. Voting against the project were Supervisors Tom Hsieh (second Chinese American), John Molinari, Richard Hongisto (later police chief), and Wendy Nelder (daughter of a former police chief). Local city officials proudly proclaimed, this will be the last, large, housing project in the city. We neighbors said to each other that we had been "screwed!"

The impacted neighborhood associations, which included BANG, ASNA, Alamo Square Homesteaders, and Mid-Divisadero Merchants Association had, in anticipation of a negative situation, joined together earlier to form a self-protective umbrella organization. The Planning Association for Divisadero Street (PADS) formed a coalition of homeowners, renters, landlords, merchants, and smaller neighborhood organizations in January 1988. The PADS articles were incorporated, in June 1988, as a nonprofit mutual benefit association. All of these groups had this in common: we wanted to see positive commercial, residential development, and rehabilitation in the Divisadero Street corridor that ran through our connected boundaries. The boundaries of the membership district were established as Sacramento Street on the north, Fourteenth Street on the south, Broderick Street on the west, and Steiner Street on the east. Several WANA and AVNA individual members, who were equally impacted, joined us in spite of the non-endorsements by their own neighborhood organizations!

The original board members were President Michael Bentivoglia, Vice President Barbara Meskunas, Treasurer Nolan Madson, Secretary Michael Manders, James Foster, Jeannette Fung, Robert Gorter M.D., Winston Montogomery, Jim Siegel, Robert Speer, M.J. Staymates, Fred Wagner, and Greg Witkoski. Mary Randall had been the interim president. The keen-witted editors of our newsletter were the married couple Winston Montgomery and Peggy Nelson, who were always perpetually articulate.

Our immediate rallying call was to stop a repeat performance of the public housing disaster with which we now lived. We proposed either rehabilitating the buildings for senior citizens with the existing units, or building cooperative replacement housing at this site. We most definitely did not want the greedy, self-perpetuating San Francisco Housing Authority involved at any level. We would attack the approval of the city on the basis of an Environmental Inspection Review (EIR) required by the California Environmental Quality Act (CEQA), of the potential effects of such an obsolete, outmoded concept of housing projects on the surrounding environment.

At their August meeting in 1988, the Coalition for San Francisco Neighborhoods (CSFN), representing forty-three neighborhood groups, voted to support the call by PADS for an EIR with only one NO and four ABSTENTIONS. Many Victorian Alliance members were voluntarily supportive, both by membership and financially.

At my suggestion, we hired Brett Gladstone of the law firm of Griffinger, Levinson, Fried, & Heinemann. As a fellow member of the then, but now non-existent, high-profile Bay Area Non-Partisan Alliance, which was dedicated to the political advancement of the gay and lesbian community, I emphasized also that he lived in the Western Addition. He was also then President of WANA and a promising attorney. Later, he became a prominent real estate attorney with his own firm, specializing in real estate matters. We filed a lawsuit on September 7, 1988, in Superior Court, against the City and County of San Francisco and the SFHA, seeking a permanent injunction against the demolition of the block and the rebuilding of the new development under the auspices of the SFHA. The lawsuit was PADS v. City and County of San Francisco. I had quickly agreed to the unenviable position of assisting the treasurer raise funds for the lawsuit!

On September 10, 1988, the *San Francisco Chronicle* quoted a letter dated September 2, 1988 to the SFHA from Arthur Kontura, director of the HUD regional office, "The authority has virtually lost control of entire developments."

With this observation in mind, we actively collected money to fund our lawsuit to counter what we knew would be an expensive public-financed legal staff. We refused to accept the new housing development with the same existing, horrendous, neighborhood impact. Wayne Corn held several fund raisers at the Alamo Square Inn at 710 Scott Street. Jim Siegel was generous with his funding and offered his grand home for PADS fundraising events. Also, a psychologist, Dr. Rodney Karr graciously opened his Chateau Tivoli Inn for a fundraiser on October 21, 1989. This fundraising event was well- attended, in spite of the Loma Prieta earthquake occurring on October 19. His flamboyant Alamo Square Queen Anne Victorian mansion (circa 1890), with corner towers, a gable roof, a double-arched entryway with a balustrade above, and wrought iron roof-decorative elements was formerly the Jewish Welfare Center. At that time, he also owned the fabulous Victorian Mansion at 280 Divisadero Street. This house was later bought by the Zillmans after a foreclosure action.

Our lawsuit was rejected by Superior Court Judge Richard Figone on the basis that this project was replacement housing, and we were told by our law firm that they would not be assisting us any further. Perhaps the political pressure had become too intense for both Brett Gladstone and his former associate Patrick Macis departed. Brett left to establish his law firm. Our law firm recommended that we contract with Pat Macias, who was now with the law firm, Ragghianti, Lusse, & Thomas in San Rafael. Pat was amiable, capable, and energetic. On August 28, 1991, the Court of Appeals affirmed the decision of the Superior Court. Pat suggested that we ask for a rehearing of the appeal before the District Court of Appeals. He gave me a schedule for the rehearing. I said, "I think everyone is worn out, and I can't honestly collect any more money with everyone so pessimistic." Barbara Meskunas, who had become the president of PADS, concurred. I would become president of PADS in1992. The reality was that the newly built housing project was soon to be occupied.

Already on August 17, 1989, David Gillmore, of the SFHA had exulted at the ground-breaking ceremony at the leveled-land site of the former Yerba Buena West Plaza. With a televised press conference to celebrate the "exciting" new, family public housing to be built here, Belva Davis (an African American TV pioneer anchor at KPIX) reinforced this new building as a positive development. Mayor Agnos and friends were all beaming and thrilled with their visionary project. The Robert B. Pitts (the first African American Regional Director of HUD) Plaza was completed in October, 1991. Eva Mae Williams, as president of the Plaza West Tenants' Association, stood gloating at us.

On August 18, 1989, Stephen Schwartz, staff writer for the *San Francisco Chronicle* wrote,

> ***"The ceremony ended when a wrecking ball made a series of relatively ineffectual taps at a wall on the east side of Scott Street, followed by a movement of the crowd toward lunch tables laden with food. As the Mayor and housing***

dignitaries ate and chatted, shouting matches broke out between protestors and the local residents, most of whom were enthusiastic about the plan for new housing. One angry woman shouted that the pickets should 'boost your property values somewhere else,' while protestors yelled that Agnos is 'building a new slum.' The Western Addition neighborhood has changed remarkably over the past five years, with widespread improvements of properties along Divisadero Street by middle-class property owners."

The Neighborhood promptly renamed it *The Pitts*. Shortly afterward, John, Ming, and I were dining at Stars restaurant near City Hall, and I saw the *progressive* Supervisor Sue Bierman. I went over to see her and mentioned the new name. She was speechless about the new name and almost drunkenly fell off her bar stool at the fashionable, and politically well-patronized, Jeremy Tower's restaurant.

President of the SFHA, Lew Lillian, proclaimed earlier, as quoted from the *San Francisco Examiner* article in July 1989, "This is the dawn of a new era for public housing in San Francisco…. It's designed to be a state of art site for public housing. All of the mistakes of the past have been considered and been avoided. We're going to screen families very well. We're making every effort to have a drug-free environment."

PADS members continued to monitor the SFHA Commission meetings until the Court of Appeals decision in August 1991. At the September1990 commission meeting, Peter Byrne, a member of the Artists' Television Access and a local independent journalist, moved to a better vantage point to videotape the commissioners when he noticed a SFHA photographer move to the front of the room. David Gilmore asked him to step back, and he refused, so two San Francisco police were ordered to escort him from the room. Margaret Verges, a PADS member and a fifty-year-old housewife interjected, according to The *San Francisco Bay Guardian* newspaper, "Why are you restraining him? He's a journalist. He has a right to be here. It's a public meeting." Gilmore placed her under citizen's arrest. The same two San Francisco police officers handcuffed her and led her to a squad car. Verges was strip-searched, fingerprinted, and photographed before her release from jail, approximately five hours later! All of the commission proceedings were videotaped by Byrne. Verges would later be quoted in the *San Francisco Independent* newspaper, "I can't believe the ordeal I went through. This is incredible that this would happen in America that you can't go to a public meeting to speak." At the December 1991 commission meeting, many public-housing tenants of different ethnic groups reinforced their opposition to the draconian tactics of the SFHA and began in earnest to complain about their wretched living conditions. Later, Margaret Verges and her husband Keith Consoer, adopted two delightful young daughters from China.

Shortly, following his arrest, the Rodney King riots in May of 1992 spread from Los Angeles to the San Francisco Bay Area. Our Police Chief Richard Hongisto was responsible for closing down the BART exits in San Francisco to stop the large numbers of outraged people from Oakland swarming here to protest. Many of the Oakland and San Francisco protestors were also intent on causing physical damage and looting the affluent downtown stores. Hongisto's overall, instantaneous actions were successful in diminishing property damage and deaths. Unfortunately, one of the personal physical casualties was John's fifty-four-year-old brother, James. Having attended a Navy reserve meeting in Oakland, he was wearing his naval uniform and walking toward North Beach to have dinner with his mother.

On that fateful evening, he was struck in a crosswalk at eight thirty at night, at Columbus Avenue and Kearny Street, by a convertible car containing five African American males, and thrown twenty feet to land on a sidewalk. The punks had just looted several downtown clothing and jewelry stores and were fleeing a pursuing police cruiser. Jim suffered extensive brain damage requiring four brain operations. He was in a coma for two days at San Francisco General Hospital, and his entire family was there! John and I visited him. I fully expected that he would die. His wife Gloria, a Mexican American Roman Catholic said, "I pray that God will save Jimmy." Ming volunteered his bedroom for their three sons to sleep. Gloria and their daughter kept a bedside vigil and stayed overnight in foster City with friends. My father had arrived at the same time to see his properties and also stayed with us, being a great comfort toward all. He had been told In Kansas City, "Dr. Speer, you shouldn't fly to San Francisco." He calmly said, "I paid for my airplane ticket and am going."

Jim miraculously recovered. Even after long, extensive, Veterans Hospital care, he is still confined to a wheelchair and has diminished mental recall. As a housing inspector for twenty-three years, he has been able to manage and provide financially for his wife and four children. All of his children obtained university degrees, mostly from Cornell University, on scholarships. Through a U. S. Navy scholarship, his oldest son, Jaime, earned medical degree from the University of Oregon. His first posting with his wife was in Cherry Point, North Carolina, in 2010, and was later deployed to Afghanistan. He and his family are presently based in Annapolis, Maryland. Two of the captured looters were never charged!

The crashed automobile was found to have been registered to a tenant in the Western Addition at Fulton and Baker Streets. The registered owner "innocently" claimed that the car had been stolen previously that day. After the accident, I immediately asked the then Supervisor Angela Alioto (daughter of the former mayor and someone that I knew politically) to help assist Jim's family.

After the completion of the $20 million (well-over the original, projected budget!) family housing Pitts Plaza, in November 1991, there was once again the constant gang cross-gunfire between the Eddy Rock gang and their rival gangs that lived in other neighborhoods, such as the projects in the Hunters Point and Bayview districts. Most neighbors who live near the Pitts Public Housing avoid driving close or walking on peripheral sidewalks. An owner of a Basilica Lofts condominium across the street had his rear automobile window shot out as he waited for the automatic garage door to open during a daylight period. At night, we again experienced the familiar series of popping noises, which we recognized as gunshots. Relocated to the Pitts Public Housing, the former gang members began terrorizing the neighborhood by riding small, motor scooters and harassing their neighbors. Their preferred pet was a snarling, pit bull dog, which they paraded proudly around the projects. The police began to more closely monitor the area, criminal activity quieted down periodically.

Later, the buildings were posted with signs stating that *Loitering is not tolerated.* These signs had little effect and were minimally enforced. Because of financial restrains, the housing authority eliminated their ineffective private-security guards.

Because the SFHA was under investigation at this time from HUD officials in Washington D. C., as usual, their funding had been diminished. Also, there was a great concern from the neighbors, since there was no genuine property management in place. All other apartment buildings in San Francisco with over twelve units are required by law to have a resident manager on the premises at all times, but the housing authority opaquely flaunted this requirement by having a manager only during the daytime! Certain gates at the rear of the interior parking lots were continuously being broken and left open so criminal activities could occur more secretly. The parking lots became ceaselessly full of loud and disturbing activity, both in the daytime and at night. The suggestion of one neighbor, that entry gates and fences be installed, was completely ignored.

Also the windows of the townhouses were gradually fitted with iron bars by various tenants, at their own expense, to protect themselves from break-ins. The SFHA had earlier assured that no window bars would be necessary. Many of the tenants, both Asian and Hispanic/Latino, pleaded for police action. These same tenants were rarely visible but constitute a good percentage of the tenant profile. As quickly as possible, many of them left for a safer environment. Within a few years some of these new townhouses were vacated through evictions by the housing authority, and the doorways and windows were boarded up. Some of these units were left vacant for a couple of years, in spite of the local politicians constantly demanding more housing for underprivileged San Franciscans. The city has some of the most-stringent, rent-control laws in the USA, but the local SFHA has its own set of rules and regulations.

Several relocated families came back to this site and became notorious for drug dealing and other criminal activities. The family of the African American president of the first resident council, and a true black racist, Eva Mae William, was a prime example. Her overcrowded "family" unit was on the southwest corner of Eddy and Scott Streets and had a vantage point to observe the presence of the police or the earlier security guards that were hired by the housing authority. Someone broke down her front door and shot her obese grandson, who did eventually recover from his gunshot wound. With neighborhood protests over all of these incidents, Mayor Gavin Newsom (2004–2012) and our reluctant District Five Supervisor Ross Mirkarimi, requested that cameras be mounted on the buildings and also on poles to monitor criminal activity. They were certainly effective in a decrease of criminal activity. But since the cameras were not monitored, they did not offer evidence of who was actually involved in criminal activity.

Cellular telephones became quickly popular for communication between the drug dealers to make personal contacts and keep each other posted on the whereabouts of the police patrols. Some dealers used the interior of the Palestinian American owned corner grocery store in the Magland Arms building as a lookout location. Another local merchant reported to us that one of the resident families was deeply involved in gang activity.

On a March afternoon in 2009, a relative of another resident African American family was killed in East Oakland. His sister, Aisha Guillory, who was then the president of the tenants association, attended his funeral. This internally related, matriarchal family was like so many that had long existed on both sides of the Bay, particularly in San Francisco and Oakland. As reported in the local news, the above-mentioned family member—Lovelle M. Mixon, who was a twenty-six-year-old ex-felon on parole, and a rape suspect, was stopped by two Oakland motorcycle officers. He killed them both and then fled to his other sister's apartment in Oakland. Someone reported the building where he fled and a SWAT team of police officers burst into the apartment. Two of the officers were killed by Lovelle, shooting with a high-powered rifle through a closet wall. Lovelle was killed instantly by the other police officers shooting into the closet. His sister was purportedly voted-out as president of the tenants' association at the end of 2009, as being incompetent. As reported in the local news, in December, 2009, his grandmother (Mary Mixon), honorably refused to let anyone in the family be used by opportunistic attorneys to sue the city of Oakland for the mental trauma suffered by her granddaughter, who was in the flat at the time of the homicide.

In October of 2010, Superior Court Judge Charlotte Woolard granted the fourth of a series of four-year court injunctions against street gangs. Previous injunctions had created "gang-safe zones" in the districts of Bayview-Hunters Point, Mission, and the Western Addition. As a *San Francisco Chronicle* article states, "Including the previous injunctions, the city has focused on 134 gang members in an effort that police and City District Attorney Dennis Herrera tout as a key measure to cutting the homicide rate in half last year and so far this year…." This injunction bars the listed gang members from engaging in a variety of activities, including menacing conduct, graffiti, loitering, flashing gang signs, and congregating with other known gangsters in an L-shaped *safety zone* surrounding three public-housing developments. The Robert B. Pitts Plaza and Yerba Buena East Plaza were singled out in the Western Addition and the gangs were identified as The Chopper City, Eddy Rock, and Knock-Out Posse. The *San Francisco Chronicle* stated, "Herrera (San Francisco District Attorney) said he sees the injunctions as one tool, not the panacea for gang violence. He said one measure of success is a dramatic reduction in contacts with police for those named in the injunctions." The article further indicates that three-fourths of the 134 gang members are from out of town.

Earlier in August of 2010, a German couple from Minden was visiting San Francisco to celebrate the wife's fiftieth birthday and their wedding anniversary. As they were searching for a restaurant, for a sunset dinner, a block from the fashionable Union Square, she was killed by a gunshot in the crossfire of a shoot-out in front of the hall used for social events, and died in her husband's arms. Most San Franciscans were horrified and tried to console the family. The police announced an intense campaign to discover the perpetrator of this senseless death. In April 2011, the family of Mechthild Schroer, who had been headmaster of an elementary school, came to question why no one had been charged. Her husband, Stefan, and two sons, asked where the investigation had led. Police refused to release further details by citing an ongoing investigation. They also met with District Attorney George Gascon, who said that he would prosecute as soon as he had a strong case.

A week later on May 5, 2011, seven reputed gang members, including two juveniles, were arrested for the crime and charged with murder. According to a *San Francisco Chronicle* article the next day, "The suspects, members of two gangs in the Western Addition and a third named for the Valencia Gardens housing project (in the Mission district), were brawling outside an end-of summer dance. Schroer was killed when at least one of the combatants open fire, police said." The father of one of the defendants, Rabeem Jackson said, "He wasn't shooting no gun. He was falsely accused. He didn't know none of those guys."

14.

San Francisco Redevelopment Agency Commercial Development In The Western Addition A-1 And A-2 Project Areas

As has been elaborated upon in earlier chapters, our neighborhood had been directly impacted and affected with the residential development by SFHA and SFRA in the Western Addition. But more importantly, the commercial development, which began in the 1950s, and the following decades of development, would determine the newly completed topography of the Western Addition. In various capacities, I was directly involved with these major changes.

The A-1 Project Area of the SFRA, consisting of the demolition of a five-block strip along Geary Street to create Geary Boulevard (an eight-lane expressway with a two peripheral lanes at the Fillmore Street overpass), accelerated in 1959, with the appointment of M. Justin Herman as executive director. New commercial projects and high-rise housing filled the vacated land around the expressway. Further future development on the newly vacated land in the A-2 Project Area of the SFRA was to complement this commercial development, particularly along Fillmore Street and Van Ness Avenue. These two project areas did not include the surrounding SFHA projects, which had been built, starting in the early 1950s, beginning with the three-story, reinforced-concrete Westside Court, which had a central courtyard with a lawn, and a large, paved, parking lot. This complex occupied a square block surrounded by Post Street on the south, Sutter Street on the north, and Baker Street on the west, and Broderick Street on the east. This area had formerly been used for truck farming with glass greenhouses. Later in the 1950s, the SFHA Yerba Buena East and Yerba Buena West Plaza (already discussed as being outside of the A-1 and A-2 Project Areas of SFRA), and finally the Yerba Buena Annex, in the early 1960s, were constructed. These public housing projects were discussed earlier.

The main commercial focuses along Geary Boulevard are in the following chronological order of construction: Cathedral Hill, Japantown, Mount Zion Hospital, Kaiser Permanente Hospital, Webster Towers, Fillmore Center, and the Jazz District. The A-1 Project Area commercial construction was the earlier development beginning with the Cathedral Hill district at the east end of Geary Boulevard, the middle segment being Japantown Trade Center, and at the west end, Kaiser Permanente Hospital. Although Mount Zion Hospital at the west end was not technically included in either project districts, I have included this area as being historically and futuristically important. The A-2 Project Area commercial/residential development along Van Ness Avenue was explored earlier, and the later commercial development along Fillmore Street, south of Geary Boulevard, is examined here with the Webster Towers, Fillmore Center, and Fillmore Jazz District.

Perhaps, the question should be asked by the reader, "Why the commercial development in the A-2 Project Area was not logically included with the commercially oriented A-1 Project Area in the overall SFRA master plan?" After we moved to the Western Addition in 1975, the A-1 Project development was almost completed, and the Webster Towers and Terrace Apartment Complex in the A-2 Project Area was being built on Fillmore Street. The later peripheral A-2 Project Area sites, the Fillmore Center and the Jazz Center, were to be the main battlefields for our neighborhood groups. The pre-existing cooperatives and senior housing are discussed earlier, as well as the powerful influence of the African American ministers in connection with these developments and the construction of new churches for their congregations.

Cathedral Hill

The commanding-view corner site at Geary Boulevard and Gough Street, which had previously been pre-earthquake housing, became the site of a new Lucky supermarket in 1960, with the approval of the SFRA Commission. But after the simultaneous destruction, by fire, of the Roman Catholic Cathedral, Saint Mary of the Assumption, on nearby Van Ness Avenue, the one-year-old supermarket, with the approval of the SFRA Commission, was demolished with a lot of influential pressure for a new cathedral there. The trade-off of another site, and possibly a cash settlement, has never been investigated to my knowledge. The earlier, red-brick Victorian German Gothic Cathedral was dedicated in 1891. The basement had been purportedly used for gambling games, such as slot machines, baccarat tables, and bingo, which brought in income for Catholic Charities.

By 1971, the strikingly new cathedral, with a four sided, 190-foot, hyperbolic parabolic roof, and seating for 2,500 parishioners, replaced the supermarket, but had no noticeable gambling in the lower level. The cathedral itself has a sanctuary of 45,000 square feet and a lower level comprising 62,000 square feet. An elevated plaza separates the two levels, with parking around the lower level. The travertine-clad cathedral has a gold-leafed, aluminum cross on top of the cruciform spire. The interior space is completely open with a free-standing, white-marble altar accented by an overhanging, scintillating baldachino composed of a silver and gold moving mobile. Dramatic stained glass windows, an outstanding electro-pneumatic pipe organ, and private-niche chapels add extra flourishes to this overwhelming, inspirational space. The architects were the renowned Pietro Bellushi of the Massachusetts Institute of Technology, and Pier Lugi Nervi of Rome. This cathedral demonstrates the mysterious politically influenced divergences that are inherent within the redevelopment project areas, which produce so many surprises for what would or could happen. One must admit that the cathedral is an incredibly dramatic focus to the current cathedral hill. Some local San Franciscans have wittily, although uncouthly, nicknamed the cathedral "Mary's breast," or the "washing machine agitator." In 2010, a ground-floor addition for Sacred Heart Cathedral Preparatory added additional space to the newer, main campus for the high school a block away on O'Farrell Street. The school is considered to be academically superior.

The surrounding, architecturally significant churches that were preserved near Saint Mary of the Assumption Cathedral make grand statements, mirrored in the modern buildings surrounding them. One such church is the grey, stone, First Unitarian Church, founded in 1850, where the original minister and an important figure in the statehood of California, Thomas Starr King is buried in an adjacent garden. Recently, a life-size marble statue of him was removed from the rotunda of the U.S. Capitol Building and replaced with a statue of Ronald Reagan. This church was designed in 1889, by George Percy, in a mixture of Romanesque and Gothic-revival elements, implying the perfect English parish church. A redwood and concrete, contemporary social center, with an inner courtyard and fountain, was added between 1967 and 1979.

Across O'Farrrell Street, which is now the inbound exit of Geary Boulevard, is the redbrick Saint Mark's Lutheran Church, with a dramatic, west, low, round, turreted tower on an octagonal base and an east, larger square, turreted tower, designed by Henry Geilfuss in 1895, with German Romanesque and Gothic elements. The interior is an incredible, wood-paneled, trussed, nave interior, painted in French ivory and gold. In the1960s, modern additions were constructed consisting of an urban-life, center, office building, the Martin Luther Square, and a nineteen-story, moderately priced, condominium tower.

On the Geary Street outbound Geary Boulevard side of the First Unitarian Church, the modern Gothic-inspired Hamilton Square Baptist Church, founded in 1881, was completed in 1958, on the foundation of a basement church dating from 1945, with relocation from Hamilton Square. The congregation had earlier owned a 1912 church, at the corner of Post and Steiner Streets on Hamilton Square, which is now Jones Methodist Church, with an African American congregation. A lovely garden, with a native plant garden, and a centrally located, bubbling, Mediterranean-style fountain, enhances their present location.

Several blocks away, at Bush and Franklin Streets, the exquisite Trinity Episcopal Church, which was founded in 1849, has a prominent location. This grey, sandstone, square English Romanesque/early Gothic-style church, with its matching parish hall, was designed in 1892 by A. Page Brown. The red-painted entrance doors open into a precious sanctuary, with Tiffany stained-glass windows and a lectern. A southern English cottage garden provides a perfect setting.

Perhaps the most significant Victorian building was Saint Paulus Lutheran designed by Julius Krafft, in 1894, as a wooden, Gothic-revival version of Chartres Cathedral, at the southeast corner of Gough and Eddy Streets. This church was tragically destroyed by a fire in 1995, started accidently by church- sanctioned charitable tenants and homeless in the basement. Cathedral Hill, nevertheless, still preserves a concentrated collection of some of the finest late Victorian ecclesiastical architecture in San Francisco, and perhaps in the United States. The congregations must have been able to intimidate the SFRA, or mediate with God, to save this historical treasure trove of Victorian architecture.

Also, there are several grand Italianate Victorian mansions that were preserved through the efforts of such well-connected personages as the leftist attorney, Vincent Hallinan (his wife, Vivian, purportedly supported the family through ownership of many apartment buildings in the Tenderloin), or other stubborn, independent owners. Purportedly, one of the condemned mansions, by eminent domain, was being demolished by SFRA contracted laborers, and they discovered gold ingots placed in the fireplace flue. Supposedly, they grabbed their loot and quit their jobs the next day. Also, there were people, for profit or preservation, who pried loose the exquisite, architectural detailing and fixtures of these magnificent mansions. The 1958 Alfred Hitchcock movie, *Vertigo*, shows several of these mansions that were later demolished by the SFRA.

The nearby high-rise buildings consist of retirement centers, such as the massive, grey, concrete The Sequoias (Life Care community/not-for-profit corporation), which is sponsored by the Northern California Presbyterian Home Services. Located on five acres, this twenty-five-story building, with roof-top gardens, many interior gardens that the individual owners tend, and a seven-story addition, was built in 1969. The architectural firm was Stone, Marraccini & Patterson. Other high-rise, cooperative complexes were built as mostly private, market-rate housing for single people and couples. One of these large complexes was circular, and the others were ponderous rectangular and vertical towers.

Nearby, low-rise, cooperative housing was built for affordable, subsidized, market-rate family housing. An example of one of the more successful of these developments is the St. Francis cooperatives, on the south side of Geary Boulevard, between Webster and Laguna Streets. This appealingly, scattered, cluster of housing in a garden setting was built in 1961, and it was designed by the architectural firm of Marquis& Stoller. These garden court units were sponsored and subsidized by the Longshoremen's Union, with an income ceiling for residents. Longtime SFRA commissioner, Leroy King (Ernest King's brother), who was a Union member, was one of the first occupants with his family.

The modernistic, trapezoidal-sided, twenty-seven-story, reinforced-concrete Cathedral Hill Tower, built in 1966, resembles a transplant design from the Los Angeles of that time. This 138-unit, high-rise building at 1200 Gough Street, with panoramic views; was a mix of the usual SFRA cooperative and rental units. The building, with outdoor balconies, is at the beginning of the Geary expressway (from the eastern confluence of O'Farrell Street and Geary Street) and Gough Street. The building is an interesting configuration to the hill, with the neighboring historical buildings and modern buildings. Former Mayor Willie Brown Jr. occupied, at different times, three of the units in the building. In 2005, the building underwent significant waterproofing and new installation of the exterior windows because of earlier defects in design. Then in 2010, the lobby was remodeled to a more luxurious quality, the hallways were upgraded, and there was a streamlining of the elevators. This now-desirable building has become condominiums and has an upscale, twenty-four-hour door service.

In 1994, the luxurious, modern, fourteen-story Post International building, with seventy-two condominiums, with both townhomes and apartments, capped off the completion of this area. The architecture is a later interpretation of the post-international style, with a dramatic, curved, curtain wall of tinted glass. This is at the juncture where Geary Boulevard reverts to the original Geary Street. The juxtaposition of the First Unitarian Church and the Saint Mark's Lutheran Church are quite dramatically reflected on the glass wall.

I sold a stunning, two-story townhouse in one of the side, low-rise buildings, Post International, to a wealthy, young, gay, Chinese American businessman.

In the early 1960s, to the west of Saint Mary's Cathedral, the innovative developer, Joseph Eichler, built his iconic, garden cooperative complexes, designed by Claude Oakland. They were called Laguna Heights. Later a high-rise tower of cooperatives, designed by Jones and Emmons, was added. Presently, these buildings are now referred to as mid-century. This complex was first managed by the earlier-mentioned John Stewart and Company.

The nearby Salvation Army headquarters building on Geary Boulevard became the Chinese Consulate in 1990, and was cater-cornered from the Japanese Consulate. This consulate is a continuing magnet for protestors of all sorts, particularly the *Free Tibet* protestors. But the consulate also processes an enormous number of tourist visas and anxious crowds in a queue around the surrounding streets.

In 1977, I purchased, with six partners, who included my father, a thirty-seven-unit, reinforced-concrete, Art Deco, circa 1926, five-story apartment building (19,836 square feet) across the street from the Eichler Developments at the northwest corner of Laguna and Eddy Streets, for an incredibly good price of $415,000. We anticipated that the new, pleasantly landscaped community across the street would improve property values in the surrounding area. Although our building at 1215 Laguna Street was 50 percent vacant, I set aside monetary reserves for improvements to the building. The owner of the building and listing real estate broker invited me out to lunch toward the end of the escrow period to discuss some concerns that I had after several inspections. He picked me up at my office in the Russ Building, and I was rather surprised, after expecting a cheap lunch, to discover that he was taking me to the most prestigious Pacific Union Club, to which his father was a member before him. The club flag is at half-staff on the day a member dies. Interestingly, I discovered the obvious fact that, even in a club you were born into, there is still a strict hierarchy of your table location in the dining room. Also, your university affiliation and fraternity affiliation are, of course, important, but your current family financial situation is most importantly assessed factor. After he reassured me over lunch about my growing concerns with regard to the defects in the building, my partners and I closed the escrow. That lunch was probably the most expensive experience ever for me, after I observed later the lack of important information that was not divulged by him about his building! But it was a good learning experience, as my sage father commented, "Experience is usually expensive."

Most of the existing tenants were behind in their rents, and some were even more delinquent. Prostitution rings were operating out of the building, as well as drug dealing. As manager of the building for the partnership, I hired two attorneys to start evictions on the tenants that were delinquent on their monthly rental payments. As they were being evicted, they vandalized the building, including breaking the elevator. They probably would have burned the building to the ground had the building not have been constructed of reinforced concrete. Because of that extreme drought year, and the unfortunate fact of only one water meter for the building, I began to convert the toilets to tank-flushed, and to replace the galvanized plumbing with copper. Then, thieves removed the new copper plumbing pipes for the increasing resale value. I contracted a security company to secure the building on a daily, twenty-four-hour basis. Their guards were often found sleeping in one of the vacant apartments by my tradespeople doing the rehabilitation. After two frustrating years, I had managed to stabilize the tenant profile in the building. But the partners, excluding my father, now wanted me to give up the property management. Rather than complicate the situation, in 1979, I said, "Just pay back my father's and my original investments, and we will give up all of our interests in the building. After an interval of twenty-six years, and several owners, the building sold in 2005 for $4,370,000!

The whole situation was untenable at that particular time because of the crime and violence emanating from the Yerba Buena East Plaza public-housing buildings, which surrounded our building. Like its sister public housing, the Yerba Buena West Plaza, which was much discussed earlier and was further west, both were fully segregated with African American tenants. Also, similarly because of rampant fires and major criminal activity, these buildings were replaced in the late 1990s by the dense, low-rise housing for families. Citywide, the SFHA has depleted much of their block grants with the rebuilding of the Valencia Gardens, with its famous Benny Bufano sculptures, and the Cesar Chavez Street housing projects. Thus, with the decreased funding, the unattractive new Yerba Buena East Plaza was built on the cheap in 2006.

The replacement housing, whose contractor was Nibbi Brothers, was cheap, faulty, and architecturally unpleasant to look at. Landscaping was not even attempted. The front porches of the townhouses are only five feet from busy street traffic. This new housing, immediately on completion, became again a center of shootings of resident gang members by rival gang members. Often, innocent, tenant bystanders were killed, as well as the gang members. Nearby neighbors became nervous driving near the projects, even in the daytime. Cameras on poles were mounted here also.

But again, since they were not monitored, they were made virtually useless. Finally, police squad cars were stationed nearby, in a quite intimidating manner, and the problems somewhat dissipated. In 2007, the Yerba Buena East Plaza was declared by a court injunction to be *a gang safety zone.*

Surprisingly, two years later, an attractive and upscale Arts and Crafts-designed condominium development (Buchanan Lane), with a mews of townhouses with garages underneath, was built adjacent to the also new Yerba Buena East Plaza. Letters to the newspapers describe the anger and frustrations of the home owners of all ethnic groups who bought these condominiums. They were experiencing the same grief of crime and violence that I had experienced earlier with our thirty-six-unit apartment building.

Another large, high-rise building, constructed like the Yerba Buena East and Yerba Buena West Plazas, was added in the early 1960s, and is located at Turk Street and Webster Street. The eleven-story building was called Yerba Buena Plaza Annex. It was visited in the late 1970s by then Governor Jerry Brown, who stayed overnight there with his guards nearby. At that time, this building was a cesspool of crime and filth and had been nicknamed the *Pink Palace* by the locals because of its color. In 1985, it was repainted a grayish-white color and completely rehabilitated with the original floor plans intact. The windy, outside balcony passageways were enclosed to make entry to the apartments more hospitable. The new senior tenants consisted of some of the original senior citizens, who illegally allowed their grandchildren to stay overnight with them. These grandchildren would often harass the other tenants.

The building was renamed the Rosa Parks Senior Center in memory of the civil rights leader. There were no fixed-rental rates, and instead, the residents pay thirty percent of their income, which leads to some interesting scenarios. Later, a few security guards were hired by the SFHA to patrol the premises; thus, some tranquility now prevails. More visible on-site management has made difference. With the increasing Russian immigration from the 1980s, the tenancy has become more and more elderly Russian couples. Their presence is now noticed on Fillmore Street by increasing numbers. They even have a social center located in the original Steiner Street post office building across from Raymond Kimball Park.

The 2010 U.S. census shows the building consisting of a population that is 41.4 percent White, 28.8 percent Asian, 21.2 percent African American, 6.5 percent Hispanic, and 2.1 percent other. Formerly, the occupancy had been overwhelmingly African American.

Japantown

The original Japantown on the north side of Geary Boulevard, and bordered by Fillmore Street on the west, Laguna Street on the east, and Bush Street on the north, was obliterated by the redevelopment agency in the early1960s. A few, outstanding, Victorian homes were nevertheless preserved by outraged property owners, mostly members of WANA. In the 1970s, through forceful preservation efforts, several Victorian row houses and commercial buildings were saved on Fillmore and Sutter Streets as a business district. The best preservation efforts were made by the owners who lived north of Bush Street, and who were not included in the A-1 and A-2 Project Areas, as mentioned earlier. This area is now designated as Lower Pacific Heights. Many gay people were actively involved in these efforts, as well as Japanese Americans who had returned to their homes from the internment camps after World War II. The core of the redevelopment renewal (A-1 Project Area) was the new Japantown Center (1968) on Geary Boulevard, which covered four large city blocks. Minoru Yamasaki and Van Bourg Nakamura designed this Japanese Cultural and Trade Center, which features a large, contemporary, two-story Japanese shopping complex, surrounding a large plaza in the center. This whole complex is over the city-owned, two-story parking garage. Next to the east-end complex of shops is a luxury eight-story hotel, with landscaped interior/ exterior gardens, and has some guest rooms with traditional Japanese baths. The two-story Japanese consulate building is adjacent to this hotel on Laguna Street, between Post Street and Geary Boulevard.

The original plaza featured a three-story, concrete Peace Pagoda, given to the city by her sister city of Kyoto, landscaped with rectangular fish ponds full of large koi fish, and planting beds with bonsai trees, rocks, and flowering shrubs. The whole effect was pleasant and tranquil. Unfortunately, the updated plaza above the city-owned parking garage continues to leak water below after a later four-year retrofit in the 1980s. Even later, expensive attempts to remedy the situation have not been able to correct the original faulty design and construction. Next to the western complex of shops and restaurants, an original Kabuki theater and more shops are connected by an overhead Webster Street shopping arcade. This interior Japanese village, with a contemporary styling, gives the visitor a feeling of having traveled to Japan and is popular with tourists.

Across Post Street, on the north side (A-2 Project Area), a more traditional Japanese village was constructed later in 1976.

Two-story, wooden buildings with shops and restaurants line both sides of the stone-paved Nihonmachi Mall. Attractive, steel origami-shaped fountains, created by our local famous artist, Ruth Osawa, offer an exciting focus to the mall. The overall effect is a positive creation by the SFRA and offers a renewed centralization for a newly invigorated Japanese community. In reality, many Nisei Japanese Americans have moved to the suburbs surrounding San Francisco. But this newly constructed Japantown became a perfect setting and focus for the annual spring Cherry Blossom festival and street parade for local, as well as the suburban Japanese Americans. During one festival, when I was president of the Japantown city Parking Garage Corporation, Francee Covington (vice-president) and I sat above the backseat of a convertible and waived to the crowds. Francee said to me, pointing to the crowds, "Look, over there is Chandler (her son) and mom!" We then went to the end of the parade and proceeded to sit with a select group in the official grandstand. The dance groups of women in kimonos were colorful, and the motorized floats were interesting. The parade always finishes with sake barrels on a hand-carried platform by a group of men, many wearing only *fiduchi* (thongs). On top are always several men dancing, and alongside the platform, other men sprinkle the crowd with sake. Along the parade route, the participants are generously supplied with sake, and the crowd is sprinkled with the same sake!

In 1975, I was asked to be on the board of directors of the Western Addition Parking Corporation (WAPC), which is a city nonprofit corporation that made decisions that affected the garage. The garage was begun in 1964, and finished in 1968.The garage was located on the floors below the Japantown center. Harry Shiffs, who owned a men's clothing store on Fillmore Street, near O'Farrell Street, and who was a corporation director, was my contact by being a part-time salesman with Roman Realty. The short, Jewish, Harry, with a beautifully clipped, white mustache was a jovial family man. He was by profession a dapper dresser. We bonded quickly and I appreciated the world to which he introduced me. This group was prosperous businessmen with connections to the community. The only Japanese American director was an accountant, and none of the other board members were women or African American. The construction of the center had inherent problems, which mainly had to do with the plaza, mentioned earlier, and water leaking through the ceiling from the fish pools and the winter rainstorms. When the garage was completed, the original contractor, stupidly, had not been held liable for this defect. Our primary purpose was to oversee the maintenance and development of the garage. We attempted to have various contractors repair this problem. Our corporate luncheon meetings were held quarterly. Our attorney, Dick (Richard) Dole, as well as department representatives from into the City Controller's office and Parking and Traffic Department, were present at these meetings. Although we were not compensated, our lunches at the local Miyako Hotel were paid for by our corporate-compensated attorney.

The meetings were always interesting; with update reports being provided by the resident manager of whichever selected parking management company. Since the garage did not provide enough revenue to pay expenses, we came up with ideas to produce more revenue and continue to provide the necessary parking for the merchants in the Japantown area and the Fillmore district. The building improvements above the public garage were owned by a Japanese American company, National Braemar, based in Honolulu. In 1979, I was elected president and made a determined attempt to bring more Japanese onto the board of directors. Several members, whom were always changing, were bank managers and the always-the-intellectual Kinokuniya Japanese bookstore managers, who were all periodically replaced with new managers from Japan. Other directors were local merchants. Also, I recruited Barbara Meskunas, of BANG (later President of the SFHA under Mayor Frank Jordan), Mary Jane Staymetz of WANA (a founder), and Francee Covington, who owned a media-production company and was African American (later President of the SFRA Commission and a SF Fire commissioner). At one point, we contracted to have a well-bonded construction company replace the plaza above to eliminate the leaking. We were involved later, during the 1990s, in negotiations with the SFRA for a subsidiary garage in the proposed new jazz district complex on Fillmore Street, south of Geary Boulevard.

In spite of our successful management, I was blindsided at our January 1998 board meeting at the Miyako Hotel. The Department of Parking and Traffic Executive Director Bill Maher said, "It is public property, and it will revert to government control. We're trying to do it with taste and decorum." He also added, "If the board does not go along, the city is prepared to take action." My response to this was quoted in the *San Francisco Observer*, February 1998 issue: "There would be less interest (by the city) in maintaining the garage. It would become just a cash machine for DPT (Department of Parking and Traffic), at the cost of keeping the garage in good shape for the public. We've seen it before." The natural termination date for the board was only two years away. The gross receipts and expenditures were annually approved by the office of the City Controller, and the board had a good relationship with them. Also, an independent auditor, Hood and Strong, provided the annual review. Curiously, the Chinese American, community-run, Portsmouth Square Garage in Chinatown was never threatened. Perhaps the inevitable local, Chinese American public, outcry was anticipated by the city bureaucrats.

The whole situation appeared to be contrived by the now-majority Japanese members of the board, as though they wanted full control of the garage corporation. I appealed to my friend, Alan Okamoto, whose family was the only Japanese real estate brokerage in San Francisco. He had been the president of the San Francisco Association of Realtors. He said, "I will try to defend the WAPC position, but you know San Francisco politics."

As a nonprofit, our attorney pointed out positively that we were exempt from paying taxes by the California Constitution. Nevertheless, as my premonition, newly elected Mayor Willie Brown Jr., in1996 (the local Wizard-of -Oz or God-Father depending on your political views), dissolved partially the WAPC as well as the Western Addition Economic Task Force (WAETF), to which I had been appointed by former Mayor Frank Jordan in 1993. The purpose of this group was to develop a jazz district in the lower Fillmore Street area and develop an enterprise zone to give tax credits to businesses that invested in underserved and low-income areas. The enterprise zones had been created by the U.S. Congress in 1984 (forty-two of these zones were in California). The task force was chaired by Naomi Gray, an intelligent and forceful African American. The Jazz Center became a reality by the end of the century and is discussed later.

Our WAPC board was involved with the SFRA in numerous discussions for building of an annex garage funded by the WAPC in the designated Jazz District at the corner of Fillmore and Eddy Streets. As a goodwill gesture, we invited, at Mayor Brown Jr.'s request, his personal barber, Reggie Pettus, a long-time Fillmore personality, to become a board member. As well as appointing a Japanese American politico, Steve Nakajo. I knew that the real reason for these abrupt changes was that money would be used to provide a pipeline for additional money to the city general fund.

Siphoning off revenues from public parking that was earmarked for the parking authority, had become a regular city accounting procedure. The money technically was to be used only for repairs and upgrading of the garage facilities. I was perhaps most disappointed that the Japanese members of the WAPC did not agree with me. On June 9, 1998, I sent my resignation as President and board member to the WAPC board. I had, in reality, fought unnecessarily for control of a non-paying advisory role with my excellent performance and pride of civic duty. This was my genetic trait!

There was no gold watch or a certification of appreciation from Mayor Brown, or a garage named after me. But I shall always be proud of my service to the city and be aware of the meanness of political spirit and ultimate unfair value of patronage. Bill Maher was soon demoted, in March of 1998, by Mayor Brown and transferred to the San Francisco International Airport as the grounds manager. Jeff Mori, and his wife Sandy, seemed to team-up in a shadowy, political backdrop. Jeff became the president of the newly formed Japan Center Garage Corporation on August 4, 1998.

Eventually, the new garage, that I had helped negotiate, was built at the corner of Fillmore and Eddy Streets in the Jazz Center. This garage became popular with the patrons of Yoshi jazz club and the upscale 1300 Fillmore restaurant.

Despite a later infusion, or possibly bribe, of city money to the new Japantown Parking Corporation to upgrade the Peace Plaza with a new design and landscaping, water continues to leak into the garage. That problem was no longer my responsibility but the problem for the newly Japanese constituted board. The sparkling, original buildings of the 1960s are aging now, and there is talk of rebuilding at that site. The original Japanese development company (National Braemar) lost control of the buildings many years ago in bankruptcy. The original Kabuki Theater failed to be profitable and was sold to the AMC theater group (AMC Kabuki 8 Cinema Theaters). The movie theaters are now the Sundance Kabuki cinema. A former AMC manager, who was one of my former board members, thought that the WAPC was the best venue to acquire movie theater screening in the proposed new Jazz District, prior to my resignation. No cinema complex was ever constructed in the new Jazz District.

Mount Zion Hospital

In 1887, a group of forty-three members of the Jewish community met with the purpose of establishing a hospital in the San Francisco area "for the purpose of aiding the indigent sick without regard to race or creed, to be supported by the Jewish community." From a temporary downtown hospital at Hyde and Stockton Streets, the first permanent hospital was established at 2311 Sutter Street in 1899. Rabbis from the congregations of Emanu-El, Sherith Israel, and Beth Israel strongly supported this dream to become a reality with the generous contributions of Baroness de Hirsh Genneth. These earlier Jewish immigrants were mostly German and Polish (some English, French, and Sephardic) and became quite successful businessmen and soon began to contribute great philanthropy—such as the funding of Mount Zion Hospital for their community. This early community was widely dispersed throughout the city, but there were two significant synagogues close by to this campus at Divisadero and Sutter Streets. In 1905, the Congregation Sherith Israel (established 1851) moved to a new synagogue at the corner of California and Webster Streets, with a large, central dome on a square base in Romanesque style, with eastern overtones, by Albert Pissis. The synagogue was restored in 2011, with, among other renovations, the removal of the garish 1950s, salmon-hue exterior painting to show the beauty of the original gray, Colusa sandstone walls The Congregation Beth Israel (established 1861), with 200 members of German and Polish descent, moved to a Romanesque-style synagogue with two towers on Geary Street, between Fillmore and Steiner Streets, in 1905. That building partially collapsed in the 1906 earthquake. The rebuilt synagogue would serve the more Eastern European Jewish community that was evolving now around Fillmore Street and have an interesting future history.

The Congregation Emanu-El (established in 1851) was well endowed by Ashkenazic members (mostly German immigrants) and some Sephardic members. After several moves from temples in the downtown area, the congregation moved into a magnificent massive temple on the corner of Arguello and Lake Streets in 1927, designed by Arthur Brown, Jr., John Bakewell, Jr., and Sylvain Schaittacher. This L-shaped, red-tile, domed building is Middle Eastern in feeling, with Byzantine-Roman and early medieval traditions. It has a sunny, enclosed courtyard with a fountain. Many members of this congregation continue to contribute significantly to the cultural and philanthropic causes in San Francisco. Interestingly, the Congregation of Ohbei Shalome, which had split off in 1872, built the fascinating Moorish-style wooden temple in the Western Addition at Bush and Laguna Streets. The building is now part of a Japanese American, senior assisted-living center.

In 1908, Isaias Hellman, the president of Wells Fargo Bank, donated $100,000 in the memory of his wife Esther, to build an additional yellow-brick hospital building (Esther Hellman Building opened in 1914) that still remains at the northwest corner of Post and Scott Streets, with exterior earthquake bracing added later. The influenza epidemic of 1918 averaged more than one hundred flu patients per day at the hospital. With a shortage of places for a nurse to live, a seven-story, nurses-residence building was opened in 1925 at the corner of Sutter and Scott Street. In 1933, Mount Zion was the first hospital in the city to offer psychiatric services. An outstanding building of paper-like concrete slabs, punctuated by decorative curving balconies, was constructed in 1950, and designed by Eric Mendelsohn. This building at2356 Sutter Street, formerly known as the Maimonedes (Unity) Hospital, was acquired by Mount Zion Hospital and became the in-patient psychiatric center.

John worked intermittently, beginning in 1975 at this newly named Mount Zion Psychiatric Pavilion, as the evening charge nurse, until his retirement in 1991. His commute on foot was only five blocks from our home. The out-patient psychiatric center remained mostly in the main hospital. A major expansion of the original Hellman building occurred in 1950 with the construction of a new building with a five-floor, L-shaped structure designed by Skidmore, Owings, and Merrill, which was located along Post and Divisadero Streets. In 1990, the Board of Directors of Mount Zion Health Systems, Inc., and the regents of the University of California, approved the integration of the Mount Zion Hospital and Medical Center into the Medical Center of UC San Francisco, with all employees becoming UCSF employees. Eventually, the psychiatric services were all consolidated at Langley Porter Institute at the UCSF Parnassus Avenue campus. In 1973, John, as the evening charge nurse was attacked by a visitor armed with a smuggled-in machete, but John was able to press an emergency alarm button. The squad team came to the rescue. Consequently, the ward was locked down. Most of the later new buildings at the

Mount Zion campus were designed or rebuilt for medical research and development.

When a new cancer treatment and research complex was planned in 1992, PADS was asked to join a task force for community input. As president, I personally approved of the new buildings and the possibility of the incredible far-reaching new biomedical research. Other community members were not so pleased with the building density and the possibility of radiological research to be conducted there. They sued in Superior Court to delay construction for a more comprehensive Environmental Impact Review (EIR). Bruce Spaulding, then UCSF vice-chancellor for planning, was quoted in the *San Francisco Examiner*, "This (complex) is very symbolic because everybody has been assuring us we can do business in San Francisco." Mayor Frank Jordan, a well-mannered and pro-business individual, was furious about the lawsuit that threatened the largest employer in the city. The EIR was approved by the UC Board of Regents. The handsome, modern complex built consists of a five-story, 90,000 square-foot, outpatient cancer treatment facility at the southeast corner of Sutter and Divisadero Streets and a four-story, 109,137 square-foot, research center at 2340 Sutter Street, with rear access to Bush Street. There is a great deal of new expansion into new facilities, and the purchase of the surrounding, newer buildings was negotiated in an extremely positive manner.

UCSF is presently developing one of the largest and foremost biotechnology centers in the world on the south bay side (Mission Bay) of San Francisco. This area was originally the site of the Southern Pacific railroad yards and ship-building industries. The lack of impact on nearby residential neighborhoods and the desirable, large, centrally located parcel of land have been noteworthy!

Along with the adjacent live-loft development at South of Market, originally proposed and initiated by Joe O'Donoghue, the entire area has become, what I refer to as, the *mushroom fields,* with rapidly exploding, exciting new development. The future development of biotechnology offers great promise for the future and perhaps it will be the new gold-rush era for San Francisco!

Near the Mount Zion campus, at the southwest corner of Divisadero and Post streets, the futuristic Osher Center for Integrative Medicine building was completed in 2010. It creates a positive concentration of medical services and a more unified Divisadero Street corridor. Curiously, UCSF did not need to issue a public EIR to the local community for this building. And the existing brick and wood funeral home building (1890s) was quickly demolished. The new building is a striking, post-modern building with a red brick and angular, artificial, light-colored, wooden façade

Opposite the Hellman building, on the corner of Post and Scott Streets, is the Jewish Family and Welfare Services, which was founded in 1850. This Byzantine-styled building, constructed in 1930, has been absorbed, at the insistence of WANA and BANG in 2000, into the well-integrated, massive, Mediterranean-styled Rhoda Goldman Plaza Senior Housing for Assisted Living at 2180 Post Street (A-2 Project Area).

Fascinatedly, an interior parlor photograph of a building that was demolished at 2265 Sutter Street (the garage entrance) was shown in a 1949 *San Francisco Examiner* a photograph with the caption, "A negro mother fans the flies away from her sick child in this crowded room…" This photograph was the distorted propaganda from the SFRA to demonstrate the poverty in the Western Addition. This eight-story, 155-unit building of 195,791 square feet, is serviced by a garage entered from Sutter Street and fronts on Hamilton Square (Park). The developers gave a considerable grant of money for the renovation of the neighboring Western Addition Public Library branch in the park, which was built in 1965 and designed by the popular architectural firm of Appleton and Wolfard.

The equally massive, concrete apartment building next door to the senior housing center was originally occupied by the University of the Pacific. With the infill of this block, and the 2000 Post Street apartment building, the historic Hamilton Square, originally surrounded by three-story, row Victorian houses has greatly changed by the A-2 Project Area development. The SFRA built the library in the park, as well as a recreation center with a swimming pool, during the administration of Mayor John Shelley (1964–1968). Both public structures were remodeled and updated in the late 2000s.

Hamilton Square (in the A-1 Project Area) is now connected to a newly created park to the south with an overhead pedestrian bridge across six busy lanes and the middle, landscaped divider of Geary Boulevard. This park is called the Raymond Kimball Park and has several beautifully low, sculpted hills, and a soccer/baseball field, which was recently covered with Astroturf. The footprint for Kimball Park had been filled previously with mostly pre-earthquake, wood-frame housing. However, also around the periphery of both parks were formerly several, large, post-earthquake, poured-in-place concrete buildings, and brick-masonry buildings, that represented the vibrant neighborhood that had existed prior to the urban redevelopment of the SFRA. One particularly important remaining structure was the 1871 Victorian redbrick Girls High School, on a large campus at the corner of Geary Boulevard and Scott Street, which was replaced in 1913 after the great earthquake and fire by the yellow-brick Ben Franklin Middle School. Ever since we moved to the neighborhood in 1975, this school was considered blight on the neighborhood, with its belligerent, mostly African American students, who painted graffiti on the nearby buildings. Today, the multi-racial school is divided into two charter schools, with one being the (elementary) college-preparatory KIPP (Knowledge Is Power Program fifteen-year-old program) and the other the San Francisco Bay Academy and the Gateway High School which is one of the top eight charter school in the United States (www.gatewayhigh.org).

The former Golden Gate Elementary School, on Golden Gate Avenue between Scott and Pierce Streets, is also a charter high school, called the Center for Creative Arts, in a newer building behind on Turk Street in the same block. The famous violinist Yehudi Menuhin attended classes in the older vacant elementary school building. The school was rehabilitated completely in 2013. The Dr. William Cobb (African American) Public Elementary School, on California Street between Divisadero and Scott Streets, became a Montessori school, over the objections of the local teachers' union. All of these schools, unlike my earlier childhood schools, are well integrated and have a wide group of ethnicities. The graffiti on the buildings in the neighborhoods around the old Ben Franklin School has disappeared, and the students seem happy and energized.

This situation is like my positive experience of childhood in the Kansas City, Kansas, school district. My father (or mother) was required, from kindergarten through high school, to read my monthly report cards and sign and date them. John and Ming also had positive experiences in the earlier San Francisco Unified

School District (SFUSD), in spite of the general, prevailing prejudice against Chinese Americans. But, with the encouragement of their teachers and the reinforcing encouragement of their parents, they became even better students. Because of the recent achievements by the charter schools, with much publicity and an energized effort by the parents of the now-majority ethnic group of Chinese American students who attend public schools, the SFUSD is now allowing students to walk to school near their homes instead of being bused to other locations. In 2008, the SFUSD partnered with Mayor Gavin Newsom and District Attorney Kamala Harris to hold accountable the parents of students who are habitually truant—missing for eighteen days or more. The next two years demonstrated that this monitoring is successful in decreasing the dropout rate of high school. The general public opinion is that the real impetus for learning radiates from family encouragement and involvement. This issue would seem to be self-evident, except for the established educational politics in San Francisco, as well as elsewhere!

Near the UCSF Mount Zion campus, at the corner of Geary Boulevard and Divisadero Street, is the distinctive Sinai Memorial Chapel, which was built in 1937 and is a cream-colored, deco, concrete building accented with bas relief limestone decorations of the Star of David and the Menorah, and palm-leaf stylized, rounded arches. This is the only Jewish mortuary in San Francisco. The earliest Jewish cemetery was within the boundaries of Broadway, Vallejo, Franklin, and Gough Streets, and dated from 1850 to1860. Temple Emanuel-El relocated the cemetery (Home of Peace Cemetery) to within the boundaries of Eighteenth, Nineteenth, Church, and Dolores Streets, and Sherith Israel (Hills of Eternity) bought an adjoining site at the same time. In 1888, the State of California prohibited further burial within city limits, and new grounds were purchased in Colma (the nearby necropolis). This previous cemetery site has spectacular views and is now the popular Dolores Park, owned by the city.

Also, along this Divisadero Street corridor are several medical buildings. The prominent African American Collins family built a handsome six-story building across from the main entrance of UCSF Mount Zion Hospital in 1989. This concrete building, with dark-green bays and a ground floor clad in red granite, has a five-story parking garage, with attractive planter boxes on each floor. There are ground-floor commercial/retail spaces, and most of the other floor space is either leased to UCSF or to Kaiser Permanente Hospital. The building was dedicated to Daniel and Dereath Collins by their family. Their son, Chuck (Charles) Collins, and his wife, Paula, are civic minded and donate to the arts (Museum of Modern Art). In. 1995, they built a four-story, glass and concrete, post-international-style building next door at 2330 Post Street.

At the northwest corner of Sutter and Divisadero Streets is a sophisticated four-story medical building of 250,000 square feet, with an underground garage, built in 1996 and developed by Richard Blum, the husband of U.S. Senator Diane Feinstein. This building is elegant and timeless in looks. Like many of the newer buildings, this building has been absorbed by the greatly expanded University of California, San Francisco, Mount Zion campus.

In contrast, an interesting historical building nearby is the presently active San Francisco Russian Center (community and social services), located at 2450 Sutter Street and built in 1911. The building is a fascinating creation, with elaborate Teutonic Baroque detailing, which bespeaks of the original German Turnverein Hall.

Kaiser Permanente Hospital

At the western border of the A-1 Project Area is the Kaiser Permanente Medical Center, which straddles both sides of Geary Boulevard and is a positive anchor to our neighborhood. Henry J. Kaiser, the major shipbuilder during World War II, established the Kaiser Foundation Health Plan as a medical health-care insurance plan for his employees. This nonprofit health plan coordinated its operations with the Permanente Group. Physician and surgeon Sidney Garfield, MD, established this group as a physician-owned collective. After the war, Kaiser reorganized his shipbuilding into an industrial empire; building dams, construction commercial towers, and manufacturing automobiles, as well as forging steel and turning out aluminum. In the 1950s, my father had owned two of the Kaiser Manhattan automobiles, but resisted the less chic and much smaller Henry-J. This nonprofit health insurance was expanded in 1946 to include any other outside patients, which included the majority of the other union workers and civil-service employees of San Francisco. Their first San Francisco hospital building, with 216 beds, opened at Saint Josephs Avenue and Geary Boulevard (2425 Geary) in 1954, and was their fourth hospital in northern California.

The Kaiser Foundation Hospital site was part of the former Calvary Cemetery, which was relocated in 1945, with the bodies, to a mass grave in another cemetery in nearby Colma. As mentioned previously, a new development of tract-housing, called the Anza Vista District, further south and west, was also created at this previous cemetery site. The new $3.2 million building was called by the *San Francisco Chronicle* "A dream-designed hospital to set new standards of patient comfort and convenience." Over the next two decades, the building was joined by new construction or acquisition of existing buildings on both sides of Geary Boulevard. By 1970, the Permanente Medical Group included 137 full-time staff physicians, most of who were board certified in their respective specialties, and an internship program. After a piecemeal renovation of the original hospital, a major expansion, called the North Wing, was completed in 1992, after twelve years of tortuous community negotiations, with opposition from neighborhood activists and opportunists. In the North Wing, there is a two-story lobby; a mezzanine level for staff meetings, records, nursing, and social services; and four stories above the laboratories, radiological services, obstetric services, surgical operating rooms, and a twenty-three-bed recovery rooms. After this extension, a new parking garage and a mechanical engineering building were constructed to the east, between Saint Josephs Avenue and Divisadero Street, on the south side of Geary Boulevard. These structures were built around the existing 1960s buildings. These additions were created, according to Kaiser Permanente Hospital, around a rainbow coalition of minority staff.

Alva Wheatley, an African American, whose family had been living in the BANG district since World War II, oversaw all of the regional construction-services work for the North Wing, and committed this project to hiring fifty percent minorities, which would be females and individuals living in the Western Addition.

As mentioned earlier, her sister had angrily struck me at a BANG meeting in the nearby Christ Bearers Church (a former mortuary), while I was expressing my negative view of the replacement housing project. The following is a review of this incident, which occurred over the issue of the building of new family public housing at the Yerba Buena West Plaza site in 1988. Robin Miller, who was president, tried to politely moderate the situation and was rebuffed. Ms. Wheatley continued struggling with me and smashed by eyeglasses. I yelled, "I am going to sue you."

She yelled, "I'll see you in court, honey."

The volatile Mary Rogers was responsible for busing-in, from outside our neighborhood, a group of public tenants to disrupt our meeting. She smiled at the meeting like the Cheshire cat, or perhaps more like a mentally disturbed person, busy knitting like Madam De Farge and sending me to the guillotine! Some neighborhood members thought that the infamous Association of Community Organizations for Reform, founded in Arkansas in 1970 (ACORN), was indirectly involved with this agitation in the background. This group has been recently defunded of government monies and has now been badly incapacitated from their previous high status of political power. Even though a family member of Ms. Wheatley was a local judge, she was required by the court to reimburse me for new eyeglasses!

To date, this expanded Kaiser Permanente medical center boasts fifteen buildings (incorporating the original French Hospital campus in the Richmond District in 1989), 4,139 employees (including physicians), 478 physicians, 1,199 registered nurses, and 73 nurse practitioners. As of 2007, the medical center serviced 972,541 outpatient visits. Culturally sensitive and competent care from their Department of Medicine includes bilingual Chinese and Spanish to provide linguistic and cultural services. It offers additional interpretation services in 56 languages, including American Sign

Language. This medical center has certainly been a stabilizing area for the western border of BANG. Our group has been actively involved with many other neighborhood groups through our input on all aspects of the new construction projects that followed, as well as other concerns, such as patient parking, and crime, such as muggings. The Kaiser Permanente Community Task Force, of which I am a member, was established in 1992 for the purpose of pursuing and voicing these common concerns at monthly meetings. When we first moved into the neighborhood in 1975, street parking was difficult because of patient parking, but BANG was able to obtain permit parking for residents only. Later, Kaiser Permanente improved the situation considerably by providing new parking garages for their patients, beginning with the new earlier mentioned garage in 1992.

After many task force meetings over the years, a new state of the-art, eight-story, medical-office building opened in 2000, on the north side of the 2200 block of Geary Boulevard. WANA had their boundary on that side, and the BANG border was on the south side facing the new building. We were quite in favor of this dynamic, new, stunning, contemporary building, with increased inpatient parking and a projected skyway over Geary Boulevard to connect the two campuses. WANA was opposed to any high-rise in their neighborhood. Much of the opposing views were a turf battle, as is everything in San Francisco. The controversial Joe O'Donoghue, who had established the Residential Builders Association, assembled a large plot of adjacent lots with houses for development of this new medical building. He was successful with a city election, in 1992, for the approval of Proposition K to obtain the necessary zoning and the merging of the lots. Barbara Meskunas and I had known Joe for a long time, and were extremely enthusiastic about his plans. The usual bureaucracy at the Department of Building Inspection and Planning Department, as well as the SFRA, of course, delayed the construction project for eight years. But this delay could have been possibly longer without the guidance of the politically influential attorney, Alice Suet Barkley. In 2001, the hospital became the only one in San Francisco to meet the year 2030 earthquake standards, as required by California's Hospital Seismic Safety Act.

This sleek and futuristic building meshes in an environmentally friendly manner with the nearby UCSF Mount Zion Campus. This building, with the maximum use of natural light and stunning views, was designed mainly by architect Keith Millay of the local architectural firm, Anshen and Allen. The out-patient building contains 260,000 square feet of useable space and an underground garage with 532 parking spaces. During the excavation of the garage, many artifacts over one-hundred-years old were discovered at various sites, such as the contents of a hand-dug well. These shards include medicine bottles, a child's metal skate, a porcelain doll's head, the brass bowl of a kerosene lantern, a white-clay tobacco-pipe bowl, broken Chinese and Japanese porcelain plates, bottles, Irish-limerick children's plates reassembled from ceramic fragments (illustrations inscribed with P is for Patrick—the wild Irish boy, and L is for Lewis—who went to see the bear), and a terracotta statue of a youth in Victorian-period clothing. These items are now exhibited in glass cases in the expansive, three-story atrium entrance court. One of my personal disappointments is that a pedestrian bridge, three stories above ground level, which would have connected the north campus with the south campus, has not been built. The San Francisco Planning Commission approved the proposal but the San Francisco Arts Commission vetoed the bridge as an eyesore, even though staff, patients in gurneys, and visitors-on-foot would have quicker, life-saving access across the busy and dangerous Geary Boulevard, a continuous, daily used expressway.

At present, Kaiser Permanente San Francisco Medical Center is almost at the point of constructing a new medical building on Divisadero Street, between Geary Boulevard and O'Farrell Street. A dilapidated plaster-covered Mission Revival circa 1920s apartment building occupied the northwest corner at O'Farrell and Divisadero Streets. After numerous task force meetings, we experienced again the same bureaucratic delays, ranging from a lengthy, in-depth, *shadow study* for a mini park on Beideman Street, and the SFRA requirement of replacement apartment housing. The sponsor for this apartment building was to be the African American Tabernacle Community Development Corporation. A consortium of five African American church ministries in the Western Addition District has developed a plot of land on O'Farrell Street, owned by Kaiser Permanente. The spokesman for the Tabernacle group is Dr. James McCray Jr., who is also the president of the San Francisco Parking and Traffic Commission. It was projected, in 2006 that the new building would cost $5 million to build, with the funding provided by Kaiser Permanente. This apartment building consists of eleven one-bedroom apartments, three two-bedroom apartments, and seven studio apartments. The Tabernacle group manages the building. The task force required Kaiser Permanente to audit their operations annually. On December 13, 2010, the handsome building was completed and dedicated with a ribbon-cutting ceremony, including a bountiful luncheon buffet. The construction crew comprised sixty-five minority workers and 3 percent female workers. Kaiser Permanete hired Alice Suet Barkley to expedite the situation and eventually canceled her legal services.

Going back in time to 1984, John, Ming, and I were visiting our friends Margaret and Jim Delameter at their ranch near Healdsburg. Sitting on their scenic deck and sipping the local Dry Creek Chardonnay wine, I said, "I presented a purchase offer for a building (the above mentioned Mission Revival building) to our neighborhood corner grocer (Eastern-Orthodox Christian Palestinian) who was my buyer. He stubbornly won't accept a $25,000 difference." Jim said, "Offer the seller an increased purchase amount for us and see whether the seller will carry a second note and deed of trust." The seller was Tom Hayes, a popular, husky, Irish American plaster contractor and an important person in the Irish American cultural community and the Residential Builders Association. Earlier he had completed some repair work to the lath and plaster ceiling of a bedroom in our home. I was amused, on completion, when he said, "It's smooth as a baby's bottom." His daughter Joanne Hayes-White is our present city fire chief. The Delameters' offer was accepted by Tom. After a previous visit to the Beverly Hills Hotel, Margaret was inspired to paint the building, named Breton Hall, with the same pink and white colors as that hotel, and she installed a green and white striped awning. Later, the building was sold by them to Kaiser Permanente Hospital for a grand profit. The pink building now owned by Kaiser Permanente, sat vacant for many years and became badly deteriorated and unsightly. Because of bureaucratic delays, new construction could not begin and the hospital was forced by the city to replace missing plaster and repaint the building a neutral tan color. An added expenditure of nearly $1 million for this façade work was spent needlessly for a vacant building, which had all of the necessary environmental protection policies in place and was to be imploded. The San Francisco Department of Building Inspection considered the vacant building to be blighted and an eyesore!

Some of the asinine issues with the San Francisco Department of Planning included: the above-mentioned shadow casting of the mini park, the requirement of many changes to an excellent exterior design, and the controversial proposed entrance off the more lightly traveled O'Farrell Street, versus the heavily trafficked Geary Boulevard corridor. Kaiser Permanente had legally evicted all of the rent-controlled protected tenants with *buy outs*, or a promise to move into the constructed new apartment building on O'Farrell Street in 2011. In spite of the "Lesser Economic Depression" and other delays, this building will hopefully be replaced soon with a 69,000 square-foot medical office and clinic building. The projected five-story building will house the hospital's outpatient pediatric and transplantation departments, physicians' offices, a pharmacy, radiological and breast/lactation services, and an adolescent clinic. In 2006, the project was projected at a cost of $40 million. With the new U.S. government health plan created by the Affordable Healthcare Act, this site could possibly remain a vacant site for many years. As a member of their health plan, I would hope that their excellent healthcare plan is kept intact!

The long-delayed, bureaucratic demolition of this building had a typical *San Francisco* incident. On April 12, 2011, the group called Homes Not Jail, which is under the leadership of Paul Boden (organizing director of the Western Regional Advocacy Project in San Francisco), broke into the building, and ten activists stayed there overnight. Their signs read: *Kaiser Thrives, People Die,* and they sang the song *The Partisan* which describes fighting hopelessly against a large warring army. The Kaiser management-staff, who had left the evening before the occupation, called the San Francisco police department the next day to evict the unlawful trespassers. The goal of the organizers of the occupation (thirty-three hours) was to stay in the building as long as possible for maximum media exposure. The senselessness of this situation demonstrates the ridiculousness of the so-called "progressives" and their enablers in the anarchy community.

A contrasting situation is the nearby UCSF/Mt. Zion campus, which constructed the new five-story Osher Cancer Center building on the site of a quickly demolished a handsome early twentieth century brick-faced wood-framed mortuary. UCSF is exempt by state law from the usually required Environmental Impact Report. Presently, Kaiser Permanente Medical Center has hired security guards to protect patients from criminal activity associated with the tenants of the nearby public-housing projects at Westside Court and the Pitts Plaza. Also, they have contracted with the two overlapping police stations (Park and Richmond) to provide extra protection. Regarding these safety precautions, BANG and AVNA have greatly benefitted. The increased pedestrian patient traffic and staff activity have added stability to our neighborhoods. Also, their attractive landscaping and fencing in the center divider strip on Geary Boulevard, at the expense of the hospital, have much enhanced the general appeal of our neighborhood.

Webster Tower and Terrace Apartment Complex

Located between the earlier-discussed housing projects, the original, commercial Fillmore Street, south of Geary Boulevard was almost completely leveled in the 1960s. Originally, a large main postal-distribution center for the whole city was planned for this two-square-block site, and Ellis Street was eliminated. This ill-conceived project was abandoned by the administration of Mayor Joe Alioto. During the 1970s and 1980s much new construction occurred here. Surrounding an existing, brick, apartment building, with commercial sites on the ground floor at the southeast corner at Geary Boulevard, was built a large market-rate apartment complex of twelve stories above a two-story commercial space, with offices above stores on the ground floor fronting on Fillmore Street. The new Webster Tower and Terrace Apartment Complex was accompanied by a parking lot and commercial development to the south. On the west side of this parking lot, a two-story commercial/office building comprising second-floor offices over ground-floor retail spaces was constructed next by the same developer, Richard Szeto, a well-respected representative of the then growing Korean-immigrant population arriving in San Francisco. At the south end of this parking lot was the Safeway grocery market, at that time purported to be the largest Safeway in northern California. At the opening reception for the grocery store, then-Mayor Diane Feinstein said, "I plan to shop here." Although, this was a great boon for the neighborhood, the scattered, small, corner grocery stores, mostly owned by Middle Eastern immigrants and predominately Eastern Orthodox Christians, seem to still flourish, even though these stores had much higher prices and a limited stock of food. Unfortunately, the parking lot often became scenes of gang activities, which most probably spilled over from the nearby public-housing projects.

In 2003, a plaza with palm trees was constructed on part of this parcel where the western side of O'Farrell Street dead-ended at Fillmore Street. Suttle Plaza was dedicated to the memory of Gene E. Suttle, who was the agile and popular African American director of the SFRA A-2 Project Area. He was a member of the gay community. Many community leaders of the Western Addition are immortalized in the inset grey granite markers with dedicated inscriptions, in the plaza. I am personally familiar with most of them, and I am both impressed and disappointed by the selections. The neglected, original, Canary Island palms in the plaza soon started to die, have been removed, and were not replaced with another species!

Fillmore Center

The most monumental construction, and an anchor for this business district, was the Fillmore Center completed in 1991, across Fillmore Street to the west from the Webster Tower. This particular assemblage of 8.95 acres had been cleared with the removal of the long-ago vibrant Fillmore District commercial buildings and had remained vacant for thirty years. This specific site between Fillmore, Steiner, Ellis, and Turk Streets was originally proposed by the SFRA for the main United States postal central distribution center, which was later built on Evans Avenue in the Hunters Point District. This complex of ten buildings, using the structural engineering firm of DMJM is an incredibly majestic anchor for the area, with its five, pastel-colored, high-rise buildings, with pitched roofs. The development would be financed and politically influenced by the city-established commercial forces. The anchor five, bay-windowed and colorful, high-rise apartment towers, with pitched roofs, are a mixed combination of nine and nineteen-stories, with three-storied penthouses in the nineteen-story buildings. Surrounding these five towers are the five other low-rise apartment towers of five- to six-stories, with ground-floor commercial spaces. There are a total of 1113 residential units and 74,000 square feet of retail space. An underground parking garage and a fully equipped athletic club, with a swimming pool, service the building complex.

A broad, open, beautifully landscaped, concrete ground-floor plaza in the middle of the complex is accented to the south by a magnificent, artificially constructed waterfall, with a collecting pool surrounded by a lawn and redwood trees. Attractively placed landscaping, both on surrounding hillocks and in concrete container boxes, add tranquility to this plaza, which exits to Fillmore Street. An original series of water channels in the main part of the plaza was replaced in 2009 with a staging area, a stunning, chrome, metal sculpture *Hard Bop*, by John Atkin, and permanent concrete benches.

The redevelopment agency required the original developer to allot twenty percent of the units for low to "middle average" income-earning tenants. These set-aside units were subsidized by section-8 certification from HUD. The building contractor was the politically and financially well-connected Turner Construction, based in Atlanta, Georgia. This construction company would quickly evolve into the most prolific builder of government-funded (SFRA) buildings in the city. The portion set aside for *affordable* rental units was thirty percent. The remaining fifty percent of the rental units were to be *market rate* units, that is, they were comparable with similar available units in the city.

In March of 1992, the *San Francisco Examiner* reported that the narcotics division of the San Francisco Police Department raided a subsidized, Section-8, newer townhouse at 1216 Turk. They arrested Soloman Mohamed, thirty-eight, and his common-law wife, Paula Polite, forty-two. They were major suppliers of drugs to nearby public-housing tenants. Police found approximately 240 pounds of marijuana, several loaded guns, $30,000 in cash, and $17,000 in traveler's checks. In addition, they found a large key ring that contained an oversized blank key that Officer Lee recognized as one similar that is used to enter the new nearby Fillmore Center apartment building at 1755 O'Farrell Street. Armed with a search warrant, the officers found approximately $1.4 million in cash in plastic garbage bags and boxes, as well as a duffel bag filled with approximately sixty pounds of marijuana, gold coins in the amount of $50,000, and a small arsenal of guns on the fourth floor. At the time, this was the second-largest cash seizure in department history. The couple was drawing welfare benefits for their eight children, ranging in age from nineteen months to twelve years. In addition to be in charged with conspiracy and drug sales, they were charged with child endangerment!

Eventually, these subsidized units were mostly vacated, voluntarily or involuntarily. Since these units were built after the rent-control laws went into effect, the rents have continued to increase because of the desirability of their central location. The penthouses now rent for $1,900 for the one-bedroom units and $2,500 for the two-bedroom units. Some of the commercial retail spaces are still vacant. Gradually the leased office space in the ground-floor retail spaces have evolved into restaurants and service-oriented businesses that are compatible with the new, revitalized, Jazz District. These buildings, through side-walk improvements, such as maple trees and street lights with old fashioned glass globes, have given the area a much-needed improved environmental and positive shopping impact. The upper Fillmore business district, above Bush Street, continues to give a completely different impact visually. I will always think, "The Fillmore Center (perhaps a Trojan Horse) became the most significant positive focus for our embattled neighborhood!"

Other Developments in the Fillmore Street Corridor

The Fillmore Center surrounds the redbrick Majestic Hall on the southwest corner of Fillmore Street and Geary Boulevard. This pre-earthquake brick building circa 1905 originally had an amusement hall on the top two floors and commercial on the ground floor. The hall became a roller-skating rink in 1947. In the 1970s, music impresario Bill Graham created the iconic Fillmore Auditorium famed for its rock music and psychedelic light shows, which John and I attended. To the west of the Fillmore Auditorium were Temple Beth Israel (partially destroyed and rebuilt after the 1906 earthquake) and the Alan Pike Masonic Hall, circa 1905. As mentioned earlier, this Masonic Hall was previously occupied by People's Temple of Reverend Jim Jones and remained vacant after the infamous mass suicide in Guyana. Later the hall with an auditorium was utilized by a Korean Protestant Church.

The earlier vacated synagogue was purchased in the mid-1980s by the world-renowned California artist, Tony Duquette who was noted for his spectacular jewelry and Hollywood set designs. He said in his book "More is More," "Beauty, not luxury is what I value." The newly dubbed Duquette Pavilion evolved over two years and included his eclectic, fabulous collection of cinema sets and clothing. The overwhelming interior was a magical fantasy of lights, brilliantly colored and whimsically placed. This set design was called *The Canticle of the Sun of Saint Francis of Assisi.* The building and its contents were tragically destroyed in a fire from a gas heater being used by the caretaker in the late 1980s.

In 2000, both buildings were replaced with a large new concrete branch post office (94115). Our former, smaller, 1550 Steiner Street branch post office is now occupied by a Russian senior social center. Although large, the new reinforced concrete building is a much reduced postal presence from the main postal center originally projected in the 1960s! Of course, to counteract the bureaucratic planning of the interior space, there was the usual political maneuvering by our neighborhood groups to acquire a more upscale service facility. This post office services not only the much reduced Western Addition but also the adjoining, extremely affluent Pacific Heights district. Pacific Heights is the present home neighborhood for the families of U.S. Senator Diane Feinstein, U.S. Representative Nancy Pelosi, Gordon Getty, Larry Ellison, etc. The post office was well-designed and is an improvement for the neighborhood.

Earlier in the 1970s and 1980s, prior to the anchor Fillmore Center development, many high-rise, reinforced-concrete towers for senior housing were built south on Fillmore Street. This new construction was sponsored by various African American churches. The SFRA offered the vacant lots at low prices and helped provide construction loans. Interspaced between these towers were several other church-owned apartment buildings. Where the amusement park, called the Chutes, circa 1909, had stood on the east side of Fillmore Street between Eddy and Turk Streets, Reverend Amos Brown's Third Baptist Church, built the two-story West Bay Center on a 16,486 sq. ft. lot space at the corner of Eddy Street in 1993, which is rented out for various public events. Willie Ballard, who was the contractor that rehabilitated our home in 1976 and his wife Ruby, contributed initial seed money for this center. They had also sold us their flats on Scott Street. Next door is the Third Baptist Church constructed in 1973, the Thelma Arms for senior citizens, which is a 13-story tower with 142 units, and commercial shops on the ground floor. This politically powerful and bombastic Baptist minister, Reverend Brown, invited the then recently elected President Barack Obama in 2009 to address his congregation. President Obama accepted the invitation.

Another developer was the much smaller congregation of El-Bethel Baptist Church on Golden Gate Avenue at Fillmore Street. In 1974, across the street on the southwest corner, the church sponsored the construction of the six-story El-Bethel Terrace for senior housing, which was over Fillmore Street retail spaces, and next door was the 13 story El-Bethel Arms for senior housing with a total of 131 units. The San Francisco tax records indicate the owner has a Silver Spring, Maryland address with an assessed valuation of $5,133,908 when it was built! Delaware incorporations also seemed to be even more popular in the SFRA project areas. The Fillmore Hotel, which catered to discriminated African Americans, often jazz performers, had originally occupied this site. The Kosher Langendorf Bakery across the street was demolished by the Redevelopment Agency and was replaced with bland, stucco-covered, low-rise, wooden-framed, subsidized housing. Around the corner, the site of the Ukrainian Bakery, located at 1125 McAllister Street, was also replaced by wooden-shingled, subsidized housing called the Friendship Village.

The prime, whole west side of the 900 block on Fillmore Street is now dominated by a non-descriptive, one-story, 1975 Uptown Church of Christ and a huge parking lot. Plastic flowers arranged artfully in standing planter boxes in the parking lot add an interesting footnote to this now very valuable 30,988 sq. ft. lot. As mentioned earlier, the charismatic bar owner, Leola King, had her Blue Mirror Night Club at this site. Notably, she, at their request, had locked up a group of the national assembly of African American Baptist ministers for a few days of frolic and enlightenment. "Goldie" King had related to me, "When I visited the French Riviera, I drank champagne out of one of my gold slippers." Unfortunately, after many other club purchases, she lost everything when her Classic Revival mansion on Alamo Square was completely gutted by an electric fire during renovations. The fire destroyed a fabulous interior, as well as her extensive collection of expensive fur coats and specially made one-of a-kind hats. She had no insurance and her electrical contractor was not licensed. The area, near her original bar, has continued from the 1960s on to have many bland buildings, which were built by the pastors of various African American churches. Thus, both new church buildings and residential apartment buildings were sponsored by their politically powerful pastors. Some people in the community referred to them as *poverty pimps*. Perhaps, this construction was mutually agreeable to the city political community for the support of each other, so that more lucrative development elsewhere in the city could be accomplished without racial tension!

In context, early San Franciscans had said that God (Ishmael and Allah) had favored the bars and liquor warehouses over the churches during the reoccurring fires of the 1906 earthquake. The later counterbalance prevailing in city political influence of the well-entrenched preachers after the Watts Riots of 1965 was reinforced by Mayor Alioto (1968–1976), who pragmatically tried to appease the African American community and justify the extreme white gentrification at the SFRA developments of the Yerba Buena Center and the Golden Gateway.

Behind the Uptown Church of Christ was a large undeveloped SFAR-leveled lot that Mary Rogers and her cronies wanted to convert in the 1990s into, "African American" very-low-senior rental housing. As if the area was not already saturated! The political upshot was that a large market-rate apartment housing complex was built between McAllister and Fulton Streets that had only somewhat better-designed buildings but with market-rate apartments. The complex consists of two addresses at 988 Fulton Street and on 1235 McAllister Street. Later, the owners considerably improved the facade design and sold the units as market-rate condominiums near the now desirable Alamo Square Historical District. At 988 Fulton Street, the wooden-frame building of sixty-three units is a mix of two bedrooms and two bathrooms, and one bedroom and one bathroom units and was built in 1999. This building was joined in 2000 with the wood frame building of forty-one units at 1235 McAllister Street above a common, above-ground garage. The one bedroom condominiums, of approximately 659 sq. ft., sell on the market for more than the original $400,000. The two bedroom condominiums, of approximately 900 sq. ft., sell now for more than the original $520,000.

As a footnote, one hundred units of *very low-income-senior-rental* housing in a building was constructed on a parcel (701 Golden Gate Avenue) located at the southwest corner of Golden Gate Avenue and Franklin Street. SFRA designated MHRSC, L.P.

and a California limited partnership, to modify the distribution of surplus cash for the development from the Citywide Tax Increment Housing Program. The site contractor was Cahill Construction. The attractive contemporary Mary Helen Rogers Senior Community is catercornered from the massive market-rate Opera Plaza (commercial and housing condominium complex) and was completed in2013. Although, I admit to agreeing with the late Ms. Rogers that the Western Addition would have been better off without the SFRA interference, I can never forgive her racism, meanness, and political opportunism.

Some other redevelopment agency developments in this area include the old Acme Brewery offices on Fulton Street, converted into the African American Art and Culture Complex. Across the street from the brewery and around it, subsidized, low-rise housing was constructed. The concrete Ella Hill Hutch Community Center was constructed in the 1980s at 1050 McAllister Street and is now covered with murals of historically important African Americans. The Center was named after the first female African American supervisor from the earlier District 4. My personal political experience with her was that Ella Hill Hutch was a black racist against whites (Asians were not even worth considering), but she was quite pleasant personally. Surrounding this center are several tennis courts and a park with a carved tree trunk, from Eddy and Divisadero Streets, of a reclining male figure, now without its African-featured head.

At the southwest corner of Fulton and Buchanan Streets is the original Central Hebrew School, which has curiously Islamic-style architecture and is now morphed into the Korean American Community Center for their cultural activities and socializing. Next door at Buchanan and Hayes Streets is one of the finest Italianate Villas with French Second Empire elements in the city. The surrounding Hayes

Valley district has undergone a remarkable transformation after the elimination of the neighborhood elevated highway following the Loma Prieta earthquake of 1989. The old cathedral, The Holy Virgin, Joy of All Who Sorrow Russian-Orthodox Church Abroad, at 864 Fulton Street still exists. This present church was preserved from a recycled Gothic Revival Victorian Church called Saint Stephan's Episcopal, designed in 1881 by Wright and Sanders. In 1930, a large Russian Orthodox community, which had fled Russia via China during the 1917–1919 Bolshevik Revolution, purchased the church. A new Russian Orthodox Cathedral was begun in 1961 and consecrated in 1977. This opulent Byzantine-style building with five gold-tiled onion domes topped by gold double crosses with footrests is an impressive major landmark at 6210 Geary Boulevard. A smaller congregation remains at the original cathedral.

Bordering upon the church, a large grouping of wooden shingled, low-rise subsidized apartment buildings in the A-2 Project Area was built in 1971 and is called Friendship Village. It features interior courtyards for the apartment house groupings and was designed by Buckley and Sazevich. This architectural firm sympathetically preserved some Victorian facades of demolished buildings into the two-square block construction area. Jonathan Buckley and Descamps were the architects for the later, much more successful, Divisadero Heights Condominium development on the 1900 block of Eddy Street, mentioned earlier. Most architectural critics probably would intellectually agree that this difference occurred because of the forceful neighborhood input and their mutually recognized concern for a simpatico design with the existing architecture.

Closer to Alamo Square at 717 to 723 Webster Street, between Fulton and Grove Streets, a pair of attached two-story late Queen

Anne Victorian cottages is politically noteworthy. The flat located at 719 Webster Street was the site of the murder of community activist, seventy-year-old Joyce Ruger in 1998. Previously, she had loudly protested the drug dealing on her street, and someone took their evil revenge. She was bound to a chair and strangled. Her home was ransacked of her valuable art collection and fine jewelry. Then, the punks set her home ablaze. In 1999, Troy Hayles (thirty-one years old African American), a parolee with a history of arrests for armed robbery, was charged with her murder, arson, robbery, and burglary. Neighbors recalled they knew a man called Troy who they thought was a drug user. Joyce had befriended him after he told her that "she reminded him of his mother." There was insufficient evidence to bring him to trial! This area was commonly called then by Realtors *the war zone*, because of the drug activity in the subsidized, low-income housing. One of these flats is owned now by our former District 5 Supervisor Ross Mirkarimi (Persian and Russian-Jewish background) and his family. He was a young, handsome, and quite popular District Supervisor. However, it was thought by many of his constituency that his only interest was promoting a "progressive" agenda. Unfortunately, he was ineffective in his earlier politically popular investigation of the continuing obvious abuses of management and financial accounting by the politically powerful SFHA. Without a garage, he has had his automobile broken into several times. He was originally against monitoring cameras at the public-housing sites. But he became later enthusiastic about their use and encouraged constant monitoring. Also, he promoted intensifying the use of police walking the neighborhood-street beats, with emphasis on high-crime areas. The police have not been particularly enthusiastic about getting out of their squad cars. But they do it now.

Unfortunately for a city that prides itself as being progressive, the SFRA allowed in the Fillmore Street corridor fast-food restaurants: Burger King at Fillmore and Sutter Streets, McDonalds at Golden Gate Avenue and Fillmore Street, and Kentucky Fried Chicken at Geary Boulevard and Steiner Streets. These establishments certainly cheapened the original concept of redevelopment from the ethnic restaurants that were destroyed.

Fortunately, Sacred Heart Church at the other end of this corridor at the southeast corner of Fillmore and Fell Streets provides an extremely more positive situation. This yellow-brick former Roman Catholic Church on a commanding city-hill site provides a showcase for historical preservation in San Francisco. The church was designed by Thomas J. Welsh in1897 and is of Lombardy Romanesque style and features a tall square campanile. The church had, originally, a wealthy congregation drawing from Hayes Valley and Alamo Square. Robert Pritchard and friends are leading a valiant effort to preserve this vacant privately-owned church!

As a real estate broker who delights in landmark architecture of all periods, I consider myself to have been dispositional fortunate in helping further the preservation of some of the finest examples of Victorian architecture in this earlier, and now affluent, Alamo Square neighborhood of San Francisco. My first experience there was listing a house for sale at 908 Steiner Street in 1974, which was the then-famous, multi-colored hippie house. This house was the first, and one of the most, colorful of the many Victorian fanciful-painted facades to follow. Michael Larsen and Elizabeth Pomada have captured these colorful facades in their noteworthy *Painted Lady* series of books. This two-story 3,600 sq. ft. Stick-Eastlake row house, circa 1888, with Corinthian pillars and a commanding bracketed cornice sold for the then remarkably high price of $35,000. The Realtors at Roman Realty could not believe that I was willing to have Sunday open houses in *that* neighborhood. This house sold in 2010 for $1,275,000.

Also later in 1974, I sold the nearby 1345–47 McAllister Street, which was an exquisite, fanciful French Belle Époque-style, three-flat building with a ballroom on the fourth floor, circa 1900, designed by James Dunn. Its roof is punctuated with two *Oeil-de-Boef* windows bracketed by female griffins, and the cornice is supported on each side by male caryatides. In front of the doorway entry is an elegant, copper-covered, clamshell canopy. The building had been constructed for a wealthy Jewish merchant in the spice trade, who lived with his wife in one flat, and his two daughters, with their families, lived in the other two flats. The top-floor ballroom was used for family entertaining, social parties, and recitals with professional musicians. Regretfully, in the 1960s, the owners divided these large flats in half, but they did keep the magnificent detailing intact. I represented both the sellers and the buyers. My buyers were a charming, older white couple, who lived in Marin County. In 1976, through my newly established real estate company, they sold with a tax-deferred exchange into a nineteen-unit Pacific Heights apartment building. The buyer for their building was a single, young, Chinese American lady from a rice-farming family in Mississippi.

Much later after many other noteworthy transactions in the Western Addition, my company sold, a block away, in 1994, three flats in an elegant Beaux Arts building, circa 1900, designed by the talented Jewish Julius Krafft, on the southwest corner of McAllister and Pierce Streets, across the street from the Third Baptist Church of Reverend Amos Brown. The sellers are a charming, distinguished, attractive couple, who are both African American physicians. Zealous Wiley had inherited the property from his family, and the interior and facade had never been altered. Brenda Spriggs Wiley was responsible for the details of a meticulous and expensive rehabilitation, which was spectacular! The flats, as tenants-in-common, were purchased for $650,000-$760,000 by three young white couples, who are mostly employed in the high-technology industry in Silicon Valley. Interestingly, our next-door neighbor, Marian Larkin's son Anthony, purchased for his own family, on the same block of Pierce Street, a pair of enormous Queen Anne Victorian flats, and he has completed an attractive rehabilitation. My firm has sold several Victorian buildings overlooking the historic Alamo Square over the years. This housing, in contrast to the redevelopment agency planned housing, is certainly significant!

To go back again to the more mundane, new SFRA-subsidized construction, many other two-story, wooden-structured, subsidized-housing complexes, as well as those mentioned above, were designed by architects of various degrees of talent but always politically connected. Good design should always be the most important factor. The quality of construction was often rather shoddy/cheap and the units have not weathered well. The redwood-built Victorian/Edwardian buildings are in comparison still viable. The SFRA, Section 8, subsidized, building complexes were generally covered in stucco or wooden shingles. Some tenant organizations of these cooperatives were more enlightened than others and utilized better property-management companies.

An effort was made in recent years to demolish and rebuild new housing for some of these complexes, but this effort was met with great resistance by the tenants, neighbor activists, and some members of the board of supervisors. The fact that the local housing authority was always on probation and surveillance by HUD, made the situation even more explosive, with various factions trying to exert their personal influence. No one wanted politically to focus on the lost tax income on these now valuable properties that could have been located anywhere. The crime-ridden Marcus Garvey and Martin Luther King Jr. bankrupt cooperatives are good examples. In 2011, they were stylishly renovated with government stimulus money legislated by the U.S. Congress and mandated by the HUD administrative staff of President Obama.

Jazz Center

The last major parcel to be developed on Fillmore Street was to be a high-rise tower with ground-floor commercial spaces and high-rise luxury condominiums above, at the northeast corner of Eddy Street. And the rest of this parcel to the east, at the northwest corner of Webster and Eddy Streets, was to be developed as low-rise housing. Chuck Collins, an African American, who came from a fine, well-educated, professional family and grew up in the wealthy suburbs of Marin County, proposed, in the 1990s, a well-conceived combination of upper market-rate housing and a first-class commercial building with luxury condominiums. His family already had a good construction track record with their earlier-mentioned professional medical office buildings on Divisadero Street, mentioned earlier. Also at this time, he and his wife, Paula, were in a partnership to develop the Metro Cinema complex next to a new urban park, with an underground parking garage, at the earlier controversial Yerba Buena Center. The site for this construction was on SFRA-cleared land near the already constructed Moscone Convention Center. Additionally, his father, Daniel Collins DDS, had been the founder of the Urban League. The Fillmore Street development of the commercial complex was predicated on an underground public-financed garage. The Western Addition Parking Corporation, a similar public-financed garage previously mentioned in the Japanese Cultural Center, was to be the sponsor for this subsidiary garage.

The usual "neighborhood activists," such as Reverend Arnold Townsend, Mary Rogers, and Randall Evans complained, "Chuck isn't part of our community." Of course, they were either being paid for their consulting services by various other developers, or political adventurers, or themselves for profits. They argued, "Chuck doesn't represent the interest of our community." I lobbied extensively for Chuck and Paula. I suggested at one public meeting, "I think an upscale southern barbecue restaurant and preferably Kansas City style would be a great addition." A rival African American developer-lobbyist yelled, "Do you think we only eat barbecue?" The politics in San Francisco gets so convoluted that any outsider, with the possible exception of a New Yorker, Los Angeleno, or Chicagoan, would be totally confused!

The Citizen Mayor Frank Jordan (1992–1996) had organized a group in 1994 called the Jazz Preservation District Committee. He had appointed Francee Covington, other concerned neighbors, and me to this committee. Naomi Gray, an African American, was elected president and did an exceptional job. As president of the WAPC in Japantown, I had already been in negotiations with the SFRA to provide a new underground parking garage that would be an extension of our Japantown garage. More parking for the Jazz District would provide secured, nearby parking at the corner of Fillmore and Eddy Streets. The AMC complex in the Japantown Center was considering an extension of their multiplex cinema complex to this location. Jim Jefferson, a fascinating, intelligent, engaging, husky African American, was a powerhouse behind the scenes. He promoted and negotiated with the popular Blue Note jazz night club to open a branch in the new building. There was much concern within our committee about making the area vibrant but also protecting visitors from the violent street crime that existed at that time. The development was to be an Enterprise Zone, which was created by the state in 1984 to allow cities to offer tax credits to businesses that invested in underserved and low-income areas. The next mayor, Willie Brown dissolved the task force in 1996.

After many extensions on contract for the development by the Collins, the contact was transferred in the late 1990s to Michael Johnson and Associates, who represented a mostly African American group. The first stage of development was, the site parcel facing Webster Street and was built as a complex of affordable Arts and Crafts-style housing and an adjoining low-rise building for financially disadvantaged senior citizens. The street-facing townhouses were constructed around the apartment building and have attractively landscaped front yards with low, wrought-iron fences covered with pink roses. An underground parking garage serviced all of the units.

At the turn of the twenty-first century, this same developer constructed, on the Fillmore Street corner, a magnificent ten-story condominium building (Heritage on Fillmore) sheathed in Jerusalem limestone above a luxurious foyer and a chic upscale and handsome restaurant called 1300 on Fillmore. The chef and owner, David Lawrence, is of Jamaican ancestry with a British upbringing and has created his own style of African American southern cuisine. His lovely wife, Monette White, is the attractive hostess. The adjacent, tastefully furnished cocktail lounge has walls lined with framed photographs of great jazz performers who have performed in the Fillmore District and elsewhere. Soon after this elegant expensive restaurant opened, John, Ming, and I dined there with friends who knew the owners, and we had excellent dinners. At a nearby table, the always impeccably dressed, former Mayor Willie Brown, with a fashionably dressed group of friends, was enjoying an animated conversation. Even though we had never formerly met, he and I exchanged mutual nods and smiles during the evening.

Next door in the same complex was a branch of the famous jazz club, Yoshi's, which includes an upscale Japanese restaurant and a night club venue for musical performances. The club is owned by Japanese American investors and attests to great interest internationally for jazz music. The underground city garage of two stories offers secure parking for the condominium owners, as well as for patrons of the Fillmore Heritage Center commercial enterprises. This capstone for the Jazz District is a testament to the good taste and foresight of former Mayor Willie Brown, as well as his powerful influence. These new improvements to the cityscape offer a most exciting, long-range potential for our neighborhood.

On January 21, 2013, the SFJazz Center, costing $64 million, was opened in the Civic Center to great public acclaim. The acoustics in the 700-seat Robert N. Miner Auditorium were pronounced by founding executive artistic director, Randall Kline, "It's unbelievable. It just sounds so beautiful," as quoted in the *San Francisco Chronicle*. SFJazz has grown in the past thirty years as a money-losing two-day festival into a major year-round arts organization that presents and commissions a wide spectrum of jazz, Latin, and other global music. The combination of the two jazz clubs provides San Francisco with a further array of superexcellent cultural venues!

The vacant retail space in the Fillmore Center is being developed with restaurants and other music lounges. The earlier mid-1990s Rasselas Jazz Club and restaurant featuring the owner's native Ethiopian cuisine is newly energized and now seems main stream. In addition, the earlier sidewalk-planted and now matured maple trees, and traditional glass-globe street lamps add a welcoming feeling and synergy to this newly created business district. The Divisadero Street and Upper Fillmore Street business corridors have both prospered in spite of the Great Recession. The new influx of younger, single adults and young families of all ethnic groups give vibrancy to the Western Addition. Many of the old timers of all ethnic groups still seem to be shocked about the changes. For me, this dramatic change is positive and appreciated after such a long interval. What a contrast this is to the isolated 1990s constructed jazz district at 18th and Vine Streets (with an American Jazz Museum at 1616 E. Eighteenth Street) in Kansas City, Missouri, with the vast, intimidating, undeveloped redevelopment-owned surrounding acreage is remarkable!

The SFRA had earlier completed their redevelopment within the A-1 Project Area. And in December of 2008, the SFRA terminated redevelopment in the A-2 Project Area.

On October 28, 2010, ground was broken for the last condominium development in the A-2 Project Area, at 1345 Turk Street behind the still-existing, brick-masonry power house for the early electric street cars. The development, called Fillmore Park, consists of thirty-two (seven one-bedroom flats, seventeen two-bedroom flats and townhomes, eight three-bedroom townhouse flats). The price range was from the mid $100,000s to the low $300,000s. The financing was through the SFRA, locally based Wells Fargo Bank, CALReUSE, and the Center for Creative Land Recycling. The building was developed by African American Michael Simmons' MSPDI Turk, LCC group. As reported in an October 31 *San Francisco Examiner* article, Supervisor Ross Mikarimi called the project, "An uplifting note for us to commemorate the conclusion of the Redevelopment Agency's jurisdiction in this area," and SFRA Commissioner Francee Covington, who said, "Thirty-two units; that's one hundred ten happy people. This will make a big impact." Simmons further added that the units would be offered to seventy to one hundred percent of the city's median income population, and to certificate holders (the original owners who lost their homes to urban renewal), and Simmons said, "The challenge is to get the word out early. A lot of low and moderate-income people don't think they can buy." "The most difficult task lies ahead," said Reverend Arnold Townsend, a long-time neighborhood activist, minutes before he joined Simmons, Mirkarimi, the African American SFRA Executive Director, and others in donning hard hats and turning over shovelfuls of ground-breaking dirt, "to see that the people who are most deserving get these homes."

"Covington cited community meeting as a wake-up call during the planning phase of this project. Murkarimi lauded 'families coming back' to the neighborhood. Blackwell stated that 'Certificate of Preference holders' would get the first opportunity to buy at Fillmore Park-if they can be found. Townsend said, 'we're not through building the community.'"

With their current mandated powers, the seemingly indestructible SFRA, with its political octopus tentacles, could simply relocate their urban renewal to other areas, such as the Hunters Point shipyards and the Bay View district, as well as the downtown blocks around the Yerba Buena Center, etc. Other future sites probably will be created out of self-interest. As long as the *pork* federal and state funding continues, the SFRA will be a looming factor in changes to the life of the city for better or worse!

15.

Epilogue

As I look back at these Western Addition events, through forty-four years of my personal looking-glass of collected memories, to the present, I have attempted to put everything into proper perspective. Sometimes this is difficult because of the old prejudices, both for enemies, as well as friends. Perhaps, this is a sign of age, not necessarily wisdom. There is the temptation to write malevolently about many events, personalities, and situations, which looked suspiciously like transparent corruption and manipulations. Dealing with the devious bureaucrats and so-called civil servants, politically appointees to commissions and some piranha-minded attorneys, was for me the most exhausting of experiences. I hope that the reader will understand my projection of the many future follies, which could continue to be perpetuated by the SFRA and the SFHA. But history can be a good learning tool. In our present twilight-zone, reminiscent of George Orwell's novel *1984*, the ever-secretive and convoluted political world is not easy to capture on the printed page. I have tried to penetrate this labyrinth through public/private meetings, personal contacts, business transactions, and my extensive collection of informative, local newspaper articles. I have endeavored to sort out the changes in the Western Addition through various developments. These changes reflect the American urban evolution and anthropography. At present, the real danger seems to be everyone or group seems to think of themselves, as *victims* of society.

The present Western Additon is now listed by the SFAR as a subdistrict, with the boundaries as Divisadero Street on the west, Gough Street on the east, Geary Boulevard on the north, and McAllister Street on the south. We are now listed as living in the Anza Vista subdistrict, with boundaries of Divisadero Street on the east, Masonic Avenue on the west, Geary Boulevard on the north, and Turk Street on the south. Although we are now in area previously the site of the Calvary Cemetery, I will always think of us "Western Additioners." The former Delameter house at 1100 Broderick Street, now in the Anza Vista subdistrict, was for resale in the summer of 2013 at an asking price of $1,895,000.

The seeds planted by earlier historical personalities, and later neighborhood activists, are now bearing fruit. *Gentrification* is appreciated by most sensible citizens of any ethnic background. How counterproductive it is today to say that the early pioneers destroyed ecologically viable sand dunes? Our present neighborhood has gone from an earlier, blighted area to a desirable and attractive area with lively shops, restaurants and tree-lined streets.

DIVISADERO STREET CORRIDOR UPDATE 2013

New building developments, which were on hold because of the Great Recession, are being constructed. A thirty-two market-rate studio condominium private development at the northwest corner of Ellis and Divisadero Streets are being marketed in 2012 to 2013 from $550,000-$795,000. The sales statement asserts, *Simply the coolest new building in one of the City's hippest neighborhoods*. The completion of this building is a great improvement over one of the many ugly gasoline stations on Divisadero Street.

Many of these stations that replaced grand Victorian buildings have now been replaced by condominium developments. Even a presently vacant lot is an improvement over a gasoline station. Due to the difficulty of obtaining a construction loan in the Great Recession, the construction was delayed nearly three years. The eagerly awaited new building (2020 Ellis Street) began construction in August of 2011. An excellent architect Stanley Saitowitz, a Russian-Jewish immigrant, designed the city-approved, futuristic metal-sheathed building that has a handsome, ground-floor pierced-metal grill façade. The studio units, with sliding doors to form a sleeping space at one end, take full advantage of the sunny, southern exposure and the landscaped garden views on the north side. He also designed a stunning building at the northeast corner of Post and Webster Streets, for the same developer John McInerney. It replaces the Japantown bowling building, a notorious "newer," 1980s-immigrant Asian American gang members' meeting place.

Outside of the Western Addition in the Richmond district, Saitowitz and his firm, Natomas Architects, designed the stylish, futuristic replacement synagogue for the Congregation Beth Sholom, at the southwest corner of Park Presidio and Clement Street. The temple is a half-moon upended in shape, clad in Jerusalem limestone. The offices and educational rooms, located in a stainless steel cube, are separated by an entryway to the courtyard and garage. This congregation is the first major conservative synagogue in northern California, tracing its beginnings to 1906.

The Divisadero Street Landscape Improvement Project, which started in September, 2009, is now completed, with funding from the American Recovery and Reinvestment Act of February 2009, at an expenditure of $2,600,000. The development area starts from Waller Street and ends at Geary Boulevard. Why does it end at

Geary Boulevard? Is it because of the artificially designated and arbitrary supervisorial districts, or lack of funding? According to the initial signage of the San Francisco Department of Public Works stated, "This (long overdue) revitalization project consists of sewer installations, roadway pavement renovation, curb ramps, and new sidewalk bulb-outs (increased corner sidewalks to slow automobile flow). In addition, the beautification improvements include handsome, traditional, new street-lighting fixtures, sidewalk and median landscaping, and benches (an extended sidewalk seating area)." These expanded areas, now with restaurant table and chair areas, are now called parklets or pocket parks. My main objection to the improvement was that the male Ginkgo Bilbao trees were not the tree of choice after PADS had earlier planted so many of them. Typical of many later civic improvements by new local committees, the planted strip lacks imagination, interest, and even more important, a necessary irrigation system.

The small San Francisco Nation of Islam Muslim Community Center, which is African American, at 850 Divisadero Street, has been closed but the KPOO African American radio station, at 1329 Divisadero Street, that broadcasts all of the Board of Supervisors meetings on FM, continues to coexist with the changing streetscape. The unrestricted, wood-smoke-polluting, southern-barbecue restaurant, with a parking lot at the northwest corner of Divisadero and Grove Streets has a For Sale sign presently. Further down, the boarded-up vaudevillian-era Harding Theater, circa 1927, has been the focus of a few newly-arrived activists who want the owners of the property to convert it back to a theater. The developers made a concession for a small theater included in their condominium complex, with the preservation of the existing building and expansion onto an adjacent vacant lot. The 300 block storefront *John* Coltrane Church, which earlier was the jazz club called *Both/And*, is now a Chinese American-owned cleaners. The church is newly located in the West Bay Center (corner of Fillmore Street and Eddy Street) on the ground-floor commercial level.

The Divisadero Street corridor has become a trendy, youthful destination, though at times a noisy venue, with crowded upscale restaurants, upscale grocery stores, electronic-wired cafes, and singles bars. Pocket parks for bars and restaurants are a magnet for social networking with the computer crowd. Many bicyclists, joggers, and babies in prams pushed by young couples, crowd the sidewalks and street. Of course, most of them are accompanied by various breeds of dogs. The golden nugget is that a few, specialized, small retail stores have remained in spite of higher taxes and fees imposed by the city bureaucrats. A good example is the fabulous Cookin' shop, which has an extensive collection of rare, old, and nearly new American and French cooking items and their accoutrements plus world-wide cookbooks. However, the best item in the store is the wonderfully witty, salty owner, Judy Kaminsky, who is not for sale, nor is her pet Lhasa apso, Tank.

Many of the newly located young residents (Gen X/ Gen Y) commute daily, both ways, on white or sleek silvery muted-colored large buses, with a designated Castro/Divisadero sign or unsigned and darkened windows, to their jobs in the nearby Silicon Valley. On the buses, they are actively programming their lap-top computers, Twittering, and using YouTube and Facebook. They are busy, well-paid, worker bees. Somehow, the earlier, less intense but gloomier, era seems like an eerie, curious time-warp!

These handsome, intelligent arrivistes are busy having families, renting newly expensive units, and buying residential housing.

Unfortunately, a few of those purchasing older properties do not appreciate historical interiors and are demolishing them to provide "open loft" spaces.

Good progressive concepts, such as Kaiser Permanente Hospital and the UCSF Mount Zion campus, along the Divisadero Street Corridor, continue to expand in a positive manner. So far, Kaiser Permanente Hospital provides a particularly positive conduit for the *Obama* healthcare program. Also, these medical centers bring more people to our community by offering excellent, advanced medical care in state-of the-art facilities.

PUBLIC VERSUS PRIVATE UTLITIES

What a difference from the earlier days of PADS when the bed-and-breakfast owner, Wayne Corn and I met great resistance to improving the appearance of the dreary, concrete, median strip along Divisadero Street from the City Department of Public Works and Pacific Gas and Electricity (PG&E), the privately owned utility company with headquarters in San Francisco. The present San Francisco supervisors continue to try to establish a municipally owned utilities company. My father had been the advisory board president to a group of civic-minded businessmen at the Board of Public Utilities in Kansas City, Kansas, which was a good alternative. When the city took over the utility company with its water filtration plant, corruption became rampant. Although, with the 2010 explosion of a PG&E gas-supply line in South San Francisco, which devastated a residential district and killed several people, the public is beginning to question the capabilities of this particular company to ensure the common safety. Also, the public is furious that California public enforcement agencies, along with company greed, conspiracy, or incompetence, have provided no restraint or oversight protection. Further insult has been elicited by PG&E in that their customers would be responsible for $2 billion or more for upgrading their supply lines!

The public owned San Francisco Water Company, with the Hetch-Hetchy water reservoir, manages well enough to provide superb Sierra Mountain water. During his administration, the then Mayor Brown supported bottling this high-clarity water for profit to the city. Most citizens realized that they only needed to sell the water from their water faucets. But the efficient, original, delivery system has been much neglected by diverting earned income from maintenance to social welfare programs and the general-operating budget of the city. The result is that the taxpayer is now being charged through bond issues and increased rates for the necessary improvements under the guise of seismic upgrading. The income was *casually* diverted in the past to the city coffers without any thought to maintaining such a valuable asset for the city. After stressing the need for water conservation, the SFPUC-Water Department (San Francisco Public Utilities) is now worried about the loss of revenue flow. The true heroes of this water system were the engineers and enlightened businessmen who were the original impetus through U.S. Congressional legislation ninety-five years ago. My eighty-two-year-old father had stated shortly before he died in 1994, "How can the present urban water systems be in such low regard and unsafe with the improvements that were made during my lifetime?"

Generally, I believe that privately owned corporations, with proper public scrutiny and appropriate governmental oversight are often much more efficient than government projects. As a basis of this hypothesis, former U.S. General and President Dwight Eisenhower wisely said that the *military-industrial* complex should always be sharply focused upon and watched suspiciously.

These earlier San Francisco visionaries provided that private enterprise, with limited and sensitive supervision, through government cooperation could provide an ideal model for a city. Our private Recology Sunset Scavenger Company, with their excellent recycling, is a role model for efficiency, reasonable fees, and courteous service. Some idiots still prefer a public, unionized company, which usually paralyzes a city with mountains of refuse from their long, painful strikes. The politics of the Progressive Movement by U.S. President Theodore Roosevelt should be used as a model today, where the government only interferes to regulate business with the promise of promoting the general good will of every American. The Liberal, so-called *progressive*, politicians' efforts to change everything through the bounty of monetary funding as identified by the often disastrous and corrupt practices of the local SFRA and local SFHA, which display a severe disorder for the common good.

SFHA UPDATE 2013

In 2009, the SFHA administered 7,409 Section 8 vouchers and received $90 million for housing-voucher assistance. At that time, they own 6,262 public-housing units, of which 2,027 are designated for seniors and disabled.

In September 2010, both the *San Francisco Examiner* and *San Francisco Chronicle* reported the SFHA had failed to collect $2.2

million from hundreds of public housing tenants, and it claimed a computer glitch. At present, they have no clear plan to fairly collect rent payments from 1,400 families that are behind! The office of the Inspector General, the investigative branch of the U.S. Housing and Urban Development department, found that eighty-nine percent of the Section 8 housing units in the city that were audited failed to meet federal quality standards, with deficiencies ranging from electrical hazards, security breaches, uncollected garbage, and debris. The SFHA (seventeenth largest in the United States) is responsible for the units that are owned by private individuals, who are required to maintain their units. In spite of this situation, the SFHA received $212 million, of which 99 percent was money from HUD!

The SFHA proposed, in the fall of 2010, the Hunters View housing project, which will replace three steep blocks of fifty-five, two-story, concrete, public-housing apartment buildings built in 1956. These are scattered along curving roads and cul-de-sacs. The site has magnificent views of San Francisco and the San Francisco Bay. It is located in the primarily African American neighborhood near the former Hunters Point shipyards. The projected new development will be 107 housing units, followed by 650 more, as part of a $400 million mixed-income housing. The San Francisco Board of Supervisors allotted a $30 million commitment to commence construction of two projects in the planning stages: Potrero Terrace on the south slope of Potrero Hill and Sunnydale in Visitation Valley. All of the sites range in size from twenty-three to forty-nine acres in our densely crowded city. Daniel Solomon has been selected as the architect, with his team of design partners, and John Stewart Co., Devine & Gong, and Ridge Point Nonprofit Housing Corporation are the *recycled* developers. Middle-income and public housing coexisting together has been demonstrated already to be highly problematic. With the same developers and concept in the Western Addition A-2 Project Area, this undesirable situation for me is clearly a *déjà.vu* moment in time with the same actors!

By the spring of 2011, the HOPE San Francisco initiative, started in 2007 by then Mayor Gavin Newsom (2004-2010), had run out of funding to complete the remodeling of six other housing projects. HOPE stands for Housing Opportunities for People. This initiative is modeled on the federal HOPE VI program, which was responsible for funding the rebuilding of several public-housing complexes from 1994 through 2006. The initiative relies heavily on developers, who would make money by building market-rate condos outside of the project areas. Some of the other sites would depend on the SFRA to provide matching funds. The city would need $127 million to start the necessary infrastructure projects, such as utilities, street paving, and drainage, prior to development. The Westside Courts at Broderick and Post Streets is one of the considered sites. The complex consists of 135 units, with HUD rating 52 units with life-threatening present conditions, such as mold, faulty electrical wiring, and rodent infestations. Thus, forty percent of the units are in deplorable condition, while two-bedroom condominiums sell in the surrounding blocks for $400,000 or more. At that time, SFHA Executive Director Henry Alvarez estimated that the total project budget for the replacement housing would cost over $1 billion. He blamed the poor conditions in public housing from years of underfunding and deferred maintenance.

At this time, there are seventy-one crime cameras located at twenty-four locations in the city. Around the SFHA projects in the Western Addition are twenty-one cameras located at eleven locations. As mentioned, they were first installed in 2005 and were not well monitored but were somewhat effective in deterring criminal activity. Finally, law enforcement is now utilizing the surveillance footage three times more as requested by defense attorneys, which has much improved security.

A citywide curfew, that applies to children of fourteen years or younger, and requires them to be indoors between midnight and 5:00 a.m., has been effective. The curfew makes exceptions for work, family, and religious or special events. As of August 2011, the Oakland Board of Supervisors has refused requests from their police chief for a similar curfew, even though the homicide rate has greatly increased, particularly by juvenile offenders.

Unfortunately, criminal activity is still a large concern of neighbors, but the drug dealers and punks are usually from outside of the city, unless they are visiting family or friends in the SFHA project complexes. They can quickly be spotted by the wearing of black-hood sweatshirts, partially covering their faces, and their low-slung, baggy, dark jeans. Cellular phones with cameras have been used to record events by technologically knowledgeable victims of the Gen X or Gen Y, particularly because their own cell phones are often the stolen.

Andrea415@yahoo.com e-mailed to neighborhoods: Subj: Just got mugged on Eddy and Broderick: Sent 6/24/2011 11:41:08 A.M. Pacific Daylight Time. The message was,

> ***I wanted to let our neighborhood know what just happened at 10:15 am today.***
>
> ***I was in front of my house getting the mail and got mugged. There were two african american guys (maybe 18–25) but just one came behind me (I did not see them at all). The guy I saw was wearing a black hooded sweatshirt and dark***

jeans. I had my back toward the street and was getting my mail at the mailbox, as I was coming in from a walk. I had my baby and stroller with me (baby in stroller). One of the men came behind me, put his hand over my mouth yelling for me to give him my cell phone. He yelled several times. I thought it was a joke at first. It just did not seem real in broad daylight (10am). I gave him my phone and he pushed me down and started running. Two of my neighbors saw this and ran after the guys and "'the [(y]" got away. (My phone dropped out of the guys hands as he ran, so the police are getting prints of it later today…there is a real CSI apparently)

I am a white woman in her mid 30's and my baby was in his stroller next to me. I really cannot believe this just happened. The police have taken the report!

Thanks to Ian and another amazing neighbor (forgot his name), who tried to run after the guy, for coming to my aid. Ian mentioned that his bike was stolen out of his garage two days ago…he lives on Broderick between Ellis and Eddy as well. Please be on the lookout, but also be very aware of who is nearby at all times.

Andrea
(1109 Broderick (at Eddy)

On July 22, 2011, an eleven-year-old girl was visiting with her cousins for a sleepover. Linda Ngo had finished watching television at her uncle's apartment at the "newer" Yerba Buena East

Plaza in the 1100 block of Laguna Street and returned to her bed. Moments later, around 11:45 p.m., a bullet crashed through the street-level window and hit her just above her heart and exited her body. She was rushed to General Hospital in critical condition. Our formerly owned, thirty-six-unit building at 1215 Laguna Street was only one block away.

A gun fight had erupted across the street in Jefferson Square Park, about two hundred yards from the San Francisco Department of Emergency Management, at 1011 Turk Street. Rival gang members randomly shot at each other and multiple shots were fired at the housing project. Her uncle Eric Holt had called 911 at the nearby emergency center.

The police arrested an eighteen-year-old man and a nineteen-year-old man in connection with the shooting. They were among three gang members wearing black, hooded sweatshirts who had been detained by the police in the park. The arresting police officer, Albie Esparza, declined to give names of the suspects or state whether charges had been filed. A July twenty-fourth article in the *San Francisco Chronicle* stated,

> ***Saturday's shooting is the latest tragedy for Holt's family. They've been burglarized several times since they moved into the public housing complex a decade ago. The 61-year-old (African American) is trying to remain strong, taking care of his daughter (who is developmentally disabled and has undergone almost two dozen brain surgeries) and his wife, Ngoc Holt who is on disability. But Friday's shooting has shaken him. 'I don't know who could have done this,***

> ***'he said. 'I didn't see anybody. The blinds were closed shut.' He is contemplating asking for a transfer to a public unit in Chinatown, where he feels it might be safer and his Vietnamese-born (wife) 'might feel more comfortable culturally. 'I'm scared now,' Ngoc Holt said.***

In the same article another tenant Cece Miller, twenty-eight years old, said, "I used to live in Double Rock," referring to the nickname for the Alice Griffith public housing near Candlestick Park. "This is Disneyland compared to that."

Why does this senselessness violence continue to happen in public-housing projects? The inherent SFHA financial corruption; inadequate maintenance and stupidity; some criminal, multigenerational tenant families; and public naiveté and apathy still exist! The housing authorities have outlived their usefulness, as our coalition (PADS) predicted back in 1984, and should be drastically reformed or abolished!

Fortunately and luckily, Linda Ngo survived the bullet through her body near her heart. She returned to the safety of her family home in the Richmond District of San Francisco.

As reported in a Business Report of the *San Francisco Chronicle* on January 11, 2013,

> ***Alice Gutierrez, a single mom of five, used to live in one of the worst public-housing complexes in San Francisco. The stench of raw sewage filled the air in the vermin-infested 1950s barracks-style buildings. Now she lives in one of the best,***

> ***a brand-new building on the site of her former residence, Hunters View, Located in Bayview-Hunters Point, 'This so beautiful I feel like I'm in a five-star hotel,' she said. Gutierrez is among the first residents to move into rebuilt housing in Hunters View, a 22-acre hilltop (a sunny area with incredible San Francisco Bay Views) that is undergoing a huge, $480 million revitalization. On Thursday, Mayor Ed Lee inaugurated the first rebuilt Hunters View building, a 25-unit public-housing structure where Gutierrez and other residents are settling into. Two more Hunters View buildings will open in spring for a total of 107 units in the first of three phases, which cost $80 million.***

John Stewart Co. will *naturally* manage the properties and has mandated strict tenant rules regarding legal occupancy and health rules.

As reported in a front page article in the January 26, 2013 issue of the *San Francisco Chronicle*, Henry Alvarez, the embattled African American executive director of the SFHA, requested a leave of absence for *personal* reasons. He indicated that he would not renew his contract, which expires that summer.

> ***Alvarez's announcement came amid mounting questions about his leadership and nearly two months after The Chronicle first revealed that he faced three lawsuits from employees accusing him of discrimination and retaliation. Alvarez is also contending with increasing frustrations***

about increasing tenant frustrations about unresolved maintenance problems, a highly unfavorable review recently by inspectors with the U.S. Department of Housing and Urban Development, and allegations that he steered two contracts to favored bidders.

The agency's own attorney accused Alvarez of discriminating against white employees in favor of black employees. Former Mayor Gavin Newsom (elected in 2010, Lieutenant Governor of California) had hired him in 2008 after heading the San Antonio, Texas, Housing Authority. SFHA Commission President Amos Brown (President of the city NAACP) and the present Mayor Ed (Edwin) Lee had earlier strongly supported Alvarez, but quickly wavered in their support for him. At this time, the SFHA oversees 6,476 units of low-income housing at 45 public-housing projects in a city, where one San Francisco tenant is paying $500/month for a closet in a house located in the impoverished Bayview neighborhood. I would predict that *finally* people will realize how greatly flawed the SFHA is!

SFRA UPDATE 2013

In September 2010, the *San Francisco Examiner* published a notice of property tax default in the city and that the SFRA owed a total amount of $331,346. Yet, HUD has been funding the SFRA with an incredible amount of money for the future development of the southern sector of the city. The agency's total spending for the fiscal year 2008/2009 totaled $337 million of which nearly $70.7 million is supported by nontax increment revenue sources (land sale proceeds, leases, grants, development contributions, i.e., San Francisco rent control *extortions*. According to the SFRA website,

> ***The agency is the city's primary housing and economic development arm, working with both nonprofit and for profit developers to advance the needs of the city and revitalize segments of the local economy. Additionally, the Agency sponsors public development within its redevelopment areas ranging from streetscape improvements to workforce development to the construction and maintenance of parks, open space, and multi-cultural arts facilities.***

The SFRA Western Addition A-1 Project Area, established in 1956, expired on March of 1973. The SFRA Western Addition A-2 Project Area, established in 1964, expired on January 1, 2010. The project areas that the SFRA is currently involved with are Golden Gateway, Yerba Buena Center, India Basin Industrial Park, Hunters Point, Rincon Point/South Beach, Bayview Industrial Triangle, South of Market (1989 Earthquake Recovery Area), Hunters Point Shipyard, Mission Bay North/South, Transbay (Terminal), Mid-Market, South of Market Expansion, Bayview Hunters Point, and Visitation Valley. Like an octopus, its tentacles continue to grasp for more land. Our present *Lesser Economic Depression* might be the determining factor for the construction of these projected developments!

In January 2011, newly elected Governor Jerry Brown (former Governor 1975–1982) and resident for one night at the *Pink Palace*, that is, the Rosa Parks Public Housing Project) proposed in a mature and intellectual manner, with his annual budget, to discontinue all the redevelopment agencies and enterprise zones in California.

Awkwardly, the city of Oakland benefited when he was mayor, but perhaps he perceived the graft of the whole system. The money collected from the property taxes of the completed project areas would be diverted tax increment money from all further redevelopment development projects to the general funds of those cities. These funds would provide the necessary money to maintain underfunded civic services in the Great Economic Recession. Also he proposed eliminating the artificial and politically lucrative enterprise business zones, such as The Jazz District in San Francisco.

The proposal created the disturbed, gluttonous, redevelopment sows, who squealed all the way to the state capitol in Sacramento, to protect their overflowing money troughs and their suckling piglets. Some cities claimed; how could they possibly finance the building of professional sports stadiums, golf courses, etc., without government funding! On the Martin Luther King, Jr. holiday weekend, some agencies greedily and quickly authorized new projects to keep more of their funding. In San Francisco, the SFRA Executive Director Fred Blackwell is quoted in the *San Francisco Chronicle* as threatening, "If you take worst-case scenario, just about everything we are working on could be in jeopardy." Finally, someone of authority like Governor Jerry Brown was agreeing with my continual criticism of the SFRA. I hope most citizens will agree that the SFHA is additionally a poverty pimp who sells itself for money for the well-connected! Surprisingly, all of the hypocritical Republican legislators would not join the anxious majority Democratic legislators to agree to this wise legislation.

On March 15, 2011, the SFRA agenda items approved by the SFRA Commission was (4h)

> ***Authorizing a Third Amendment to the Tax Increment Loan Agreement, and a Second Amendment of the Disposition and Development Agreement, with Armstrong Townhomes, LLC a California Limited Liability Corporation, to modify the schedule of performance, and to modify and increase the budget by $9,630,088, for a total amount not to exceed $34,117,133: in conjunction with the development of 124 low-and moderate-income ownership units; 5600 Third Street: Bayview Hunters Point Redevelopment Project Area; Citywide Tax Increment Housing Program. (Resolution No. 29-2011).***

Also the SFRA commission approved agenda Item (4j):

> ***Authorizing the execution and delivery of a Multifamily Housing Revenue Note, in an aggregate principal amount not to exceed Forty One Million and no/100 dollars ($41,000,000) to assist HV Partners 1, L.P., a California limited partnership, for the financing of the acquisition and construction of affordable residential rental facilities known as Hunters View Phase I at Middle Point and West Point Roads (Block 4624, Lots 3, 4,& (and Block 4720, Lot 27) authorizing and approving related actions and authorizing the execution and delivery of related documents and adopting environmental findings pursuant to the California Environmental Quality Act (CEQA): Bayview Hunters Point Redevelopment Project***

> ***Area: Citywide Tax Increment Housing Program (Resolution No. 31-2011).***

Also the SFRA commission approved agenda Item (4i):

> ***Authorizing an Agency Payment Obligation Agreement with HV Partners 1, L.P., a California limited partnership, and Citibank, NA, a National Banking Association, to guarantee an amount up to $9,631,252 in construction loan payments to Citibank, NA, for construction of 80 public housing units and 27 low-income rental units known as Phase 1a of Hunters View: Middle Point and West Point Roads (Block 4624, Lots 3, 4 & 9 and Block 4720, Lot 27); Bayview Hunters Point Redevelopment Project Area; Citywide tax Increment Housing Program. (Resolution No. 33-2011).***

These are significant amounts of money and, added to the lesser amounts of expenditures, are staggering! I was surprised that these were California limited partnerships instead of the usual registered Delaware limited partnerships. Greed has no bounds!

Tax increment moneys for new development and the future of city general obligation bonds backed by the city's full faith and credit are seriously at risk in this political shell game.

In May 2011 as quoted in the *San Francisco Chronicle*, Oakland Mayor Jean Quan proposed the following:

> ***The General fund (is), to sell the vacant Henry J. Kaiser Convention Center (a beaux Arts building dating from 1914 on the edge of Lake Merritt) for $28.3 million to the city's redevelopment agency and divide the revenue over the next three years. The move eases the budget crisis while potentially siphoning more money out of the hands of Gov. Jerry Brown who wants the state to redistribute redevelopment money and assets directly to the general fund of cities. Although the building has held numerous famous events, it is not physically within an established redevelopment area and certainly does not remove blight or create jobs….***

In a July 5, 2011 *San Francisco Chronicle* article by the excellent African American columnist Chip Johnson stated,

> ***It's not as if the city's (Oakland) elected leadership doesn't recognize the sleight of hand used to patch up the city's finances and approve a budget for the next two years. In May, Oakland Mayor Jean Quan referred to the sale of the convention center as "one of the last gimmicks" left in the city's bag of tricks. The convention center sale will not be repeated. The structural cracks in the city's finances are still there, and the city is running out of tricks….By signing such a pact, the council would break its contract with the resident-voters who elected them. Remember the part about pledging to serve the people first? If you refer to the oath you took. I'm sure you'll find it.***

On the west side of San Francisco Bay, SFRA Executive Director Blackwell stated in June 22, 2011 in a telephone interview with the *San Francisco Chronicle*,

> ***The hit in San Francisco would be pretty substantial....noting threats to efforts such as business revitalization on Third Street in the Bayview district and a push to revamp the mid-Market Street neighborhood. Some of the city's bigger developments are safe, such as the plan to add 5,700 new homes at "Park Merced," because they are being financed through private capital. Funding for the massive Treasure Island project also should be safe since officials restructured its financing to avoid relying on these funds. Plans to build 10,000 new homes at the former Hunters Point Naval Shipyard hinge mainly on redevelopment funds, but Karen Finn, a manager in the governor's Department of Finance, said in April the project would be safe because Brown has no intention of killing "projects that were under contract, under way."***

Steven Greenhut (editor of www.calwatchdog.com), in the *San Francisco Examiner* viewpoint column on June 19, 2011 stated,

> ***Previous efforts to kill local central planning fiefdoms (redevelopment agencies)—which run up debt, divert existing tax dollars from traditional public services such as schools and public domain and dole out subsidies to politically savvy developers—failed after Republicans rallied to***

> ***save the agencies, their free-market rhetoric notwithstanding. But on Wednesday (June 18th), the Legislature (California) voted to end its reign of terror, with a handful of Republicans joining Democrats in doing the right thing....In reality Republican legislators are more interested in being pro-business than pro-freedom.... Obviously, Democrats didn't vote to shut down redevelopment agencies for the right reasons. They don't mind central planning and subsidies. If they didn't like those things, they wouldn't be Democrats. They were looking for cash to close the budget hole. But who cares? However this plays out redevelopment is on the ropes. That is a reason to celebrate.***

Earlier on Monday, June 16, Democratic Governor Jerry Brown had vetoed the state budget as being unbalanced and unworkable.

After State Controller John Chiang stopped the legislators' pay, the majority party Democrat legislators passed a (2011–12) budget with compromises to the governor on June 27, 2011. A *San Francisco Chronicle* article on June 28, 2011, stated, "....Redevelopment agency supporters maintain that the plan to eliminate and replace the agencies-and move $1.7 billion into state coffers this year-is illegal, and they vowed Monday (June 27th) to take the issue to court."

The SFRA on their regular meeting Agenda on July 5, 2011, included Item 4 (d) Workshop on the Effects of State Legislation Suspending New Redevelopment Activities but Allowing the City and County of San Francisco to Take Steps to Continue the Redevelopment Agency. The SFRA will need approval on November

1, 2011, to allow the release of $24 million to comply with this survival option. Thus, city leaders will be asked by the SFRA to contribute funds from the general fund rather than directly from SFRA funds to the state-funded services in the city. The SFRA simply does not want to die! As usual, the SFRA will begin their deceptions in the shell game that they have played since 1945, and the taxpayers will be screwed again!

Both the state government and the redevelopment agencies claimed victory on August 11, 2011, when the State Supreme Court agreed to review a plan to dismantle redevelopment agencies in California. However, the Court decided in mid-January of 2012 the elimination of the redevelopment agencies was legal and barred the agencies from starting any new projects, issuing bonds, or transferring any property.

However, regardless of the future of the SFRA, the spectacular San Francisco redevelopment-initiated boondoggle on Treasure Island will most likely move forward. It was the original site of *Golden Gate International Exposition* of 1939 built from dredged bay sand, and later became a Naval Station beginning with World War II. The city negotiated to acquire the abandoned Naval Station from the U. S. Government over a decade ago for $150 million. The purchase price was later reduced to $55 million in 2010. The construction funding was to be provided by the SFRA. A target completion date of 2040 is projected for the completion of a new neighborhood for a community of 19,000 people. This scenic 400-acre development site, as well as 135 acres on the natural Yerba Buena Island is in the middle of the San Francisco Bay. It is overseen nominally by the Treasure Island Development Authority. The project is slated to include 8,000 new units of housing including: 2,400 affordable housing units; three hotels; high rises with one 450 foot; 450,000 sq. ft. of retail space; a 400-slip marina; a new ferry terminal; an urban farm; and 300 acres of park and open space.

The developers' basic plans, which were unveiled in 2005, have been tweaked to offer a pedestrian-friendly scale community in an environmentally sustainable, full service community. The developers include Wilson Meany Sullivan, Lennar Urban (Hunters Point Shipyard), and Kenwood Investments. In April of 2011, the San Francisco Planning Commission narrowly approved the environmental impact report for this project. An article in the *San Francisco Examiner* at this time noted, "Earlier in this month, planners freed the project from funding through The City's Redevelopment Agency in response to Gov. Jerry Brown's efforts to eliminate the agencies statewide. Instead, an infrastructure financing district would be set up to allow The City to borrow against future tax revenue that comes from redevelopment."

Both the *San Francisco Examiner* and *San Francisco Chronicle* newspapers, as well as the Mayor's office, strongly endorse supporting this development. The politically powerful Sierra Club rejected claims that the project would not harm the environment and exacerbate traffic problems. On June 7, 2011, the Board of Supervisors, who rarely agree with one another, voted 11 to 0 to support the proposal. This huge $1.5 billion construction project will be built on seismically unstable landfill (as well as nuclear radiated soil), which will be glaringly obviously for the awaiting seismic disaster and perhaps an ensuing tsunami. However, the developers claim boldly that massive weight will compact the soil and keep the island stable during earthquakes. They also claim that a seawall will protect against any possible tsunamis. The present warnings of global warming, causing the sea levels to rise, appear not to be in the way of great financial profits. Perhaps, a nuclear power plant for self-sufficiency is the only missing ingredient for this imminent disaster!

An article in the July 21, 2011 *San Francisco Chronicle* states, "Mayors from around the East Bay said Wednesday that Gov. Jerry Brown's elimination of redevelopment agencies amounts to theft by the state that strips cities of millions of dollars that would have improved neighborhoods and produced tens of thousands of jobs....' We can't print money like Washington, Quan (Mayor of Oakland) said. And we can't take money from other agencies, like the state of California apparently can.' Oakland would lose $40 million if officials decide to continue running a redevelopment agency. Gov. Jerry Brown, who as the mayor of Oakland mayor spearheaded a transformation of the city's downtown by using redevelopment money, advocated the eliminating of redevelopment, saying it was the right thing to do in the worst economy since the Great Depression."

Another factor for the Great Recession of 2008 *Lesser Economic Depression* was that an overwhelming number of people applied with the SFHA and Oakland Housing Authority for Section 8 vouchers, which HUD oversees at the federal level. With the encouragement of HUD, banks made risky loans to new home buyers with no down-payment and dangerous variable loans. Even private investors, such as us, agreed to refinance income properties to obtain cash equity at lower initial interest rates, which quickly escalated. We had refinanced our former Scott Street property with the much discredited Countrywide Mortgage Co. but sold before the housing market collapsed. Other homeowners and property investors were not so lucky—particularly in Oakland rather than in San Francisco. The SFRA continued to construct more low-income public housing units during this period. At the same time, many applicants for the existing public housing projects refused to move into the crime infested, and often derelict public housing units. Until the economy improves, there could be disastrous consequences, such as riots due to the frustrations of these renters and increasingly new numbers of applicants.

Catastrophically, banks such as Bank of America, Wells Fargo & Co., Citigroup, JP Morgan Chase & Co., and Fannie Mae are offering to donate, to local agencies, foreclosed homes in large cities to be demolished and the remains removed to landfills. They are even paying for the demolition costs for the glut of foreclosed and abandoned houses that they cannot sell. Cities such as Cleveland and Detroit are primary targets. *Bloomberg News* reported in the *San Francisco Chronicle* on July 29, 2011, that Bank of America, founded in San Francisco, had 40,000 foreclosures, mostly from Countrywide Financial Corp., in the first quarter. Our well-constructed 1928 Tudor-style Kansas City family home is affected by this horrific nonsense and obscene waste of viable real estate. In San Francisco, funding for new public housing is meantime available from these same lending institutions. People are homeless and starving worldwide. Why is this happening? The hedge-fund operators made fortunes and had the last laugh!

In 2013, both Mayor Quan and Mayor Lee are currently trying to discover means by which to use city revenue to build more low-income housing and public-housing projects in their respective cities. Obviously, they have many willing accomplices to achieve their goal.

Curiously, Mayor Quan hired the newly unemployed SFRA Executive Director Fred Blackwell to be the Assistant City Administrator of Oakland.

WESTERN ADDITION UPDATE 2013

Through energetic and cooperative neighborhood group efforts and private development with the earlier SFRA financing, the new Fillmore Jazz Center looks promising, even with new competition. With the Fillmore Center newly privatized again, the overall prospects for a revitalized Fillmore Street are exciting and well worth our early struggles. The Marcus Book Store is still present at its relocated Victorian building at 1712 Fillmore Street serving *Black People Everywhere* for fifty years. It is the oldest established African American bookseller in the United States. Its website is www.marcusbookstores.com. In 2011, a large senior development honoring the founders, Drs. Julian and Raye Richardson, has been constructed at the southeast corner of Fulton and Gough Streets by Cahill Construction Company. The nearby Mary Helen Rogers Senior housing is also a high-tech building and also constructed also by Cahill Construction Company.

The Upper Fillmore Street privately owned retail stores and restaurants continue to offer a resonating very up-scale shopping focus, in spite of the turn-over of stores during the Great Recession. Surprisingly some of the chain stores, such as Smith and Hawkins garden store have closed. But Brooks Brothers Clothiers has opened a boutique called Black Fleece. Unfortunately, between California and Sacramento Streets, the Italian ristorante and delicatessen Vivande Porta Via, under the affable, talented chef/owner Carlo Middione has shuttered their windows after thirty-five years. The unsinkable Mrs. Dewson, the unofficial *Mayor of Fillmore Street*, who owned a hat shop, at 2050 Fillmore Street, closed her store in 2012. This African

American lady, who offered her over-the-top Sunday millinery to her fellow church-going ladies and other ladies regardless of their ethnic background, will be missed. Her fedoras were sold to male patrons, such as our former "Lord" Mayor Willie Brown. Mrs. Dewson's late debonair husband lived alone, by their own mutual agreement, in an apartment building behind our home.

The Western Addition has now returned to its nineteenth century and early twentieth century roots and is becoming again a more peaceful/civilized environment. Also, the police are more effective in preventing crime. The dangerous Pitts Plaza has monitoring cameras that are hopefully going to be reviewed at all times in the future, unlike the insufficient viewing in the past. The number of pit bull dogs, crack-cocaine dealing, and red stoplight robberies of automobile drivers, has lessened. Periodically, police squad cars can be seen monitoring the group activity of young males, dealing various drugs. Their concentrated transactions have been, more or less, stopped. Sometimes, on Saturdays, a squad car can be seen on the slope of Eddy Street in front of our home. But still, individual punks steal purses and iphones from persons walking nearby or at local bus stops. These punks from the *hood* occasionally beat them up for no good reason!

One late afternoon in 2011, I had started to wheel our recyclable containers out to the sidewalk curb, when I saw two teenage African American punks in white T-shirts and baggy jeans (Levi Jeans invented in San Francisco during the Gold Rush) hanging below their hips coming up the street. Cautiously, I waited for them to pass by our gate. I later looked up and down the street; they were not visible. So I pushed the containers up to the gate and they suddenly appeared.

The older, fat, male juvenile pointed a small stun gun with a flashing red light at me and said, "We'll help you."

I said, "No thanks," and turned my back on them and walked up the steps to the front door. Immediately, I telephoned the police emergency line (911) but, even though they arrived rapidly, the police did not catch them. During my gardening later, I found their same *gun,* thrown into the front bushes, which was only a cigarette lighter! Perhaps, the best summing up of the situation is that a former famous superior court judge lives in a condominium on our block. Home burglaries have decreased. The police have the new added duties of assisting the increasingly homeless of all backgrounds passing through the neighborhood, in addition to dealing with the affluent, young drunks exiting the new bars and restaurants.

But the depressing reality of the Pitts Plaza is still there, as the SFPD Park Station reported in its newsletter:

> ***March 11, 2011, Serious Incidents-1100 block of Scott St. 11:45 PM kidnapping: A man went to his estranged wife's residence on Addison Street, kidnapped her at gunpoint, and fled with her in his car. Ingleside Station officers investigated and asked Park Station officers to check the man's residence on 1100 block of Scott Street (Pitt's Plaza). Sergeant Pasquinzo found the suspect's car parked nearby and no answer to the suspect's front door. Lt. Cota took over the scene, surrounding the suspect's residence with officers, and tried to contact the parties inside. Believing that the woman's life***

was in jeopardy Lt. Cota ordered a SWAT team to enter the residence. The team entered the residence, arrested the suspect, a 46 year old Western Addition man, and freed the woman. Inspector Martinez of the Domestic Violence Unit took over the case.

As a follow up in November of 2010, Jelvon Helton (twenty-two years old), an alleged member of the Western Addition gang called the Knockout Posse, was slain by numerous shots to his chest at a club in the fashionable swinger Marina District by an alleged gang member. A related article in the *San Francisco Examiner* made this statement:

In 2006, Helton was convicted of being an accessory to a felony for threatening a security guard at Eddy and Pierce Streets, according to authorities. At the time of his death, Helton wore gold teeth with the letters 'KO' in his mouth and a gold earring with the letters 'KOP,' the initials of the gang, police said. Helton was among about 100 people named in court approved injunctions baring suspected gang members from associating with each other or loitering after 10 p.m. in certain parts of the city. Earlier in 2008, his brother Andre had been shot to death in a parked car near the University of San Francisco.

The Gravity Room, the scene of the event leading to Jelvon's death, was soon afterward closed down by the city.

A good maxim is that no San Francisco neighborhood is an island unto itself. I think often of the much admired Atlantis by the ancient world as being San Francisco experiencing a disastrous tsunami. Supervisorial Districts should be observed as a whole part of the city. The city needs to return to citywide elections. Former Supervisor Ross Mirkarimi had had a somewhat credible beginning in spite of some of his unrealistic and "progressive" ideas, such as not enforcing loitering laws due to human rights issues for free association. The San Francisco Supervisory Districts either fall into irrelevance or elevation of themselves according to the attributes, such as topography, historical relevance, central location, good weather, or just dumb good luck. An enlightened and more active neighborhood group can make a tremendous difference in their particular neighborhood with benefits to all. As an example, the Coalition for San Francisco Neighborhoods (CSFN), founded in 1972, with forty-seven representatives of neighborhood associations, is generally a prism for the better being of the city. BANG was proud that the competent Barbara Meskunas was president for several terms. Because of petty differences that always seem to be present, BANG dropped our membership.

On December 31, 2012, Ross Mirkarimi caused a political fury when he grabbed and bruised the arm of his wife (Eliana Lopez), a movie actress from Venezuela, in their car in front of their two-year-old his son. Mayor Ed Lee suspended him and filed official conduct charges, seeking Mirkarimi's permanent removal from taking his newly elected post as Sheriff of San Francisco County. The San Francisco Ethics Committee voted to remove him from position but the San Francisco Board of Supervisors voted to acknowledge him as sheriff by the deciding one vote of his former, District 5, Supervisor Christina Olaque, who had been appointed by Mayor Lee. She would lose her position in the 2012 election to African American London Breed, who was reared in the original Yerba Buena Plaza East public housing. As sheriff, Ross Mirkarimi appears to be reforming and improving an already efficient department.

I hope our neighborhoods will survive the pressures of the local city government, state government, federal government, and the nonprofit foundations, which can be extremely profitable for their executives, employees, and cronies. The aggressive, opportunistic, tenant organizations; the self-aggrandizing politicians; some greedy merchants; and some equally greedy property owners are additional burdens; but perhaps we expected such. The worst threat to San Francisco, or any other city, is the misuse and misappropriation of funding at all levels of government. As a comfort for the future without our contemporary economic, racial, and religious prejudices, William Shakespeare wrote in his play *As You Like It*, "All the world's a stage, And all the men and women merely players, They have their exits and their entrances…."

OSCAR GRANT III TRIAL

I have used trial records and multiple news reports (newsprint and television) to document this trial of our former African American tenant on Scott Street. The trial (People vs. Mehserle) of twenty-seven-year-old, white Johannes Mehserle, the BART Policeman, involved in the death of twenty-two-year-old Oscar Grant III, was moved to the Superior Court in Los Angeles County. Oakland (Alameda County) was considered too controversial for the first-degree murder trial due to the extensive local newspaper coverage and the resulting riots at the Fruitvale station of the Bay Area Rapid Transit (BART) the day after the murder. Los Angeles County was a similarly integrated, large, populated county. It was chosen over the defense preference for San Diego. San Diego was considered controversial because of a low African American population versus a higher Latino and White population. Another BART police officer named Marysol Domenici, twenty-nine, who helped detain Oscar Grant III on January 1, 2009, at 1:30 a.m. at the Fruitvale Station of the Bay Area Rapid Transit, had been fired in March of 2010 by the interim BART Police Chief Dash Butler, on the recommendation of the law firm representing BART. Butler refused to go into details because of privacy issues. As witnesses, she and her other partner Anthony Pirone, who thereafter was fired, were given paid leave after the incident. Pirone was the first officer of the three officers to detain Oscar Grant and his four hostile friends on the train for "disorderly conduct." Pirone struck Grant at least once and made the decision to arrest him for allegedly resisting officers. He was holding down Grant's upper body while he was flailing around trying to escape. Pirone called Mehserle, who arrived later as a back-up officer to help him.

As Mehserle was trying to handcuff Grant, he shot Grant, who was unarmed and face down on the station platform. Grant was with his latest girlfriend and four male friends, after a short visit to Fisherman's Wharf in San Francisco for a New Year's celebration. Grant's girlfriend Sophina Mesa and mother of his daughter spoke briefly with him after he called on his cell phone inside the Fruitvale Station. She would later testify in court that he sounded scared and said he was being beaten for no good reason. He had promised their daughter that he would take her to Chuck E. Cheese restaurant for pizza on New Year's Day. Mehserle testified that he thought he was using his Taser (stun gun) not his handgun.

The whole incident was videotaped on cellular telephones by other passengers at the BART station. Six days later, after the attempted arrest and consequential shooting, scores of downtown businesses and cars were damaged in a protest rally. Later in January of 2010, BART agreed to an out-of-court settlement of $1.5 million for Grant's five-year-old daughter, Tatiana, which was negotiated by Sophina Mesa, who was raising Oscar's and her daughter in Hayward. The co-plaintiff, Wanda Johnson, his mother, did not settle on the initial $50 million lawsuit. According to a *San Francisco Chronicle* article, "John Burris (attorney), who filed the suit for the Grant family, said all of the money will be invested, with payments until Tatiana's 30th birthday." A follow-up *San Francisco Chronicle* article in May of 2010, said that Grant had been employed as a supermarket worker in Hayward and hoped to be a barber after cutting the hair of inmates at Santa Rita Jail in Dublin. He dropped out of high school and was arrested five times between the age of eighteen and his death. He supposedly was close to his grandfather Johnson and was quite upset when Johnson had a stroke in 1997. According to news reports, his father Oscar II had shot a man a month after his birth and is serving a life time sentence in prison.

The prosecuting attorney was David Stein, who is the Alameda County District Attorney and the defense attorney was Michael Rains. In May of 2010, Los Angeles County Superior Judge Robert Perry granted a defense motion to allow some details about the arrest history of Grant. According to the *San Francisco Chronicle*, "Perry read from a police report accusing Grant of running from San Leandro officers during a traffic stop in October 2006. He was shot with a Taser stun gun and resisted arrest as officers tried to handcuff him. The report says Perry however refused to allow testimony at Mehserle's trial that Grant had a .38 caliber handgun which was found twenty feet from arrest site where he had been seen with the handgun during the San Leandro incident or that he was on probation when he was killed." Grant had been sentenced to sixteen months in prison on a gun possession charge. On June 8, 2010, the trial began with no African Americans being included (eight women and four men).

In a *San Francisco Chronicle* article, Grant's uncle, Cephus "Bobby" Johnson, Jr. said, "He would have preferred that some African Americans be included on the panel out of fairness". But the uncle said that he was more concerned about decisions on evidence by the judge, including a ruling that allows the defense to tell jurors that Oscar Grant resisted San Leandro police during the 2006 arrest. A direct quote from Johnson was, "This case is about the evidence produced." In final pretrial rulings, Judge Perry, agreed to allow all video footage by train passengers. One video, according to a *San Francisco Chronicle* article recorded, "Just before Mehserle took Grant to the ground and shot him….Pirone shouted at Grant, 'Bitch-ass n-, right? Bitch-ass n-, right?'" Pirone was responding to being called that name by Grant, Michael Rains later said in the trial." Also, Judge Perry allowed, as evidence, testimony from Mesa regarding her brief cell phone call to Grant, as she had exited the platform after the initial confrontation of rowdiness by the BART police.

Michael Rains argued his case before the jury; that having fired his Taser in a six-hour, classroom training session a month before, Mehserle was ill equipped to use his Taser. Also, Michael Rains profiled his client as an immigrant from Germany at the age of four, a person who had a talent for computers before going into police work in 2006, and who was a "lovable" person. After extensive testimony from the prosecution witnesses, the first defense witness, former officer Anthony Pirone, testified that Mehserle shouted to him, "I'm going to Tase him" before he fired a pistol shot into Grant's back. Pirone added that Mehserle had earlier cried out, "I can't get his hands," and "His hands are in his waistband."

On June 24, Mehserle (6 foot 5 inches, 250 pounds) took the stand and testified (upon arriving at the station to assist), "I said, 'Calm down, we'll figure it all out.' I think I got them to settle down for a little bit of talking." He said that the Taser was new to him and he was inexperienced in its use and grabbed the wrong gun. Michael Rains asked, "What kind of shape were you in?" Mehserle responded "I really don't remember not crying." On June 25, Mehserle said," I didn't think I had my gun. I remember the pop. It wasn't loud. It wasn't like a gun shot, and I remember wondering what went wrong with the Taser." Michael Rains asked, "What he remembered after that and the former officer now crying, struggled with the words, and said I remember Mr. Grant said 'You shot me.'" According to a *San Francisco Chronicle* article, "Grant's mother , Wanda Johnson, quickly left the courtroom as a Bay Area man identified by friends and authorities as Tim Killings, twenty-four, stood and yelled 'Maybe you should save those f— tears, dude.'"

On July 8, the jury found Mehserle guilty of involuntary manslaughter but acted so recklessly that he showed a disregard for Grant's life with gun enhancement. As a *San Francisco Chronicle* article stated, "The verdict was an all-but unprecedented instance of a police officer being convicted for an on-duty shooting. But Grant's relatives, who said the video-recorded shooting was a murder and that Mehserle deserved a sentence longer than the one he is likely to receive." Within hours of the trial decision, riots with one thousand angry protestors of the verdict occurred in Oakland. The results were that one hundred downtown shops were looted, and car windows smashed, which intensified after dark. Among the seventy-eight protestors arrested, three-quarters came from outside of Oakland, but two female Oakland Supervisors who were involved certainly did not necessarily provide a positive situation. One of them Jean Quan, a leading advocate of Ebonics (colloquial American African conversation) being taught in public schools, explained at that time that she was only trying to pacify the mob.

As a backdrop to this trial, Ms. Quan was elected the mayor of Oakland in November of 2010. She was the first female and Asian mayor of Oakland. Oakland has the fourth highest murder rate in the United States. This city was infamous for being a major center for the Black Panthers/Black Muslims in the 1970s and the crack (cocaine) trafficking, which was endemic in the 1980s. Her predecessor Ron Dellums, an African American, radical, former Democratic U.S. Congressman was probably the most inept mayor in the history of Oakland. Upon being elected, he immediately increased his salary and was later indicted for not paying his personal income tax. The churlish former Mayor Art Agnos, a *progressive* liberal Democrat, holds that same inept position in the history of San Francisco. Agnos perpetuated the scams of public housing as the regional director of HUD, after his one term as mayor. The current mayor of San Francisco is Edwin Lee (first Chinese American mayor), who was designated in January, 2011, by Mayor Gavin Newsom, to complete his term through 2012. Although Ed Lee initially declared no interest in a full term, he was elected in 2012 to a full term. The charismatic, young Mayor Gavin Newson was elected Lieutenant Governor of California and brings popular, innovative ideas for the environment and technological advancement.

Earlier on July 4, 2010, prior to the jury decision, Mehserle had given a letter to his attorney Michael Rains while the jury was still deliberating. The letter asked for forgiveness from Oscar Grant's family and was released after the verdict. Family members were unsympathetic and unmoved.

On July 20, 2010, hundreds of supporters of Mehserle staged a rally at the exurban Walnut Creek BART station to support him and all other law enforcement officers. The crowd included off-duty officers and Mehserle's father, Todd Mehserle. After the Internet publicized the event by his supporters, nearly twice the number of counter protestors also arrived and laid in the street with their hands behind their backs to illustrate the unarmed position of Grant when shot. The disagreements were mostly verbal, and the officers, some wearing riot gear, were able to maintain a relatively peaceful atmosphere.

In October, Michael Rains filed papers with Judge Perry that related a Taser incident in Nicholasville, Kentucky, where an officer with the same model Taser as Mehserle carried had meant to end a fight in April 2008 and had instead withdrawn his pistol from the opposite hip and shot and wounded a man. A grand jury declined to indict the officer. Michael Rains stated this precedence should have been presented to the jury.

On October 24, the Bay Area longshoremen union led a peaceful rally to support the Grant family, who is asking for a maximum term of fourteen years for Mehserle. The job action caused the ports of Oakland and San Francisco to be closed during the 8:00 a.m. to 5:00 p.m. shift.

On November 5, 2010, Judge Perry said, as quoted by the *San Francisco Chronicle*, "Mehserle would have been justified in using the Taser because Grant was resisting the attempts to handcuff him. Mehserle's 'weapons confusion' was owing in part to BART's poor training of its officers and to 'near riot' conditions at the train station. Mesherle, he added, showed 'tons of remorse.' Perry's remarks suggested that, had the prosecution won the murder conviction it sought, he would have overturned it because he found 'no intent to kill.'" Another direct quote from Judge Perry said, "Mehserle's muscle memory took over in this moment of great danger and stress. No reasonable 'trier' of fact could have concluded that Mehserle intentionally fired his gun." Predictably, a two-year sentence by Judge Perry brought forth immediately an Oakland riot that disbursed beyond the city center, which resulted in property damage. The arrest of 152 protestors by a well-defended position by the police was quite effective. Afterwords, the defense attorneys filed for dismissal of the verdict and later a request for release on bail. They noted that the jailed Mehserle is devastated that he has not seen his son who was born on January 2, 2009. The politics and prejudices on both sides will never be satisfied.

On December 3, 2010, Judge Perry ruled on the defense attorneys' argument that Mehserle posed no danger while on bail and had legitimate grounds for overturning the July 8 guilty verdict. He denied bail. With credit for time served. Mehserle could be eligible for release in about seven months.

On December 17, 2010, an arbitrator ordered BART to reinstate former officer Marysol Domenici, thirty years old, without restrictions and full back pay. The Grant family had been incensed when she said on the witness stand referring to Oscar Grant and his friends, "If they would have followed orders, this wouldn't have happened."

On May 10, 2011, a federal judge ruled that BART, as an organization cannot be held responsible for the shooting death of Oscar Grant III. He, however, ruled most of the issues in a $50,000,000 federal lawsuit filed on behalf of Grant's family against BART police officers would be decided by a jury trial.

On June 13, 2011, Johannes Mehserle emerged quietly from a Los Angeles jail after serving half of a two-year sentence. On the same day in Oakland, a few hundred people protested his release. Among the protestors was Wanda Johnson, Oscar Grant's mother, with Oscar Grant's seven-year-old daughter, Tatiana. The *San Francisco Chronicle* of June 14, 2011 stated, "Mehserle, now a parolee, is not in the clear. Xochitl Hinojosa, a spokeswoman for the U.S. Justice Department, said the agency's civil rights division was still reviewing the shooting to see if it warranted federal prosecution."

On June 28, 2011, Wanda Jackson reached a settlement with BART at the conference in U.S. District Court in San Francisco. She agreed to a settlement of $1.3 million, which includes no admission of fault by BART or any of the officers. John Burris, her African American attorney, stated at a following press conference, "The loss was unnecessary, and I just pray that as officers go around, and they have to make decisions, that they would choose the right decision. It didn't have to be this way." Settlement talks are scheduled to continue with Grant's incarcerated father Oscar II and five of Grant's friends who say that they were mistreated by BART police on the night of the shooting.

On July 3, 2011, at 9:45 p.m., an intoxicated man named Charles Hill, forty-five years old, was shot with a handgun by a BART policeman at the Civic Center BART station in San Francisco and died an hour later at San Francisco General Hospital. He had being holding a bottle of liquor, which he smashed and advanced menacingly with a knife toward the two BART policemen with handguns and a Taser on the platform. As a *San Francisco Chronicle* article dated July 5 stated, "Sensitive to claims that the Grant shooting had a racial element—Mehserle is white, Grant was black—BART said that the man shot at the Civic Center was white, and the two officers who responded were white and Asian." Although there were supposedly forty witnesses on the platform, no videos have been produced, including BART camera videos. The incident was investigated by BART internal affairs, the new BART independent police auditor, the San Francisco Police Department, and the District Attorney's office.

On July 16, 2011, Johntue Caldwell, twenty-five years old, the best friend of Oscar Grant who was at the BART station that deadly night, was shot and killed at a Hayward gas station about 5:35 p.m. by a fleeing assailant, as he sat in his Cadillac. He was the father of two young sons and the godfather to Grant's daughter, Tatiana. According to an article by the excellent journalist, Henry K. Lee in the *San Francisco Chronicle* on July 17, 2011,

> ***In 2010, Caldwell filed a $5 million federal civil rights lawsuit, saying he was mistreated by a second BART police officer, Marysol Domencici, before Johannes Mehserle shot Grant in the back...Caldwell's suit, which is still pending, said Domenici ordered him to the ground, threatened him with a Tazer. Touched the stun gun to his face and cursed him using a racial slur. Caldwell was 'mentally and emotionally injured,' his attorneys wrote.***

Further this *same article* stated, "Dale Allen, an attorney for BART, said after the suit was filed that Caldwell had a 'significant criminal history' and was one of three men who cursed at and physically challenged officers as they detained Grant and three others after a fight on a train." John Burris, the Grant's family attorney is quoted as saying, "Johntue was a wonderful young man. He had career objectives. He and his mother were very, very close. He and Oscar had been friends since early childhood. They were as close as brothers could be, and this is a tragedy of the highest order. It's hard to imagine that another young man of that relatively small group of people is dead."

Another well-known Bay Area trial attorney verified for me that Nathan (Nathaniel) Burris, forty-nine years old, was the son of the above mentioned, John Burris. He shot-gunned down his ex-girlfriend of a thirteen-year relationship, toll-taker Deborah Ross, and her favorite friend Ersie Everette III, a Golden Gate Transit driver and aspiring church deacon from San Leandro, at the Richmond-San Rafael Bridge, on August 11, 2009. At his trial beginning on November 5, 2012, Nathan Burris is quoted in the *San Francisco Chronicle* on November 6, 2012, "…Burris said he wanted to plead guilty. 'I'm still alive, they're not, and that's all that matters,' he said in court. 'I'm ready to roll on the road.'" He refused legal counsel and was eventually sentenced to life in prison by the judge. Earlier on November 20, 2012, the infuriated jury had handed down the death penalty.

In January 2013, a movie called *Fruitvale* premiered at the Sundance Film Festival and won the top prize. Weinstein Co. purchased the rights to begin filming, for a reported amount of $2.5 million and retitled the film *Fruitvale Station.* Written and directed by Ryan Coogler, a young film-maker from Oakland, the film depicts the final twenty-fours in the life of Oscar Grant III.

Oscar was played by Michael B. Jordan to rave reviews. The film opened to the public in July of 2013.

KANSAS UPDATE 2013

Certain developments in Kansas give an interesting perspective of our changing world. In 2009, Bernadette Gray-Little became the new Chancellor of the University of Kansas. She is the first female as well as African American. A former native of North Carolina, she was formerly the popular provost at the University of North Carolina. She attributes her career goals to positive, quiet guidance from her mother. At this time her husband, who is currently associate dean of academics services, U.N.C, and both her son and daughter-in-law, Maura Garcia, are presently residing in North Carolina. I was introduced to her in San Francisco at a K.U. alumni party on January 10, 2013, at One Leidsdorff Place, and was impressed with this tall, regally splendid lady.

In 1997, the Kansas town of Nicodemus, settled in 1877 by African American setters from central Kentucky, was designated a National Historical Site by the National Park Service. The population once neared six hundred people, but has declined, like so many other small Kansas towns. Today, the town claims fewer than twenty-five residents.

Unfortunately, the delusional Pastor Fred Phelps, Sr., of Westboro Baptist Church in Topeka, continues the traditional contradictions of Kansas, with his hatefully homophobic ravings, much like the horrific Reverend Jim Jones. Incredibly, the U.S. Supreme Court voted eight to one to reject the judicial fines against his church for unchristian protests at a funeral for a dead gay American soldier killed in Afghanistan. Freedom of speech is a sacred constitutional law in our country.

In Kansas City, Kansas, the downtown commercial district of eighteen blocks on Minnesota Avenue and surrounding residential districts has become even more devastated and vacant with the exception of newer bank buildings and federal and state buildings. There has been some revitalization by Mexican Americans. The entire focus of development is now in the western part of Wyandotte County (Kansas City, Kansas is restricted by state law to the county borders), and is adjacent to our leased, still-productive family farm. The family farm house, of so many delightful summer moments, is almost completely collapsed, but the magnificent hilltop setting still exists. Nearby, the gigantic 2001 Kansas Speedway with NASCAR races (Sprint Cup Nationwide and Craftsman Truck Series), caused a rerouting of US Highway 40, on which our farm still fronts. The speedway seats 825,000 people and hosts a variety of other smaller racing events. Overlooking the speedway is a most popular 95,000 square-foot Hollywood (gambling) Casino, built in 2012 for $411 million. Across, to the north of the highway, the continually expanding, major regional-shopping magnet called Village West, financed by Kansas STAR (sales tax and revenue) bonds, is like a new city. A 2011 major-league soccer stadium, seating over 18,000; several, large, resort hotels; the Nebraska Furniture Mart owned by Warren Buffet; the regionally (states) popular Cabella's outdoor sporting supply store; the Legends Discount Shopping Center with one hundred stores; a multi-movie theater; and the Cerner office complex are only part of this dynamic urban center. A new four-lane highway, Interstate 435, services this area. Combined with the nearby Interstate 70—which is the 1950s Kansas Turnpike that my father bought to finance the construction—this area is an ideal crossroads for interstate travel and trade. The newly constructed Schlitterbahn water amusement park of 300 acres is east and across from our farm. Perhaps, the vacuum created by the vacant downtown will be reinvigorated to the east by private investment in the future, unlike the hapless earlier redevelopment agency, which created a nonstarter reconstruction.

Presently, the magnificent, brick masonry building, in a lovely, green, parkway location that is over a hundred-years old, named Westport High School, in Kansas City, Missouri, has been closed. This school is among the one-half of the fifty-seven existing schools that were closed. My father's high school was earlier considered academically superior. Although he lost his two front teeth in an ice hockey game there, he always had a charming smile, helped with handsome replacements. After my fiftieth high school reunion in June 2010, I wonder about the fate of my completely restored Wyandotte High School, which has become another major high school with a rapidly declining enrollment, anemic academic standards, and even inferior athletic teams. The majority of the student population is both African American and Hispanic.

SAN FRANCISCO AND CALIFORNIA UPDATE 2013

Regarding schools in San Francisco, there is a distinctively different situation from most other major American cities. We now have productive charter schools, and the teachers unions are perhaps more responsive than previously. Because of our unique city/county borders, the increased Internet technological industry, and biotechnological industry, the property values have continued to remain the highest in the United States. The former mayor, Gavin Newsom was not only a gay rights crusader but dedicated to making the city the most environmentally green in the nation. But at my age, I am not getting back on a bicycle with the growing crowd of riders, nor will I be raising vegetables in my backyard. Originally, I had a vegetable garden, and John said, "I'm not going to clean off the snails from the lettuce anymore." We once tried preparing the snails in a broth for the expensive escargot. We were not at all happy with the results.

An anomaly in San Francisco is the Willie L. Brown, Jr. College Preparatory Academy (fourth through eighth grade), established in 2006, which was declared as the place *Where Students' Dreams Come True*" This Silver Terrace/Bayview district school was originally Fremont Elementary School, built in the late 1950s. Then it became the Police Academy, and, in 1992, the 21st Century Academy. This building complex, on an idyllic, large, sunny campus of four acres, with hilltop views of the San Francisco Bay and downtown, previously had signs that were posted stating that it was a *Safe and Drug Free School Zone*. Various "bungalows," or mobile classrooms, were added to the larger, sprawling buildings, including an auditorium near many various sports-playing fields. In 2011, the school was declared by the State of California, Schools Superintendent to be "consistently the worst of the worst schools statewide on standardized test scores of 188 schools" in California and was closed. The voters agreed in the November 2011 election to provide school funding, through a $531 million bond issue, which provided funds to demolish the school and rebuild a new school at an expense of $50 million. The waste of viable buildings in the United States is obscene!

In the summer of 2011, next to our neighborhood in the Anza Vista district, the alternative Wallenberg High School, in a campus setting, was retrofitted and reroofed. This building, at 40 Vega Street, also dates from the late 1950s!

Despite the inherent problems in large, major cities such as the controversial public school systems, more people are attracted to the more-cultured, livable, and viable large, American cities, such as San Francisco, New York City, Chicago, Los Angeles, Phoenix, and Atlanta. However, these new immigrants to large cities must constantly avoid the increasing number of homeless, mentally ill, and economically displaced persons on city streets and parks. Added to this mix are the crazed, sometimes non-law abiding, bicyclists and skate boarders. And always in the background are the criminals and drug dealers from the remaining housing projects or suburban, depressed, regional areas, ready to prey on unsuspecting citizens or those citizens with drug habits.

For the only combined California city and county, with a restrictive 46.7 square-mile footprint, San Francisco has a rapidly growing, dense population. This *city state* continues to have an increasingly multiethnic population. Of all American cities over 250,000, the city has become like most American Cities, the proverbial *American Melting Pot*. With the largest Chinese American population of 19.6 percent, and one of the smaller African American populations of 6.5 percent, the ethnic diversity is unique. The Hispanics or Latinos population of 14 percent represents conversely less than half of that of the state. According to the 2010 U.S. census, San Francisco has a population of 805,235. Thus, it becomes the thirteenth most populous city in the United States (fourth most populous in California), and the second most-densely populated large city (greater than 200,000) in the United States. In the San Francisco Bay region of more than 7.4 million people, San Francisco has become the most important center of finance, cultural institutions, historically preserved districts, culinary industry, well-planned civic events, and biotechnology research. Further, the mild weather and overwhelming tourist approval indicate a most viable, exciting city!

According to the 2010 U.S. Census, the specific demographics for the Western Addition contained within a roughly four hundred-block area are 52,575 San Franciscans; the racial profile is 52.67 percent White, 17.13 percent Asian, 13.24 percent Black (African American), 10.20 percent Hispanic or Latino, 6.76 percent Pacific Islander, Native American, Eskimo, or of mixed race. Of these four-hundred blocks, fewer than fifty were twenty percent African American, eighteen were over fifty percent, and only three were over seventy percent. These three blocks are located between Laguna and Buchanan Streets, directly north of Ivy and Grove Streets, and Golden Gate Avenue. This area is mostly occupied by SFHA projects. Regarding the Asian population, Koreans outnumber the Japanese, and most likely the Chinese are the largest ethnic group. Thus, the ethnic evolution of the Western Addition continues to change as previously.

Many new immigrants are arriving here from Africa (Ethiopia, etc.), Russia, Eastern/Western Europe, Australia, Middle East, India, and China. They are generally well-educated and moderately wealthy. They are settling in the city and buying both homes and businesses.

OVERALL VIEWPOINT

Summing up, I suspect, in spite of the overwhelming positive changes in the twentieth century, the domination of the world by the United States ended with the worldwide Great Recession of 2008. Our expansive and expensive involvements in global wars have added to this decline. Through the increasing individual greed of the employee's union officials, at the expense of their members, and some large global corporations, as well as the rampant corrupt governance, this dire situation has escalated. The formerly prosperous European colonies of Rhodesia, Kenya, and the Republic of South Africa, in spite of great natural resources, seem to be in a downward spin. In the Middle East, Israel, with mainly American and European support, seems to be in an even more unobtainable and untenable political situation with its neighboring countries. The uprisings in Tunisia, Egypt, Syria, and Libya make the situation even more volatile.

In Asia, the financial dominance of Japan seems limited, with the recall of many Toyota automobiles and with the Sony electronic industrial empire's much-reduced revenues. The dreadful tsunami and 9.0-magnitude earthquake in March 2011 resulted in the destruction of the Fukushima Dai-Ichi nuclear- power plant. The total economy is devastated, and nuclear-power plants will not be as popular worldwide. India vs. Pakistan, with the increasing Islamic confrontation, may bring on a new, nuclear war. India, with its huge underclass, is another obstacle. The prediction is that in the near future the population of India will exceed that of China. The economic and political differences between North Korea and South Korea are difficult to contemplate. Even the European Union and Russia appear dysfunctional. At this time, China, with its ancient civilization, seems poised to become the next global superpower with its monopolistic, capitalistic empowerment of its population. Corruption there is dealt a quick death sentence, but corruption remains endemic.

Is the apocalypse emanating? One wonders whether the conflicting, various, religious beliefs are the problem, or whether the problem is of human nature in general? Can anyone predict, even among the so-called experts, the future state of our world—Earth?

Is protecting a populace with a safety net more important than outer-space exploration? The American suburbs, as well as the exclusive exurbs, which exploded in the Anthony Burgess' novel, *Clockwork Orange* seem to be in decline. As such an important target for terrorists, we hope international relationships will improve, and this city, where the first United Nations conference was held in 1945, will be preserved.

The controversial WikiLeaks, founded by Julian Assange, might perhaps provide the transparency that most of us desire from our government and expose the corruption of our present global situation! The unfortunate situation of the court martial of the gay U.S. Army Pfc. Bradley Manning, who leaked official government documents, poses an enigma to the public. Edward Snowden poses another quite revealing documentation of spying by the United States. National Security Agency (NSA) Are we now living in George Orwell's *Brave New World?* Revealed future documentation may hopefully expose, among other problems, the Byzantine domestic situation of the enormously expensive, wasteful, HUD block grants etc. All mankind will benefit from more disclosure by our leaders! As my wise father said, "Scratch the veneer of civilization, and you will find greed and corruption." As a physician, he also said, "Genetics determine so much about the actions of an individual." Biogenetic technology may give us more insight and possibly reverse aging, with people becoming immortal. Various scientists are predicting that in thirty years, *singularity,* which is defined as "The moment when technological change becomes so rapid and profound, it represents a rupture in the fabric of human history," will occur. Highly developed artificial intelligence in the form of robots, as well as computers, may revolutionize the way we think. Perhaps, even now, we are mentally overwhelmed with too much conflicting information and stimulation!

Perhaps the supposed Chinese curse, "May you live in interesting times," sums up the world today. Ming, John, and most Chinese American friends are not familiar with it. After Googling, I discovered that in 1936, Sir Austin Chamberlain, brother of a former English prime minister, heard from English diplomats in China about the curse. The curse means, "May you experience much upheaval and trouble in your life." The clear implication is that 'the uninteresting times' of peace are tranquility and are more life enhancing.

The effects of the *Lesser Economic Depression* are even-higher unemployment, obvious corporate greed, bipartisan political graft, and a financial tailspin for the American middle class. The corporations expand overseas and not generally in the United States. The financial institutions encourage consumer spending, but are reticent to extend credit for infrastructure spending.

But, as an unrepentant, perpetual optimist, with my personal front-window viewpoint of what was accomplished by the united effort of many residents in the Western Addition is reassuring. With my equally important personal relationship with John and Ming, I continue to predict a bright future with even more open communications in a positive, intellectual, Internet world-wide movement. It is a wonderful life! We saved our home from destruction by the SFRA.

I remember reminiscing with an English male traveler, on a train in India several years ago, about the beautiful countryside of Devon, where he lived and I had visited twice. He said, "Our home is a single-story long house, dating from the twelfth century. The walls are mud with wattle, and daubed with white-painted plaster, and a reed-thatched, wattle roof." Comparing, I wonder how we

Americans can be so wasteful with our housing resources, and I hope that the green environment will encourage a new approach.

The best way to conclude is to say that most of my friends and I have survived. My inspiring father had said, "I lived through the golden age of medicine with penicillin, aspirin, and few government regulations." He would undoubtedly be pleased that his two granddaughters are physicians and his grandson is potentially becoming a physician. I suspect he would be worried about their future world dedicated to our government socialized medicine. My loving, gracious mother, who, as always, was the optimistic *Hostess in the Sky*, said positively, "We are all young!" To our family's great loss, she died at the age of ninety-eight years and was buried, at a private family service, next to her beloved Leland, on 12/12/12, in the Olathe City Cemetery.

As I look around the Western Addition with much satisfaction at what all continuing neighborhood activists have accomplished for the present and future citizens, I feel gratified. Our home, one-hundred years of age in 2012, which is architecturally magnificent, situated in a hidden, glorious, private garden, and the greatly improved neighborhood location because of our various groups and my efforts, continues to give John, Ming, and myself much happiness. Our camaraderie has created a wonderful life together. I am sure of the positive future of our fabulous, energetic, and frantic City of San Francisco. As well, the future of our great nation, with a melting pot of increasing ethnic populations, will continue in its usual, inventive manner to be fascinating and environmentally viable.

16.

Acknowledgments

Ever since I moved with John to our home in 1975, I have kept a continuous file of newspaper articles at my offices from the *San Francisco Chronicle*, the *San Francisco Examiner*, and other local, neighborhood newspapers. My favorite present-day writers, such as the local radical Warren Hinckle, and the late internationally famous radical Christopher Hitchens (newspapers, books as well as magazines), are among the journalists that inhabit the battlefront of the local and foreign news, with their own, valuable, editorial contributions. The late James Wilde of *Time Magazine*, a dear friend and an unforgettable Irishman (Canadian), was a crazed inspiration. Forget the hot journalism on television, as exposed by Marshall McLuhan many years ago, and the newer electronic technology. I have relied on my memory, as well as my preserved agendas/minutes of the SFRA and the SFHA, and various committees/boards on which I have served, as well as neighborhood association notes and personal information.

As a person who is much aware of academic credibility and acceptability, this narrative has been, of necessity, free-flowing—to enlighten the reader to the reality of urban life. I used Google and Wikipedia, but was sometime disappointed in minor mistakes. But then, personal interpretations are always questionable. The continuing changes in the Western Addition as well as my newly adopted city are always fascinating in perspective of the past. I am sure that many personalities will disagree with my analysis of the Western Addition and its strong connection with many districts in other major American cities. With an extensive library on San Francisco history, I have borrowed from these books, and I am thankful for their personal contributions. Although I have never agreed completely with these books, I have given my best interpretations. My creed is that narrative in the written form will always be invaluable to humanity.

Many early neighborhood edited newspapers, such as the *New Fillmore* published by the late David Ish, the *Western Edition* published by Michael Martin, and the *San Francisco Independent* published by the Fang family; were diligent, improvising, and forceful in provided unbiased reporting on the Western Addition.

However, I would particularly like to thank the journalists of the *San Francisco Chronicle* and *San Francisco Examiner* (see glossary) for their exemplary reporting—there are so many. I would particularly commend and thank *San Francisco Examiner* journalist, Jerry Adams, and *San Francisco Chronicle* journalist, Marshall Kilduff, and Stephen Schwartz, for their early reporting of the SFRA and SFHA. Later *San Francisco Chronicle* journalists, such as John King, Debra Saunders, John Cote', and Heather Knight have been great inspirations for me. Congratulations for your brilliant grunt work!

May the God-of-All-Faiths preserve the United States of America from any insidious president or crooked politicians of all parties and their apostles!

17.

Glossary

A-1 PROJECT AREA of SFRA—Borders projected with a map of this mostly commercial area in the Western Addition

A-2 PROJECT AREA of SFRA—Borders projected with a map of this mostly residential area in the Western Addition

ANTHROPOGRAPHY—A branch of anthropology dealing with the distribution of man as distinguished by physical character, language, institutions and customs

ASNA—Alamo Square Neighborhood Association

AVNA—Anza Vista Neighborhood Association

BABY BOOMERS—American Generation born from 1946-1964

BANG—Beideman Area Neighborhood Group

CCBH—Concerned Citizens for Better Housing

CEQA—California Environmental Quality Act

CITY (the)—City and County San Francisco, California

CSFN—Coalition for San Francisco Neighborhoods

DPI—Department of Building Inspection

E.I.R.—Environmental Impact Review

ENTERPRISE ZONE—Government funded development of urban business districts

GENERATION X—Gen X-American Generation born somewhere from late 1960s to the late 1970s

GENERATION Y—Millennial Generation-American Generation born somewhere from late 1970s to the late 1990s

GREAT RECESSION of 2008=Lesser Economic Depression=" Economic Downturn" beginning in December 2007

HERITAGE—Foundation for San Francisco Architectural Heritage

HUD—Department of Housing and Urban Development

HOA—Home Owners Association

HOPE—U.S. government program "Housing Opportunities for People Everywhere" in public housing projects

LCCSF—Log Cabin Club of San Francisco

LGBT—Lesbian, gay, bisexual, transgender community

MARKET RATE VALUE—The value of property in the marketplace, which is the price a willing buyer would pay a willing seller, would accept

NIMBY—Not in My Back Yard- a person who protests about new housing in their neighborhood

PROGRESSIVE—Teddy Roosevelt's Bull Moose Party versus SF Democratic Party Liberal representatives

PADS—Planning Association for Divisadero Street

SAN FRANCISCO—San Francisco, California

SAN FRANCISCO CHRONICLE—Early newspaper founded in San Francisco in 1865-bought and expanded by Charles and Michael de Young-purchased by the Hearst Corporation in 2000

SAN FRANCISCO EXAMINER—early newspaper founded in San Francisco in 1863-bought in 1880 by U.S. Senator George Hearst and given in 1887 to his only son William Randolph Hearst-became the "Monarch of Dailies" one of many Hearst national publications-sold in 2000 to the Fang Family and later resold

SFAR—San Francisco Association of Realtors

SFHA—San Francisco Housing Authority

SFRA—San Francisco Redevelopment Agency

SIR—Society for Individual Rights

SPOSFI—Small Property Owners of San Francisco Institute

SUBPRIME LOAN—A loan that has a starting interest rate for several years below the government established prime loan interest

TAX INCREMENT MONEY—Funds collected by redevelopment agencies for completed building projects from developers

VA—Victorian Alliance

WACAC—Western Addition A-2 Citizens Advisory Committee

WAETF—Western Addition Economic Task Force in the Jazz District Enterprise Zone

WANA—Western Addition Neighborhood Association

WAPAC—Western Addition Project Action Committee

WAPC—Western Addition Parking Corporation

www.ingramcontent.com/pod-product-compliance
Lightning Source LLC
Chambersburg PA
CBHW052030090426
42739CB00010B/1846

* 9 7 8 0 6 1 5 8 6 3 7 9 5 *